W9-CCL-674

POWER
RELIGION

POWER RELIGION

THE SELLING OUT OF THE EVANGELICAL CHURCH?

CHARLES COLSON • J.I. PACKER
R.C. SPROUL • ALISTER McGRATH

AND OTHERS

Michael Scott Horton, Editor

Editor of The Agony of Deceit

MOODY PRESS

CHICAGO

All Scripture quotations, unless noted otherwise, are from the *Holy Bible: New International Version*. Copyright © 1973, 1978, 1984 International Bible Society. Used by permission of Zondervan Bible Publishers. All rights reserved.

Scripture quotations marked NASB are from the *New American Standard Bible*, © 1960, 1962, 1963, 1968, 1971, 1972, 1973, 1975, and 1977 by The Lockman Foundation, and are used by permission.

ISBN: 0-8024-6774-1

1 3 5 7 9 10 8 6 4 2

Printed in the United States of America

Contents

88563

List of Contributors

MICHAEL S. HORTON
is the editor of *The Agony of Deceit* and the author of *Mission Accomplished, Made in America,* and *Putting Amazing Back into Grace.* He was educated at Biola University and Westminster Theological Seminary in California. He has also studied at the International Institute of Human Rights in France and at Cambridge University in England. The founder and president of Christians United for Reformation (CURE), Anaheim, California, he is currently engaged in doctoral studies at Wycliffe Hall, Oxford, England.

JOHN H. ARMSTRONG
is founder and director of Reformation and Revival Ministries in Carol Stream, Illinois. A Baptist minister, he pastored for twenty-one years before becoming a conference speaker and editor of *Reformation and Revival Journal,* a quarterly publication for church leadership. A frequent contributor to numerous publications, he was educated at the University of Alabama, Wheaton College and Wheaton Graduate School of Theology, and Luther Rice Seminary.

JAMES M. BOICE
is pastor of the historic Tenth Presbyterian Church in Philadelphia and was the chairman of the International Council on Biblical Inerrancy. He is the author of numerous books, including *Foundations of the Christian Faith*, *The Foundation of Biblical Authority*, and a series of volumes on Genesis, the minor prophets, John, and Romans. Dr. Boice is also the chairman of the Philadelphia Conference on Reformed Theology and the speaker for "The Bible Study Hour." He was educated at Harvard University, Princeton Theological Seminary, and the University of Basel, Switzerland.

D. A. CARSON

is research professor of New Testament at Trinity Evangelical Divinity School in Deerfield, Illinois. Having earned his Ph.D. in New Testament Studies at Cambridge University, Dr. Carson is the author of many books and research articles, including such important studies as *Exegetical Fallacies, How Long O Lord?*, and *Showing the Spirit.*

CHARLES W. COLSON

is founder and chairman of Prison Fellowship, a ministry to prisoners, ex-prisoners, and their families, as well as to the victims of crime and those involved in our criminal justice system. Dr. Colson was special assistant to former President Richard Nixon and is a noted speaker and author of many books, including *Born Again, Loving God, Kingdoms in Conflict*, and most recently, *Why America Doesn't Work*, co-written with Jack Eckerd.

BILL HULL

is the author of *The Disciple-Making Pastor,* one in a series of books he has written to encourage greater commitment to discipleship and disciple making in the contemporary church. In addition, he is working to develop an international training network for leadership teams from local churches. He is the director of church ministries for the Evangelical Free Church of America (EFCA).

DON MATZAT

is the author of *Inner Healing: Deliverance or Deception?*, *Christ Esteem,* and *Truly Transformed* (forthcoming). He hosts a daily radio program, "Issues, Etc.,"® broadcast over the Jubilee Radio Network. He holds the M.Div. from Concordia Seminary in St. Louis and has been in parish ministry in the Lutheran Church–Missouri Synod for twenty-seven years.

ALISTER E. McGRATH

has gained international reputation as a historian of the Reformation through his many books and articles for both academic and popular audiences. His books include *Luther's Theology of the Cross, The Making of Modern German Christology, The Intellectual Origins of the European Reformation,* and *The Genesis of Doctrine.* More popular works include *The Sunnier Side of Doubt, A Cloud of Witnesses, Understanding the Trinity,* and *Justification by Faith.* He is lecturer in historical and systematic theology at Wycliffe Hall, Oxford, England, a member of the Oxford University faculty of theology, Bampton Lecturer at Oxford, and Tipple Visiting Professor of Theology at Drew University, Madison, New Jersey.

KENNETH A. MYERS
is a producer for Berea Audio and was for eight years a producer and editor for National Public Radio, working for much of that time as arts and humanities editor for two news programs, "Morning Edition" and "All Things Considered." He was formerly the editor of *This World: A Journal of Religion and Public Life,* a quarterly journal whose editor-in-chief was Richard John Neuhaus, and the executive editor of *Eternity.* He is the author of *All God's Children and Blue Suede Shoes: Christians and Popular Culture.* He is a graduate of the University of Maryland and of Westminster Theological Seminary in Philadelphia.

TOM NETTLES
is professor of church history at Trinity Evangelical Divinity School in Deerfield, Illinois, and the author of *By His Grace and for His Glory* and coauthor of *Baptists and the Bible.* Educated at Southwestern Baptist Theological Seminary, Dr. Nettles taught at that institution and at Mid-America Baptist Theological Seminary. A major focus of his study and writing has been the theological foundations of Baptist life.

J. I. PACKER
is Sangwoo Youtong Chee Professor of Theology at Regent College in Vancouver, British Columbia. An Anglican theologian, he has played a major role in English and North American evangelicalism, having written such works as *Fundamentalism and the Word of God, God's Words,* the best-selling book *Knowing God,* and more recent works, such as *Keep in Step with the Spirit, Hot Tub Religion,* and *The Pursuit of Godliness.* He was educated at Oxford University and served in a number of academic posts before coming to North America.

DAVID POWLISON
is a lecturer in practical theology at Westminster Theological Seminary in Philadelphia and a counselor at Christian Counseling and Educational Foundation, Laverock, Pennsylvania. He was educated at Harvard University (A.B.), Westminster Seminary (M.Div.), and the University of Pennsylvania (M.A.; Ph.D. candidate). He is the author of a number of articles on the relationship between biblical faith and psychology.

KIM RIDDLEBARGER

is vice president of Christians United for Reformation (CURE), based in Anaheim, California. He is also dean of the CURE Academy, "the layperson's seminary." He is associate professor of apologetics at the Simon Greenleaf School of Law and has wide experience in the Christian bookselling industry. He was educated at California State University, Fullerton; the Simon Greenleaf School of Law; and Westminster Theological Seminary in California. He is currently engaged in doctoral studies at Fuller Theological Seminary.

R. C. SPROUL

is founder and president of Ligonier Ministries in Orlando, Florida, and a popular author and communicator. Some of his recent books include *Chosen by God, The Holiness of God,* and *Classical Apologetics.* He is also professor of apologetics at Reformed Theological Seminary in Orlando. He was educated at Westminster College, Pittsburgh Theological Seminary, and the Free University of Amsterdam, the Netherlands.

EDWARD WELCH

is director of counseling for the Christian Counseling and Educational Foundation, Laverock, Pennsylvania, and is a licensed psychologist. He received the M.Div. from Biblical Theological Seminary and the Ph.D. from the University of Utah. He is the author of *Counselor's Guide to the Brain and Its Disorders* and numerous journal articles.

Acknowledgments

The editor would like to thank the staff of Moody Press, especially Jim Bell, Duncan Jaenicke, and Anne Scherich.

Also to be thanked are the overworked and underpaid staff members of CURE. Without them this project, and many others, could not have been completed.

I am not ashamed of the gospel, because it is the power of God for the salvation of everyone who believes: first for the Jews, then for the Gentile. For in the gospel a righteousness from God is revealed, a righteousness that is by faith from first to last, just as it is written: "The righteous will live by faith."
Romans 1:16-17

Introduction

What This Book Is and Is Not

Michael S. Horton

L ord Acton's famous remark, "Power tends to corrupt and absolute power corrupts absolutely," has become something of a cliché after a century of "the will to power" in the wake of the alleged
"death of God." Friedrich Nietszche, the German philosopher of the
last century, predicted this era and argued that from now on power,
not persuasion; ideology, not religious doctrine, would fill the vacuum left by the emptying of Christianity's meaning.

We moderns are clever—there's no mistaking that. Our
technological sophistication has created marvels of modern medicine and has taken us to the moon. Like the builders of the Tower of
Babel, we too live, think, and speak as though "nothing will be impossible" for us. Even in the Christian world, there is a tremendous
spirit of self-confidence and pride: our church growth projects will at
last usher in the kingdom; or we will do it by performing signs and
wonders, what some proponents even refer to as "magic," or perhaps
we will rule by taking over the public institutions and exerting political, social, and economic pressure on the enemies of Christ; others
may wish to achieve power through tapping the inner resources of
the individual through the latest offerings of pop-psychology; some
will demonstrate this self-confidence by reinforcing personality

MICHAEL S. HORTON is the founder and president of Christians United for Reformation
(CURE), Anaheim, California, and is currently engaged in doctoral studies at Wycliffe Hall,
Oxford, England.

cults, legalistic restrictions, and peer pressure; finally, some will appeal to the power of fear and paranoia to gather followings, as if they had an inside track cn such divine secrets as the date of our Lord's return. Evangelical gatherings are often marked by a certain smugness about the uniqueness of our generation in God's plan.

The culture is bathing in the quest for power—power ties, power lunches—as the naked and unashamed obsession with personal and corporate power marginalizes competing motivations. Similarly, the church now advocates "power ministries," "power evangelism," and "power healing." A popular group of Christian weight lifters even travels from arena to arena breaking blocks of ice, breaking chains, and tearing phone books in half as a testimony to their central gospel: Christ as a power-source. The group is called The Power Team.

Power has become a familiar word in Christian circles. Unlike the small church down the street we used to go to, the new megachurch in a neighboring town has *powerful programs,* and its buildings often compete with corporate office buildings for the impressive architecture of power. Or, the healing service last week was *powerful:* we all felt the power. Or, we can hear brothers and sisters refer to another form of power: "We're really gaining power in Washington. We're a powerful voting block."

It is quite possible that most readers will find in this something that hits too close for comfort. However, it is not our purpose to merely cast stones in this book. In fact, every section concludes with a "Better Way" chapter, offering constructive solutions.

Every issue we address in this volume is a matter for debate within the Body of Christ. None of the authors suggests that those who support Christian political activism, the signs and wonders movement, the church growth movement, the therapeutic movement, or sensational or potentially authoritarian schemes, are non-Christians or enemies of the faith masquerading as disciples of Christ.

So, the issues are of immense importance (it's not just a matter of different *emphases*), but are to be addressed in a spirit of humility, reconciliation, and love of both the truth and of our brothers and sisters. In fact, none of us suggests that there is nothing to learn from these various movements. Speaking for myself, I know that my own Christian faith and life would be the poorer without interaction with some of my close friends who are charismatic, for instance. Likewise, I have admired the zeal of some church growth leaders I have met. It is refreshing to see Christians talking about real-life political, economic, and social issues as though being "salt" and "light" is actually possible. And yet, we seem to have rushed headlong into the lure of it all, often leaving important doctrines behind—no time for theological reflection in the last days. And yet it was the challenge of the last days that led the apostles and our Lord to warn us to be particularly careful about telling the truth.

This book, therefore, is not meant to draw lines in the sand between true and false brethren. Rather, its goal is to point out what we believe to be serious distractions from the core mission and message of the Christian faith.

Although there will be the expected documentation for specific claims or criticisms, we are looking at movements and emphases that seem to raise concerns. At the outset, I will admit that we are painting with wide brushes—in places, *brooms*—in order to make a point! This is because we are analyzing movements within evangelicalism rather than clear denials of the Christian message.

As our perceived concern is for movements *within* evangelicalism, the tone is meant to create an atmosphere of thought-provoking reflection and debate. We do not presume to offer official declarations or final answers, but we hope that this book will be a starting point for serious discussion. It is our hope that others will write more detailed volumes in the future, as each section in this book could easily become a major subject on its own.

Through the following pages we will argue that the goal of Christian mission is not success, but faithful witness; not power, but proclamation; not technique, but truth; not method, but message. We will argue that Christ's Person and work are being obscured by ideology, subjectivism, pragmatism, legalism, carnal conservatism, and carnal innovationism. Let the following serve as the guide for where we intend to take the reader.

POWER POLITICS

Pagan morality, the sort endorsed by Plato, Aristotle, Virgil, and Cicero, can establish the kingdoms of this world, but never the kingdom of God. Such civic morality can even be informed by Christian revelation, but even that is not the same as proclamation.

The kingdom of Christ is not advanced by the legislation of ideology but by the proclamation of theology, namely, the gospel of God's grace in Christ. When moralism replaces confidence in the saving work of Christ, the church not only fails to transform the moral life of the culture, it actually serves the process of secularization by leaving its central affirmations and settling for the moral victories of paganism when the greater spiritual victory of Christianity appears to them beyond reach.

Not unlike Adam and Eve's fig leaves, that sort of "righteousness" may paper over personal or national shame, but it cannot save and it cannot extend the kingdom of God. One would not be surprised if the average person on the street regarded the basic message of evangelical Christianity in terms of moral legislation, narrow political agendas, and national self-righteousness.

But that does not mean that Christians ought not to be engaged in civic life. It is even worthwhile to engage in political and social improvement as "salt" and "light," and as part of our command to love our neighbor, but as important as our involvement in civic life is, that is not how the kingdom comes. Therefore, we can look after our neighbor's interests without ulterior motives, as though we thought that the only ends worth mounting campaigns for we those in which the interests of evangelicals were at stake. By replacing the core of Christian activity with its theological center, we will not only be better equipped to proclaim the gospel but will also have a rich reservoir of spiritual understanding in order to interpret areas of concern and involvement with greater wisdom and maturity.

POWER EVANGELISM

Spiritual warfare is real but often misunderstood these days. If the evangelical determination was "to know nothing among you but Christ and Him crucified" (1 Corinthians 2:2, NASB), the new central proclamation for many seems to be "Our struggle is not against flesh and blood, but against the rulers, against the authorities, against the powers of this dark world and against the spiritual forces of evil in the heavenly realms" (Ephesians 6:12, NIV). And yet, even this spiritual warfare Paul describes in Ephesians is not a matter of anything more than proclamation and defense of the gospel of Christ crucified. This is clear when the weapons and armor are described: the belt of truth, the breastplate of righteousness, feet prepared "with the readiness that comes from the gospel of peace" (v. 15). "In addition to all this, take up the shield of faith, with which you can extinguish the arrows of the evil one." Finally, "Take the helmet of salvation and the sword of the Spirit, which is the word of God" (v. 15). Earnest prayer and vigilance is added. Notice that this warfare is not vague; it centers on truth and error rather than a mere display of force in "power encounters." The devil wishes to destroy the gospel, and the church is fighting to preserve and proclaim it until it buries the demonic fortresses in obscurity. No weapon is offered here for the saint's use that compares with the sort of "spiritual warfare" one often sees in rallies in which the demon of this or the spirit of that is "bound." Paul is simply using a metaphor of earthly battle to represent the real spiritual battle for the success of the gospel.

As Satan is "the father of lies" (John 8:44), we are to arm ourselves with truth, not experience. As marvelous and assuring as Christian experience often is, it can be easily duplicated by the devil, and its subjectivity renders it vulnerable in battle. We are to take up our defense with righteousness, presumably in terms of justification (the declaration that we are righteous because of the imputation of Christ's holiness) and sanctification (the process of growing in personal righteousness because of the impartation of Christ's holiness). In other words, if we offer our own righteousness as a defense against Satan's accusations, we stand condemned already. We are further commanded to take "the helmet of salvation and the sword of the Spirit, which is the word of God" (Ephesians 6:17); again, these weapons are objective and external, not subjective and internal. Salvation, not mere signs of spiritual power, sends the demonic community into confusion and disarray.

Therefore, the war is to be viewed in terms of a battle for the truth of the gospel, not primarily as a cosmic, dualistic struggle between the "dark side" and "good side" of the force. Warfare of the latter type has more in common with pagan mysticism and popular science fiction than with biblical faith. "The god of this age has blinded the minds of unbelievers, *so that they cannot see the light of the gospel* of the glory of Christ, who is the image of God. For we do not preach ourselves, but Jesus Christ as Lord" (2 Corinthians 4:4-5, italics added).

POWER GROWTH

Church growth, in Acts 2, is a matter of spreading the word about the great acts of God in Christ for our redemption. One searches in vain for a successful marketing strategy behind the amazing spread of the Christian faith in Acts.

After Pentecost the very next report is Peter's sermon, and it was not a "Do I Have a God for You!" sermon, either: "This man was handed over to you by God's set purpose and foreknowledge; and you, with the help of wicked men, put him to death by nailing him to the cross. . . . God has raised this Jesus to life, and we are all witnesses of the fact" (Acts 2:23, 32). Even the coming of the Holy Spirit and the wonder of Pentecost was explained as the empowerment of the people of God for their great task of proclaiming that "God has made this Jesus, whom you crucified, both Lord and Christ" (v. 36). Thus, the believers "devoted themselves to the apostles' teaching and to the fellowship, to the breaking of bread and to prayer" (v. 42).

Imagine average people, many without any advanced education, station, or wealth, sitting up until all hours of the night learning theology! Whenever they met, they broke bread, which is usually taken as a reference to Holy Communion. How many strategies, programs, "celebrations," and church activities today have replaced the unparalleled experience of the true fellowship we share together with Christ at the Lord's Table? And as for prayer, compare the amount of time given to prayer in our worship to the amount of time spent on announcements, entertainment, and special events. Imagine what would happen if the millions of evangelicals in America alone who claim to be "born again" became devoted once again to the apostles' teaching!

We are agreed that the purpose of the church is not to grow but to proclaim Christ, and as we do that, we should expect the same success the Holy Spirit gave the early church: "And the *Lord* added to their number daily those who were being saved" (v. 47, italics added).

POWER WITHIN

Psychological well-being depends significantly on facing the truth about ourselves and coming to terms with our guilt and shame, turning to Christ for our acceptance and freedom from a guilty conscience.

Self-justification is not only the road to eternal loss, it is a shabby substitute for relieving guilt and anxiety here and now. We know that those who offer congregations and consumers shallow assertions such as "I'm OK and you're OK" are like the false prophets of Jeremiah's day "who dress the wound of [God's] people as though it were not serious. 'Peace, peace,' they say, when there is no peace. . . . The word of the Lord is offensive to them; they find no pleasure in it. . . . [They] do not even know how to blush. So they will fall among the fallen" (Jeremiah 6:14, 10, 15).

When secular psychologists such as Karl Menninger ask the church, "Whatever became of sin?" we think it's time to ask some tough questions.

POWER PREACHERS

Authority is derived from the Word, not from the office. If a minister is not faithful to the Word and to the gospel it proclaims, he is a usurper. There is no such thing as "the Lord's anointed," preachers who are above the Word with whose protection they are entrusted. Any claim to divine authority for commands, expectations, "revelations," or guidance that are not stated in the pages of Holy Scripture are marks of a spiritual tyrant and Pharisee.

The tyranny we see in legalism, carnal conservatism, and purveyors of paranoia (regarding the New Age conspiracy, "secular humanism," fear-inspired devotion to modern "prophets," or specially gifted teachers) must be replaced with the clear vision of One who "did not come to be served, but to serve, and to give his life a ransom for many" (Matthew 20:28).

In short, this book is a warning about the uncritical adoption of paths to power that seem for a time to lead to greater spiritual vitality but in reality lead away from the One who is the Way, the

Truth, and the Life. It issues a challenge to believers to refocus their gaze upon the only worthy obsession—"Christ and him crucified."

So read on, carefully and in the spirit of the Bereans, who were not content to accept even the apostles' testimony if it conflicted with Holy Scripture. May God use this volume to His glory and the greater good of His church.

Soli Deo Gloria

PART 1

POWER POLITICS

"Not by might nor by power, but by my Spirit," says the Lord Almighty.

Zechariah 4:6

Jesus said, "My kingdom is not of this world. If it were, my servants would fight to prevent my arrest by the Jews. But now my kingdom is from another place."

"You are a king, then!" said Pilate.

"You are right in saying I am a king. In fact, for this reason I was born, and for this I came into the world, to testify to the truth. Everyone on the side of truth listens to me."

John 18:36-37

POWER POLITICS

1

The Power Illusion

Charles W. Colson

Our culture's drive for power has captivated even many well-meaning believers—particularly as it touches on the political arena. In the first half of this chapter I want to address the lure of power and position, and in the second we will turn our attention to specific questions concerning evangelical political involvement.

John Naisbitt observed in *Megatrends* that significant movements begin from the bottom up, not from the top down.[1] Truly important changes in culture begin not from officials or celebrities, but through ordinary people. Every person can—and should—seek to make a difference in his or her corner of the world by personally helping those in need.

Beyond this, some people are called to work through government structures and by political means to bring Christian influence into the culture. Those who do, however, need to be forewarned: the everyday business of politics is power, and power can be perilous for anyone.

I learned about the perils of power firsthand. Within a short time after I came to the White House as a presidential aide, my brusque get-it-done-at-all-costs approach won the favor of Richard

Adapted from chapters 19 and 22 of *Kingdoms in Conflict* (New York and Grand Rapids: William Morrow and Zondervan Publishing House), by Charles Colson. © 1987 by Charles Colson. Reprinted by permission of William Morrow and Company, Inc., Publishers, New York.

CHARLES W. COLSON is founder and chairman of Prison Fellowship.

Nixon, and I began to work directly with him. With that kind of clout I had little difficulty rearranging several Secret Service agents and secretaries so that I could occupy the office immediately next to the president's.

Though the evidence of my change in status was visible in the attitude of my visitors when they realized that the president himself was just on the other side of the wall, the move was symbolic of something much more important. It meant I had passed an invisible divide. I was now *inside.* A *Newsweek* feature article heralded my arrival with the news that I was now on the top of every Washington hostess's guest list (ironic, since I never attended parties) and that the mere mention of my name "makes the tensions come in like sheet rain."[2] In Washington that means power.

In *The Masters,* British novelist C. P. Snow tells the story of a man who chooses not to be king but kingmaker, the ultimate achievement power affords.[3] Snow might well have been writing about me.

I entered government believing that public office was a trust, a duty. Gradually, imperceptibly, I began to view it as a holy crusade; the future of the republic, or so I rationalized, depended upon the president's continuation in office. But whether I acknowledged it or not, equally important was the fact that my own power depended on it.

Although power may begin as a means to an end, it soon becomes the end itself. Having witnessed Watergate from the inside, I can attest to the wisdom of Lord Acton's well-known adage: Power corrupts; absolute power corrupts absolutely.

It is crucial to note, however, that it is power that corrupts, not power that is corrupt. It is like electricity. When properly handled, electricity provides light and energy; when mishandled it destroys. God has given power to the state to be used to restrain evil and maintain order. It is the use of power, whether for personal gain or for the state's ordained function, that is at issue.

The problem of power is not limited to public officials, of course. It affects all human relationships, from the domineering parent to the bullying boss to the manipulative spouse to the pastor who plays God. It is also wielded effectively by the seemingly weak who manipulate others to gain their own ends. The temptation to abuse power confronts everyone, including people in positions of spiritual authority.

The much-publicized corruption of some television evangelists several years ago can easily be traced to an inability to handle power. It's a heady business to run worldwide ministries, multi-million dollar television shows, or wealthy amphitheater churches. Leaders who rise to prominence in the religious world are placed on the precarious pedestal of Christian celebrity. When the celebrity is magnified a million times over by the electron tube, the dangers of falling increase dramatically.

Take the case of Jim and Tammy Bakker. When I first visited their ministry in 1976, their shoestring operation was housed in an old building. They were, I was convinced, sincerely concerned with reaching others. A year later I was invited to their new, modern facilities and was immediately struck by the change in their demeanor. I did not return.

I witnessed the same phenomenon with one of the country's most popular daytime interviewers. The first time I was a guest on his show, before he had begun to soar in the ratings game, the interviewer was humble, keenly interested in the subject, well-prepared, and congenial. Two years later, when this man had become the sensation of the television world, he breezed into the room flanked by obsequious aides, was woefully unconcerned with what his guests had to say, and was arrogant and rude on the air—to the delight of his audience.

It's ludicrous for any Christian to believe that he or she is the worthy object of public worship; it would be like the donkey carrying Jesus into Jerusalem believing the crowds were cheering and laying down their garments for him. But the perks and public adoration accompanying television exposure are enough to inflate nearly anyone's ego. This leads to the self-indulgent use of power some have dubbed the "Imelda Marcos syndrome," which reasons, "Because I'm in this position, I have a right to whatever I want," with total selfishness and disregard for others. Power is like saltwater; the more you drink the thirstier you get.

POWER VERSUS SERVANT LEADERSHIP

The lure of power can separate the most resolute of Christians from the true nature of Christian leadership, which is service to others. It's difficult to stand on a pedestal and wash the feet of those below. It was this very temptation of power that led to the first sin. Eve was tempted to eat from the tree of knowledge to be like God and acquire power reserved for Him. "The sin of the Garden was the sin of power," says Quaker writer Richard Foster.[4] Power has been one of Satan's most effective tools from the beginning, perhaps because he lusts for it so himself. Milton wrote of Lucifer in *Paradise Lost*, "To reign is worth ambition, though in hell. Better to reign in hell than to serve in heaven."[5]

In the process of announcing the kingdom and offering redemption from the Fall, Jesus Christ turned conventional views of power upside down. When His disciples argued over who was the greatest, Jesus rebuked them. "The greatest among you should be like the youngest, and the one who rules like the one who serves," He said (Luke 22:26). Imagine the impact His statement would make in the back rooms of American politicians or in the carpeted boardrooms of big business—or, sadly, in some religious empires.

Jesus was as good as His words. He washed His own followers' dusty feet, a chore reserved for the lowliest servant of first-century Palestine. A king serving the mundane physical needs of His subjects? Incomprehensible. Yet servant leadership is the heart of Christ's teaching. "Whoever wants to be first must be slave of all" (Mark 10:44).

His was a revolutionary message to the class-conscious culture of the first century, where position and privilege were entrenched, evidenced by the Pharisees with their reserved seats in the synagogue, by masters ruling slaves, and by men dominating women. It is no less revolutionary today in the class-conscious cultures of the East and West where power, money, fame, and influence are idolized in various forms.

The Christian understanding of power is that it is found most often in weakness. This paradox has been a thorn in the flesh of tyrants. The Christian teaching that man is vulnerable to the temptations of power has also caused democracies and free nations to build restraints and balances of power into their structures.

The most important restraint on power, however, is a healthy understanding of its true source. When power in the conventional sense is relinquished, one discovers a much deeper power. Prisoners often discover this, as did Aleksandr Solzhenitsyn. In his memoirs of the gulag, Solzhenitsyn wrote that as long as he was trying to maintain some pitiful degree of worldly power in his situation—control of food, clothing, schedule—he was constantly under the heel of his captors. But after his conversion, when he accepted and surrendered to his utter powerlessness, then he became free of even his captors' power.

The apostle Paul said, "My power is made perfect in weakness," and concluded, "When I am weak, then I am strong" (2 Corinthians 12:9-10). And throughout Scripture God reveals a special compassion for the powerless: widows, orphans, prisoners, and aliens. Though the message of the kingdom of God offers salvation for all who repent and believe, God does not conceal His disdain for those so enamored of their own power that they refuse to worship Him or to acknowledge His delight in the humble.

A culture that exalts power and celebrity, that worships success, dismisses such words as nonsense. Strong individuals rely on their own resources—which will never, ultimately speaking, be enough—but the so-called weak person knows his or her own limits and needs, and thus depends wholly on God. Perhaps this is why God so often confounds the wisdom of the world by accomplishing His purposes through the powerless and His most powerful work through human weakness.

I first learned this in prison. When the frustration of my helplessness seemed greatest, I discovered God's grace was more than sufficient. And after my imprisonment I could look back and see how God used my powerlessness for His purposes. What He has chosen for my most significant witness was not my triumphs or victories, but my defeat.

Similarly, Prison Fellowship's work in the prisons has been effective not because of any power we may have as an organization, but because of the powerlessness of those we serve. During an unforgettable trip to Peru in 1984, for example, I visited Lurigancho, the largest prison in the world. There seven thousand inmates, including a number of terrorists, were crowded in abysmal conditions: hatred, hostility, and despair seeped out of the cellblocks. Yet within the darkness of Lurigancho is a thriving Christian community—men who have found Christ and experienced renewed hearts and minds.

After visiting with these brothers, I went directly from the prison to meet with a number of government officials in downtown Lima. Covered with prison dust and marked with the sweaty embraces of Christian prisoners, I addressed these officials at the highest level of government—and they listened intently. Had I gone to Peru specifically to meet with the key government leadership, I would have likely been stymied. They wanted to meet me not because of any power or influence I had, but because of our work in the prisons. They knew that, in the chaos of Lurigancho, Prison Fellowship was doing something to bring healing and restoration. Therefore, they were eager to listen to our recommendations, ready to discuss a biblical view of justice and prison issues. Whatever authority I had in speaking to these powerful men came not from my power but from serving the powerless. I have experienced this in country after country. It is the paradox of real power.

Christian activists who lobby for various evangelical causes run the risk at times of violating this principle by seeking power in the conventional, worldly way. How many unbelievers think first of the Christian political activist as a servant of the weak and powerless?

Nothing distinguishes the kingdoms of man from the kingdom of God more than their diametrically opposed views of the exercise of power. One seeks to control people, the other to serve people; one promotes self, the other prostrates self; one seeks prestige and position, the other lifts up the lowly and despised. Sometimes it is not even for our own personal use that we seek power, but for the prestige and position of a very worthy cause—the advance of the kingdom of God itself. And yet, if that advance is pursued along the lines of power followed by the kingdoms of this world, the kingdom we build may end up being our own.

None of this means that Christians cannot use power. In positions of leadership, especially in government institutions to which God has specifically granted the power of the sword, the Christian can do so in good conscience. But the Christian uses power with a different motive and in different ways: not to impose his or her personal will over others but to preserve God's plan for order and justice for all. Those who attempt the biblical view of servant leadership treat power as a humbling delegation from God, not as a right to control others.

Moses offers a great role model. Though he had awesome power and responsibility as the leader of 2 million Israelites, he was described in Scripture as "a very humble man, more humble than anyone else on the face of the earth" (Numbers 12:3). He led by serving—intervening before God on his people's behalf, seeking God's forgiveness for their rebellion, and caring for their needs above his own.

The challenge for the Christian in a position of influence is to follow the example of Moses rather than fulfill German philosopher Friedrich Nietzsche's prophecy concerning the "will to power" as the motivating force of twentieth-century life. In doing so the citizen of Christ's kingdom has an opportunity to offer light to a world often shrouded by the dark pretensions of a devastating succession of power-mad tyrants.

EVANGELICALS AND THE POLITICAL SOLUTION

After describing the illusion of power promised by this world, it is important that we make more of an application to the contemporary obsession some evangelicals seem to share with the power-brokers of Washington.

Christians *can* make a difference. But in recent years many Christians have urged a more direct approach for bringing needed social change than the service to the community that marked earlier evangelical involvement. And what is that more direct approach? Simply elect Christians to political office. One spokesman has even suggested a religious version of affirmative action; if, for example, 24 percent of the people are born again, then at least 24 percent of the officeholders should be born again. Others have argued that Christians should "take dominion" over government, with those in public office speaking "for God as well as for the American people."[6]

On the surface this shortcut might seem to some an appealing answer to America's declining morality. It is, however, simplistic and dangerous triumphalism. To suggest that electing Christians to public office will solve all public ills is not only presumptuous and theologically questionable, it is also untrue.

Today's misspent enthusiasm for political solutions to the moral problems of our culture arises from a distorted view of both politics and Christianity—too low a view of the power of a sovereign God and too high a view of the ability of man. The idea that human systems, reformed by Christian influence, pave the road to the Kingdom—or at least, to revival—has the same utopian ring that one finds in Marxist literature. It also ignores the consistent lesson of history that shows that laws are most often reformed as a result of powerful spiritual movements (not vice versa). I know of no case where a spiritual movement was achieved by passing laws.

In addition, history puts the lie to the notion that just because one is devout one will be a just and wise ruler. Take the nineteenth-century leader who forged a unified Germany from a cluster of minor states. Otto von Bismarck-Schönhausen was a committed Christian who regularly read the Bible, spoke openly of his devotion to God, and claimed divine guidance in response to prayer. "If I were no longer a Christian, I would not serve the king another hour," he once declared.[7]

Yet Bismarck was also the ruthless architect of *Deutschland Uber Alles* (Germany Over All), a chauvinistic worldview that laid the foundation for two world wars. Historians describe Bismarck as a Machiavellian master of political duplicity who specialized in blood and iron.

As we have said earlier, power can be just as corrupting—or confusing—to the Christian as to the non-Christian. And the results in some ways are more horrible when power corrupts men or women who believe they have a divine mandate. Their injustices are then committed in God's name. This is why an eminent conservative historian has suggested that "religious claims in politics should vary inversely with the power or prospects for power one has."[8]

It's a fair distinction: Prophets should make religious claims. Political leaders should not—otherwise they can become ayatollahs.

So the first test for public office should not be a spiritual one. The celebrated claim that "the ability to hear from God should be the number one qualification for the U.S. presidency"[9] is dangerously misguided. Politicians, like those in any other specialized field, should be selected on the basis of their qualifications and abilities *as well as* on their character. Even in Israel's theocracy, Jethro advised Moses to select "capable men . . . who fear God" to help in governing the Jewish nation (Exodus 18:21). Jethro's advice makes sense. If terrorists were to take control of an airport, would we want policemen who were merely devout Christians handling the situation, or would we choose those who had specialized training in hostage negotiations? Luther had it right when he said he would rather be ruled by a competent Turk than an incompetent Christian.

THE CHRISTIAN AS CITIZEN VERSUS OFFICE-HOLDER

The triumphalist mind-set also fails to make the crucial distinction between a Christian's function as a private citizen and as an officeholder. As private citizens, Christians are free to advocate their Christian view in any and every form. In America that is a fundamental constitutional right. Christian citizens should be active about their faith, striving by their witness to "Christianize" their culture—not by the force of the sword, but by the force of their ideas.

But Christians elected to public office acquire a different set of responsibilities. Now they hold the power of the sword, which God has placed with government to preserve order and maintain justice. Now they act not for themselves but for all whom they serve. For this reason they cannot use their office to evangelistically "Christianize" their culture. Their duty is to ensure justice and religious liberty for all citizens of all beliefs.

This does not mean they can compromise their faith or their first allegiance to God; they should speak freely of their Christian faith and witness Christian values in their lives. But they cannot use their offices to seek a favored position for Christianity or the church.

A Christian writer has summed this up well: "The 'Christian state' is one that gives no special public privilege to Christian citizens but seeks justice for all as a matter of public principle."[10]

At the turn of the century a towering Dutch theologian, Abraham Kuyper, was elected prime minister of the Netherlands. His opponents voiced fears of theocratic oppression. Instead, his administration was a model of tolerance and public pluralism as Kuyper affirmed proportional representation, that the legitimate rights of all be fully represented.[11] Kuyper left office as the most celebrated Dutch statesman of his time (or since). If Christians today understood this distinction between the role of the private Christian citizen and the Christian in government, they might sound less like medieval crusaders. If secularists understood correctly the nature of Christian public duty they would not fear, but welcome, responsible Christian political involvement.

THE DANGERS OF UTOPIAN ACTIVISM

But Christians should not unwarily plunge into the political marshlands, thinking they will drain the swamp.

There are traps. I know; I used to set them.

My first assignment as President Nixon's special counsel was to develop strategies for his 1972 reelection. A tough task. He had been elected by only a small margin in the three-way 1968 election against Hubert Humphrey and George Wallace. Not only was the Republican party a minority, but Nixon had inherited an unpopular war and a hostile press. Added to this, he himself projected something less than a charismatic presence for the television image-makers just beginning to dominate politics.

My first memorandum to the president outlined what I called "The Middle America Plan": write off the minorities, but reach out to traditional supporters in business and farm groups; pick off some conservative labor unions; cultivate Southern evangelicals; build a new coalition among Catholic, blue-collar voters of the Northeast and Midwest. It was cynical, pragmatic, and good politics, designed to exploit whatever allies would let us cultivate them. Nixon loved it.

The memo was returned a few days later with his markings all over the margins: "Right. . . . Do it. . . . I agree."

I took all kinds of groups to see the president, from friendly cattlemen to sophisticated educators enraged over budget cuts or the Vietnam war. It was always the same. In the reception room they would rehearse their angry lines and reassure one another, "I'll tell him what's going on. He's got to do something." When the aide came to escort us in, they'd set their jaws and march toward the door. But once it swung open, the aide announcing, "The president will see you," it was as if they had suddenly sniffed some intoxicating fragrance. Most became almost self-conscious about even stepping on the plush blue carpet on which was sculpted the Great Seal of the President of the United States. And Mr. Nixon's voice and presence —like any president's—filled the room.

Invariably, the lions of the waiting room became the lambs of the Oval Office. Ironically, none were more compliant than the religious leaders. Of all people, they should have been the most aware of the sinful nature of man and the least overwhelmed by pomp and protocol. I frequently scheduled meetings for evangelical groups, denominational councils, and individual religious leaders. Henry Kissinger's briefings in the Roosevelt Room across the hall from the Oval Office were always a big hit.

The church services Nixon scheduled most Sundays for the East Room provided great opportunities as well. To select the preacher, we determined who would give us the greatest impact— politically, that is, not spiritually. At the time I was a nominal Christian at best and had no way to judge the spiritual. And there were always two hundred or more seats to be filled, tickets that were like keys to the political kingdom. I could give many similar examples of how easily duped some Christian leaders were by the lure of power.

I am not advocating that religious groups or leaders boycott the White House or the palaces and parliaments of the world. That's where the political action is, and Christians need to influence policies for justice and righteousness. That is in the best biblical tradition of Jeremiah, Amos, Micah, Daniel, and a host of others. But Christians (and others as well) need to do so with eyes open, aware of the snares. C. S. Lewis wrote that "the demon inherent in every [political] party is at all times ready enough to disguise himself as the Holy Ghost."[12] Tolstoy made a similar point: "Governments, to have a rational foundation for the control of the masses, are obliged to pretend that they are professing the highest religious teachings known to man."[13]

Consider several of the most dangerous pitfalls awaiting the unwary.

THREE PITFALLS OF POLITICIZATION

The first is that the church will become just another special-interest group. When President Reagan was challenged by the press during the 1980 campaign for mixing religion and politics by attending a meeting of the Religious Right activists, he responded that the church was like any other special-interest group, after all—like a union, for example.[14] Reagan was refreshingly candid, but dead wrong.

A second danger is that politics can be like the proverbial tar baby. Christian leaders who are courted by political forces may soon begin to overestimate their own importance. The head of one large international relief agency mistakenly came to believe that heads of state welcomed him because of who he was rather than what he represented. It wasn't long before his work and his personal life failed to measure up to his delusions of power. He left his family and was eventually removed from his position—after doing great harm to the cause he had served for much of his life.

A side effect of this delusion is that rather than lose their access to political influence, some church leaders have surrendered their independence. "If I speak out against this policy," they reason, "I won't get invited to dinner and my chances to minister will be cut off." Although such rationalizing is understandable, the result is exactly the opposite; they keep their place but lose their voice and thus any possibility of holding government to account.

In this way the gospel becomes hostage to the political fortunes of a particular movement. This is the third and perhaps most dangerous snare. Both liberals and conservatives have made the mistake of aligning their spiritual goals with a particular political agenda.

One Christian New Right leader, when asked what would happen if the Democrats won the 1988 US election, said, "I don't know what will happen to us."[15] After the 1980 election, a Methodist bishop wrote, "The blame [for Reagan's victory] ought not to be placed on all the vigor of the Right, but maybe on the weakness of saints." A better day will come, he said, "if the people of faith will be strengthened by defeat and address themselves to the new agenda which is upon us."[16] The implication was clear: If you disagreed with the bishop's partisan politics, you were not among "the people of faith." But this is done on both sides of the aisle.

Inevitably, this kind of political alignment compromises the gospel. German university professor Father James Schall writes, "All successful Christian social theory in the immediate future must be based on this truth: that religion be not made an instrument of political ideology."[17] Because it tempts one to water down the truth of the gospel, ideological alignment, whether on the left or right, accelerates the church's secularization.[18] Many German churches in the thirties allied themselves with the new nationalistic movement. One churchman even described the Nazis as a "gift and miracle of God."[19] It was the *confessing* (i. e., witnessing to the truth of the gospel) church, not the politically-minded church, that retained its orthodoxy and thus resisted the evils of Hitler's state.

Again, none of this means that Christians ought to remain aloof from political challenges. Christians will find themselves side by side with those who are not Christians, fighting for justice. In World War II, for example a devout Christian might have fought to stop the evil of Nazism and the Holocaust because he believed God commanded that the state is to restrain evil. Next to him in the same foxhole might have been a soldier fighting solely for national pride or honor. Both would have been shooting at the same enemy, but for different reasons.

Today Christians may find themselves suspect—I have experienced this myself—by the very people on whose side they are fighting. But that is the price they must pay to preserve their independence and not be beholden to any political ideological alignment.

Only a church free of any outside domination can be the conscience of society and, as Washington pastor Myron Augsburger has written, "hold government morally accountable before God to live up to its own claims."[20]

NOTES

1. John Naisbitt, *Megatrends: Ten New Directions Transforming Our Lives* (New York: Warner Books, 1983).
2. *Newsweek* (September 6, 1971), p. 16.
3. C. P. Snow, *The Master* (New York: Scribner's, 1982).
4. Richard J. Foster, *Money, Sex and Power* (New York: Harper & Row, 1985), p. 175.
5. John Milton, *Paradise Lost and Paradise Regained* (New York: New American Library, 1968), p. 54.
6. Quoted in *Christianity Today* (September 5, 1966), p. 54.
7. Vernon Grounds, "Authentic Piety," *The Other Side* 21, no. 7 (October 1985), pp. 56-57.
8. George Marsden, *Reformed Journal* (November 1986), p. 3.
9. Quoted in *Christianity Today* (September 5, 1986), p. 54.
10. James Skillen, "The Bible, Politics and Democracy," a speech delivered at Wheaton College (November 7-8, 1985), p. 5.
11. McKendree Langley, *The Practice of Political Spirituality* (Jordan Station, Ontario: Paideia, 1984).
12. C. S. Lewis, *God in the Dock* (Grand Rapids: Eerdmans, 1970), p. 198.
13. Quoted by Colman McCarthy, "For Bennett, a Failing Grade in History," *Washington Post* (September 22, 1985), p. G-8.
14. Interview with Ronald Reagan after his meeting with the Religious Roundtable in Dallas (August 22, 1980).
15. *Time* (September 2, 1985), p. 58.
16. Kent R. Hill, "Religion and the Common Good: In Defense of Pluralism," *This World* 83 (Spring 1987), p. 83.
17. James V. Schall, "The Altar as the Throne," in Stanley Atkins and Theodore McConnels, eds., *Churches on the Wrong Road* (Chicago: Regnery, 1986), p. 233.
18. Donald Bloesch, *Crumbling Foundations* (Grand Rapids: Zondervan, 1984), p. 39.
19. Ibid., p. 40.
20. Myron Augsburger, *Christianity Today* (January 17, 1986), p. 21-I.

2

A Better Way:
Proclamation Instead of Protest

Kenneth A. Myers

In 1988, MCA/Universal released a film by director Martin Scorsese based on Nikos Kazantzakis's 1960 novel, *The Last Temptation of Christ*. Millions of American Christians were outraged, most of them without ever having seen the film, or knowing anyone who had. They protested bitterly that the film, its director, and its distributors were guilty of blasphemy, of shameless and public scorn toward the truth about Jesus.

Christian leaders who were spearheading the attack on the film saw the controversy in clear-cut terms. Their side, committed to holiness and truth, was victimized by the profit-hungry, cynical, and impious Hollywood establishment, with the rest of the mass media siding with their L.A. colleagues. Although that characterization has elements of truth, there are many ironies in *The Last Temptation* affair that make it a microcosmic example of the great temptation facing American evangelicals. Stated simply, that temptation is to become so preoccupied with power *in the service* of holiness and truth that holiness and truth become eclipsed. As more and more Christians succumb to that temptation, a further problem is increasingly evident: theology, the biblically rooted study of God, His Word, and His will, is gradually replaced by ideology, a system of assertions, theories, and goals that constitute a sociopolitical program.

KENNETH A. MEYERS is a producer for Berea Audio and was a producer and editor for National Public Radio.

Of course, it is not intrinsically wrong for Christians to secure and exercise temporal power, whether political, economic, or cultural. But Christians can too easily be tempted to throw their political or economic weight around when other responses would be more prudent. The dominant response by Christians to *The Last Temptation of Christ* (or at least the most well known and hence most public response) can be characterized as attempts at economic coercion, with the most publicized being an offer to raise millions of dollars to buy the film from MCA/Universal in order to burn the negative and all the prints.

Meanwhile, a group of evangelical leaders banded together and called for a boycott of all MCA-owned businesses, the principal intent again being to prevent the film from being seen. It was reported that a number of Christian leaders "are mounting a nationwide effort involving hundreds of Christian groups and costing millions of dollars to mobilize national pressure to stop the release of the film. They don't want impressionable viewers to receive a twisted view of Christ that will keep them from faith in the historic Jesus."

Some even suggested a boycott of the film's distributors. One boycott advocate argued: "We must send this unmistakable message to the producers and directors at Universal: 'If you continue to assault the Christian system of beliefs and undermine the morality of our children, it will cost you dearly at the box office. It will decrease the profits of every business you own for years to come.' There's nothing unchristian about that position in a free enterprise system."

At the time of the protest, I wondered whether such tactics might unwittingly attract more attention to the film than it could have hoped to gain on its own. The nature and style of the protests against the film were clearly intended to get maximum publicity; after all, a boycott is not at all effective unless it is well publicized. If it is true that consequences matter at least as much as intentions, and if the goal was to minimize the spiritual damage done by the film, its militant critics must be willing to entertain the question of whether they did more harm than good, whether more people saw the film than would have if a large public protest had *not* been staged.

The Hollywood sages know that there is no such thing as bad publicity, that being banned in Boston or anywhere else is much more likely to increase box office revenues than reduce them, and that the worst thing that can happen to a movie is to be ignored. I have since heard reports that MCA/Universal executives, fearing a huge loss on a boring and esoteric film, deliberately leaked advance information about it to Christians, hoping for exactly the sort of response they received. Whether or not that report was accurate, surely it is possible that evangelicals played right into the hands of the publicists for *The Last Temptation of Christ.*

If the goal of the Christian protestors was to remove stumbling blocks to acceptance of the gospel, one must ask whether the protests themselves did not produce a significant and unnecessary obstacle for many. "Here come the 'born againers,' again," one can hear the cynical pagan sigh. "All they ever do is tell us what we can't do, can't see, and can't believe. They just want to control everybody." That outcome might have been avoided if the organizers of the protest had been receptive to *proclamation* as an alternative to *power* and *pressure.*

An alternative way of preventing the film from becoming a source of deception would have been to *explain* to people who the real Jesus is. The most powerful activity of the church in this world is the proclamation of the truth, even if that brings persecution, as it has again and again throughout history. The apostle Paul *could* have organized a boycott of the craftsmen who manufactured the idols that populated the Athenian cityscape (Acts 17). His response, however, was more creative, in the fullest, life-giving sense of the word. In many ways, organizing political and economic pressure does not require nearly the amount of energy, time, and commitment to the long-term success of the gospel as being "prepared to give an answer [*apologia,* meaning "reasoned defense in a court of law"] to everyone who asks you to give the reason for the hope that you have" (1 Peter 3:15).

That approach was taken by a few Christians in the furor over *The Last Temptation of Christ.* Erwin Lutzer, pastor of Moody Memorial Church, in Chicago, wrote a clearly reasoned pamphlet about the movie (Moody Press; now out of print), but such efforts were few in number. I seriously doubt that many Christians agitated about the film gave greater attention to the history of the church's effort to formulate the biblical doctrine of the Person of Christ. How many adult Sunday school classes examined the debates that culminated in the definition of the council of Chalcedon in A.D. 451, or Anselm's argument about the God-man Jesus? I have little confidence that many Christians took the challenge this film represented seriously enough to gird up their intellectual loins to be able to explain to their neighbors or colleagues the significance of Jesus' humanity or the reality of His temptation *and* His sinlessness. It is not enough to cry, "Blasphemy!" when one does not understand exactly what is wrong and what true statements ought to be put in its place. Because of that doctrinal ignorance, many who publicly denounced the film as blasphemous were also thoroughly unsuccessful in explaining to the public what blasphemy *is,* the sad result being that blasphemy was interpreted as being "what those born-again Christians don't like."

Public exposition of biblical teaching on blasphemy, on what in God's character proscribes it, as well as the necessary explanations of why our beliefs require such strong conviction on the matter, could have accomplished much in demonstrating the seriousness with which Christians regard the Word of God, and might even have served as a means of conversion.

Long before Christians had time to become engaged in such creative responses, many Christian leaders were thinking about a civic and commercial reaction instead of a spiritual and ecclesiastical one. A fact sheet gave guidelines for participating in the "protest." The first injunction was to pray, but the second and more emphatic tactic was to create pressure. Late in the document, there was a three-line mention of organizing a prayer vigil and sharing "materials that give the true picture of Christ" at theaters that showed the film. But generally, the response was framed in terms of protest rather than proclamation. The goal of spiritual damage control was quickly understood to mean the exertion of economic pressure.

That may have been because most of the leaders of the protest were publicly identified with parachurch organizations, a fact that reflects one of the greatest weaknesses of modern evangelicalism. One cannot properly speak of "the evangelical church." It is a *movement,* and it tends to adopt the sort of strategies that all movements prefer, adding prayer at the top of the list to ensure a Christian identity.

When the church condemns blasphemy, it is acting in its authorized role as a unique spiritual agency established by Jesus Christ, a role that transcends political and cultural boundaries. The church represents God's interests, not its own. It is never merely one power bloc among other interest groups, jockeying for position in society. Whenever it has behaved as such, it has always lost sight of its ultimate ends.

When Christians band together to try to boycott a film or prevent its release, they are acting as (and will only be perceived as) members of one of the many special interest groups in the political order. Such an action is civic and commercial rather than spiritual and ecclesiastical. It is a resort to power over persuasion, to pressure over proclamation. The means it employs (press releases, demonstrations, and boycotts) are political and economic means. Although such actions may well be *permissible,* given the dynamics of our culture, they may not be *beneficial* (cf. 1 Corinthians 10:23), as matters spiritual and transcendent are all too easily obscured by a public relations firefight.

Many commentators at the time of *The Last Temptation*'s release noted the hypocrisy of Hollywood and its allies in championing the cause of a film so offensive to Christians, when it would never tolerate a comparable assault on the sensibilities of blacks, Jews, homosexuals, or other American "communities." Why can't Christians be accorded the same "sensitivity" the media and other cultural elites extend to various minority groups? That argument may be sound, but it is also unwise. For by defining Christians merely as an interest group (better suited to a movement than to a church), one thereby legitimizes opposition to Christianity by other interest groups. The truth of the gospel, including the truth about who Jesus was, is thus perceived as partisan instead of transcendent and universal. In that way, ideological concerns, the concerns of "our group," supplant transcendent, theological concerns. Such an approach unwittingly gives encouragement to those hardcore ideologues who maintain that religious matters are mere expressions of political and economic interests. Thus, the secular cynics simply see our commercial pressures as nothing more than an economic power grab.

THE BOYCOTT APPROACH

Frustrated with MCA/Universal's "callous indifference to the Christian faith," the Office of Information of the National Association of Evangelicals (NAE) eventually escalated the conflict by issuing a call to their constituency to boycott the purchase of videocassettes of another MCA/Universal release, the popular *E.T.: The Extraterrestrial*. The reasoning was that Universal's release of *Last Temptation* would be punished by taking it out on sales of *E.T.*

The National Association of Evangelicals explained the strategy: "If we can significantly impact the profits that MCA/Universal expects from the *E.T.* video, that should get the film industry's attention. We believe MCA/Universal should be held accountable for their intolerance and insensitivity. It's altogether appropriate for evangelicals to express their displeasure by refusing to purchase MCA/Universal products. . . . We are acting in the spirit of the First Amendment."[1] But, of course, so was MCA/Universal.

In adopting this strategy, the objective of condemning blasphemy was effectively preempted. Christians ought to denounce blasphemy not because it offends *them,* but because it offends *God.* By defining the issue in terms of intolerance and insensitivity, especially by appealing to "the spirit of the First Amendment" rather than the spirit of the first and second commandments, the NAE's statement made the *Last Temptation* affair into a matter of competing civil rights: under the First Amendment, Christians have the right to protest, but Martin Scorsese also has the right to make the film. Everyone is entitled to express an opinion, and Scorsese's opinion is procedurally as valid as the NAE's. By choosing the strategy of commercial coercion, the NAE put its position on equal footing with the heresy it detests.

The proposed boycott apparently had no effect on sales of *E.T.* What's more, I'm not sure that anyone really expected it to. Instead, it seems that evangelicals were eager to assert their rights as one of many pressure groups with offices lining Washington's K Street. That makes a *certain* sense, given the nature of American democracy. As columnist Charles Krauthammer observed at the time, "American pluralism works because of a certain deference that sects accord each other. And in part, deference means respecting special sensitivities, also known as taboos. In a pluralistic society it is a civic responsibility to take great care when talking publicly about things sacred to millions of fellow citizens."[2]

Not only does that strategy fit the requirements of civility in the American polity, it is entirely appropriate given the necessary theological limitations of parachurch groups. A parachurch group does not administer sacraments. It does not proclaim the Word of God with the binding authority that Christ has granted to the church of the apostles and prophets. A parachurch group serves the legitimate (but limited) end of representing the interests of its constituents in the civic realm. When its officers and representatives speak, they do not speak with the authority that Christ has given to the church, but as individual Christians and as representatives of an association. So it was fitting that the NAE, a parachurch group, adopted a strategy that emphasized a limited, civic goal: that of assuring political and social room for its constituency.

But here we should see how the *civic* goal of minimizing offense to a sector of the population easily overshadows the *spiritual* goal of prophetically proclaiming the truth regardless of the consequences. In other words, the dynamics of an ideology, of interest-group thinking, replaces the dynamics of theology, of thinking rooted in transcendent truth.

WHAT IF . . .

What would have happened if MCA/Universal held a press conference and announced their willingness to produce and distribute a film about Jesus that satisfied the evangelical market? Their decision is a combination of public- and profit-mindedness. The evangelical community takes the company up on its offer and uses the money raised to buy and burn *The Last Temptation of Christ* to finance instead a film based on the gospel of John. Two years later, the film premieres at a gala opening in Wheaton, Illinois. But the film's debut is tarnished in the press by reports of anti-Semitism in the script. The Anti-Defamation League and the American Jewish Committee strongly protest certain scenes in the film that are extremely offensive to Jews. As a result of the protests of the Jewish community, most theaters refuse to show the film.

It seems the script included much of the episode recorded in John 8, where Jesus confronts the Pharisees and challenges their identity as children of Abraham. "If you were Abraham's children, do the deeds of Abraham. But as it is, you are seeking to kill me, a man who has told you the truth, which I heard from God. This Abraham would not do. You are doing the deeds of your father. If God were your father, you would love me; for I proceeded forth and have come from God. But you are of your father the devil, and you want to do the desires of your father." And so on.

This movie would not meet Charles Krauthammer's criteria any more than *The Last Temptation* did. If you live by the boycott, you may die by the boycott. If you present yourself merely as one of many patches in the pluralist American crazy quilt, you must behave with the same decorum you require of others. If you try to use coercive economic means to prevent a false Messiah from being presented in 70 millimeter Dolby stereo, then you should not expect the economic freedom to present the true Messiah in cinematic glory, if *that* presentation is as offensive to some fellow citizens as Scorsese's presentation is to you.

As compelling as the case might be for Christians to adopt the tactics of Cesar Chavez, it seems that there are great risks in encouraging the perception that they are just another special interest group. Although one might respect the intentions of people who promote them, the use of boycotts in the name of Christ is always liable to distract attention from the prophetic, authoritative proclamation of truth and repudiation of error that is the first duty of the church of Jesus Christ. It suggests that Christians are to be identified essentially as part of a political movement, rather than as part of a spiritual body.

Some Christians confronting our culture have adopted the slogan of "taking every thought captive for Christ." They rely on that slogan as a mandate for the establishment of coercive mechanisms that prevent the public display of unchristian thinking. But that slogan is only a partial quotation of Paul, who spoke of "taking every thought captive to *the obedience* of Christ." The captivity Paul has in view is not cultural hegemony, but repentance that produces obedience. It is achieved not by political coercion, but by the power of the Spirit. Earlier in that passage, Paul also noted that "though we walk in the flesh, we do not war according to the flesh, for the weapons of our warfare are not of the flesh."

If the tactics of the parachurch dominate Christian activity as it confronts a post-Christian culture, protest and politicking will loom larger *in the public mind* than the proclamation of the church. If public protest gives the impression that Christians are principally concerned about power and about their own standing in society and in the political order, it will become that much more difficult to take thoughts captive to the obedience of Jesus Christ. The *E.T.* boycott attempted to render judgment on MCA/Universal by a jury of angry consumers. That is a fine way to distract New York and Hollywood executives from contemplating a judgment that will render all profit and loss statements meaningless.

WHEN IDEOLOGY REPLACES THEOLOGY

The reaction to *The Last Temptation of Christ* is a relatively minor matter, more a missed opportunity than a horrifying scandal. My critique is in no way a *defense* of the film. But that I felt compelled to write that sentence might be a signal that the dynamics of movement are ever-present among evangelicals. Movements succeed by maintaining solidarity and are not friendly to reflective attention to nuance, to the statement of exceptions to generalities, or to criticism within the ranks. Instead of judging one's orthodoxy by his or her understanding of the Person and work of Christ (theology), the movement mentality judges orthodoxy by one's position on a particular policy or ideological principle. Hence I had to add the disclaimer, making clear that I was not defending the film.

But what happens when, within a Christian movement, one believer feels compelled to raise theologically based objections to some action or statement made within the movement? I have heard Christian people say, for example, that it is unwise to raise theologically based (i.e., biblically based) criticism of Operation Rescue because "they're on our side." I suspect that such sentiments are common within the pro-life movement, which often depicts itself as a Christian movement. But isn't that to allow ideology to replace theology? Doesn't that involve the eclipse of truth by the pursuit of power?

Christian journalists have been known to fabricate "facts" in the interest of making a story more compelling, more motivating, more powerful to Christian readers—in other words, to build the momentum of their movement. Some Christian magazines have been known to censor stories that depict Christian movement leaders in an unflattering light, and writers for Christian publications have been disciplined for reporting indisputable facts about Christian celebrities that made them look bad. Of course, there is no excuse for uncharitable scandal-mongering, and there might be theologically compelling reasons for a Christian reporter to maintain silence about the subjects of their report. But Christian journalists should never distort the truth in the interest of maintaining the power of "our side."

In some ways, such a pragmatic devaluation of truth is not surprising. Within the evangelical subculture, there has always been more concern with quick, practical solutions than with careful theological definition; more emphasis on personal testimonies than on apologetics; a tendency to interpret Christian experience in terms of a subjective "commitment to Christ" rather than as the life of faith as an elected gift of a sovereign God. Within evangelicalism, there is more regard for extemporaneous prayer than for creeds and confessions, more respect for believers who are practical successes—such as Christian fullbacks or Christian rock stars or successful Christian businessmen—than for Christian thinkers.

So modern evangelicalism has always tended to be a subculture concerned more with doing than with knowing, or, in the language of the liberation theologians, with orthopraxis (that is, right practice) rather than with orthodoxy. Evangelicals have disagreed on the nature of the atonement, on the meaning of the sacraments, on whether or not one could lose one's salvation, on eschatology, and many other doctrines significant to the lives of individual believers and to the church. Yet they agreed that to be a good Christian meant that you didn't play cards, go to movies, or drink alcoholic beverages. Behavior patterns not even discussed in Scripture become more "the tie that binds" than belief systems that *are* the entire substance of Scripture. One is most trusted in evangelical leadership if he adheres to social, cultural, and political conservatism, regardless of whether of not he can define "justification," which, according to Martin Luther, was "the article by which the church stands or falls."

Writing in 1966, Addison Leitch warned of the dangers of avoiding sharp theological distinctions:

> Try the following exercise on any denomination and consider its relationship to its own creeds. What, for example, is a Presbyterian? . . . Either a Presbyterian is one who is loyal to the Westminster Confession or he is something else. If he is not loyal to that confession, in what way shall he be defined? The answer is usually as follows: "Don't put us in a theological straitjacket; let's not have theological witch-hunting." This kind of response I consider to be an "out" rather than an answer. But suppose we accept the freedom from definition as a principle. After all, the important thing is to be a Christian, not a Presbyterian. Very well, a Protestant or a Romanist Christian? Will not the attitude that refuses to draw lines between Presbyterians and Baptists or between Protestants and Romanists eventually blur the distinctions between Christians and Buddhists and Moslems? It will, and it does.[3]

Leitch was concerned about the erosion of theology because of a hollowing out of the theological center by liberalism or neo-orthodoxy. But the movement dynamics of evangelicalism could easily have the same effect.

It is one thing to *put aside* theological differences about sacraments, spiritual gifts, church order, or the nature of sanctification for the purpose of a joint evangelistic campaign. That is how modern evangelicalism has grown, whether through Billy Graham's ministry or through groups such as Campus Crusade, InterVarsity, or Young Life. But what has happened too often is that evangelical Christians have wrongly concluded that what one believes about sacraments, charismata, and other controversial issues does not matter (at all), that it is really more Christian not to have any opinion on such things. Thus, there is no sacrifice involved in putting aside theological differences for a common cause; doctrinal distinctives are simply treated with indifference.

Today people calling themselves evangelicals also disagree on more fundamental matters such as the reality of hell, the soteriological exclusivity of Christianity, the necessity of a substitutionary atonement, and the eternality of God, just to name a few of the next levels of biblical doctrines that are up for grabs. Just as long as one maintains *ideological* evangelicalism, *theological* evangelicalism may be set aside for practical reasons. Will the dynamics of the movement encourage agnosticism on these core matters, too? If so, what is to prevent the evangelical movement from becoming as theologically vacant as the liberalism it once denounced?

Among theological liberals, ideology replaced theology because of a failure of theological nerve. Once naturalistic presuppositions had eaten away the core of Christian truth, *something* had to replace theology if the theologians were to keep their jobs. As the promotion of social change replaced gospel proclamation and spiritual transformation as the raison d'être of the church, it was inevitable that some form of ideology, dressed up with a lot of traditional theological terms, would come to dominate liberal theological discourse. Liberation theology, rooted in Marxist ideology, was thus a very natural and almost necessary development of the social gospel.

But lest evangelicals gain any self-confidence from this folly, let them beware of following the same course of replacing theology with their ideology and politics with a thin coating of Bible words and traditional theological jargon. Of course, the agenda may be very different (since it is doubtful that evangelicals will be launching a campaign of Marxist revolution). The problem is not so much with the specifics of this or that political agenda, but with the subversion of theology by *any* ideology that elipses the Christian witness. One can already witness the extent to which theology is a less significant binding force among evangelicals today than it was even ten or twenty years ago. Increasingly, evangelicals unite around causes of one kind or another: hunger, abortion, pornography, offensive television, codependency. Of course there is nothing wrong with activism on such matters, but one must ask to what extent evangelicals of all political stripes are following the same route as advocates of the social gospel or of liberation theology, propelled not by the corrosive effects of naturalistic assumptions but by the taming necessities of movement building.

Peter Leithart, a Presbyterian pastor, has written that evangelicalism is "maintaining high political visibility" while it is "increasingly doctrinally pluralistic." The early church was accused of cannibalism and incest, because it took its sacramental life and its fellowship so seriously. "Today," writes Leithart,

> the world views the Church as an interest group, intent on seizing political power. That is certainly a gross distortion, but it tells us something important not only about the world's own obsessions, but also about the "face" that the Church is presenting to the world.
>
> By contrast, the ancient slander shows that pagans, if they knew anything at all about the Church, knew that the Church gathered to eat and drink the flesh and blood of her Savior and greeted one another with a kiss of peace. The world perceived the Church as a liturgical, not a political, community because the Church's public presence was primarily liturgical.[4]

Leithart suggests that the church will know it has recovered a proper sense of its mission when "the accusation of cannibalism regains currency."[5]

THE DEATH OF CHRISTENDOM

In addition to the dynamics of being a movement, a number of other factors are tempting evangelicals to replace theology with ideology. One of the most profound is the sense of loss at the death of Christendom, the rapid decline of Christianity as a force that shapes the culture. We are living, many have argued, in a post-Christian age. Our culture is a post-Christian culture. That doesn't mean that there are no longer many Christians; there may in fact be more believers now than ever before, especially in non-Western nations. What the term *post-Christian* refers to is the fact that Christianity no longer plays a dominant role in shaping social and cultural life. Christian beliefs and commitments no longer have the *public* presence they once did.

Christianity influenced "Christendom" by encouraging a worldview and institutions compatible with the dissemination of Christian truth. Thus everybody, even those who did not hold Christian convictions, lived under the canopy of Christian truth. Both general beliefs and convictions and specific ideas about specific things were understood within a Christian framework. In Christendom, questions that now occupy only technical theologians were of interest to all educated people. Once, in the West, kingdoms were founded, wars were fought, and people suffered martyrdom gladly for convictions that scarcely attract passing attention in modern culture. Crusades were part of the social life of the West and were at least as much an effort to convert the "barbarians and infidels" to Christendom (i.e., Western culture) as to Christianity. But by the late nineteenth century, forces that first built momentum in the Renaissance and in the Enlightenment had brought about the widespread conviction that the power of reason and science could solve all human problems. The West had become secularized. In Nietzsche's terms, God had died; that is, the *idea* of God no longer lived in the hearts and minds of the culture-shapers.

Most Christians, however, have continued about their lives and their ministries as if nothing had happened, and to this day, many Christians do not appreciate the revolutionary changes of the last two hundred years. People are still surprised when, for example, artists receive government grants to depict and display obscenity and blasphemy. Christians are baffled at the breakdown of families, at the rise of pornography, at the militancy of advocates of homosexuality.

But we should not be surprised at any of this. Nietszche warned us about it a century ago. As far as most of the culture is concerned, God *is* dead. Why should the culture be other than hostile to God and to His truth? The problem is a lot more complicated than a movie here or an abortion clinic there. Those are symptoms of a secularized culture, and just as the problem is complicated, so the solution must be long-term and serious. There must be a renewed commitment to Christian discipleship, particularly with regard to the life of the mind as we wrestle with the intellectual idols of our time. The church had well over a century to prepare for this moment, a time when the only cultures that act from religious motivations are Islamic. But instead of preparing, instead of praying and weeping for the awful tragedy of an atheistic society and developing reasoned defenses, we sported bumper stickers that taunted, "My God Is Alive. Sorry About Yours."

There are people who dismiss the idea that we live in a post-Christian culture. They cite statistics about how most people still believe in God, or statistics about church attendence. But people can honor God with their lips while their hearts are far from Him.

Spend an evening flipping through TV and cable channels to find evidence of belief in God that isn't limited to isolated ghettos of religious programming. Spend a week reading newspapers and magazines from around the country, both the news and the editorial pages, and see how many articles and essays are written with the assumption of God's existence and the assumption that we are His creatures, made in His image, and commanded to serve Him. Spend a month in Hollywood watching movies being made, and look for Christian assumptions at work. Spend a semester in graduate departments at Stanford or Duke or the University of Virginia, and see if Christianity is even competing in the war of ideas with radical feminism, left-over Marxism, or sheer skepticism. The political and economic power plays we have seen in recent evangelical approaches do absolutely nothing to undermine secularism; if anything, they intensify the image of the goddess Reason overthowing the superstitions of a church struggling for vestiges of cultural power.

Religion in general and Christianity in particular have been marginalized, segregated from our public life. Religion is regarded as a purely private matter, not something that should shape our laws and our art, our journalism and our entertainment. And when religion is conveniently separate, even Christians are willing to pretend that God doesn't exist. When they are on the job, reading the paper, going to the movies, voting: wherever they are active in their society, it is too convenient to forget God.

In the face of the loss of cultural hegemony, conservative Christians are easily tempted to try to recover lost cultural ground by winning elections rather than arguments. Christianity once had cultural power. It has lost it. Therefore, we need to try to get it back, to recapture the culture. The means that are suggested for doing that are almost always political organization and the consolidation of power. Like most Americans, we believe that political solutions are ultimate solutions. But politics is more an effect of culture than a cause. People do not want easy access to abortions because laws are liberal; the laws are liberal because people want easy access to abortions. Of course, law does have some tutorial effect; the law is one piece of data that forms public opinion. But compared to, for example, the mass media, the law is not that powerful or persuasive and is rarely a decisive factor in shaping public opinion, especially in an egalitarian democracy.

When evangelical Christians bemoan the state of their culture, and leap to the conclusion that there are political solutions, they are in fact behaving as ideologues. They are preoccupied with power rather than with persuasion. Instead of nurturing within the church publicly provocative sources of wisdom and truth about human nature and human society, the politicized Christian assembles mailing lists, circulates petitions, and threatens boycotts.

Consider, for example, a possible alternative response to *The Last Temptation of Christ*. Some churches organized picket lines at theaters showing the film. But surely, in our culture, a picket line defiantly throws down a gauntlet; it does not invite moral reflection. Even if the slogans displayed by the picketers are true, angry placards are part of the arsenal of power, not truth; they have more to do with the projection of might than the assertion of right. Syndicated columnist Terry Mattingly has suggested that churches in large cities where the film was showing could have organized simple productions of part of Dorothy L. Sayers's drama on the life of Christ, *The Man Born to Be King*. Complimentary tickets to those productions could have been passed out to people attending Scorsese's film as they left the theater. That approach would have been persuasive rather than coercive. It would have engaged precisely those faculties that the film engaged, but with Christian resources at work.

CONCLUSION

The defenders of the tactics of power argue that we are in a war, and that wars require fighting. The question, however, is not whether or not we are in a war, but what *kind* of war and what kind of *weapons* are likely to be successful.

The church is always at war, but its spiritual battle requires spiritual weapons; the weapons of our warfare are not of the flesh.

But Christendom was a *cultural* phenomenon, not simply a *spiritual* one. The death of Christendom is not the death of Christianity. Christendom was not the church; it was a generally friendly cultural setting for the church. What we are seeing now is only the death of a culture with a mixture of Christian and pagan assumptions. In fact, one could argue that the death of Christendom (or the death of a supposed "Christian America") is an opportunity to preach Christ clearly without the confusion of cultural assumptions. However, that means that the church has lost a long-time friend whose tutelage was repaid with defense and an honored seat at the head of the cultural table. It is sad, but not fatal.

Though the spiritual war *involves* the culture and intersects with cultural issues, it is not a war for the civilization or for the country that most concerns the Christian. It is not the struggle for the customs, morals, laws, and politics of Christendom, but the struggle for the minds and hearts of men and women, many of whom have never heard an intelligent presentation of Christianity throughout the course of their lives.

At the same time, the struggle for the mind and heart of our culture will have an unavoidable effect on the culture. In this secondary sense, we are engaged in a battle for civilization. Civilization is not the kingdom of God, but civilization serves the kingdom of God. Harry Blamires, author of *The Christian Mind,* has written:

> Surely organized Christianity presupposes civilization. It is preached and practiced effectively within an ordered polity. In a jungle, where cannibals dine on missionary stew, where men prey bestially upon one another, certain preliminary steps toward minimal restraint, hygiene, and the guarantee of continuing survival have to be taken before a prayer meeting can be arranged and the gospel proclaimed.[6]

Not only is the advance of the gospel served by civilization; establishing institutions that are ordered and that reject barbarism is also an important way of loving our neighbors, and hence obligatory for all believers even if Christian discipleship is not served by it. Surely we ought to be more preoccupied with serving our neighbors than with ruling them. The involvement of Christians in cultural and civic life ought to be motivated by love of neighbor, not by self-interest—not even by the corporate self-interest of the evangelical movement.

But Blamires insists that the battle for civilization is not the same thing as the battle for the kingdom of God and warns against identifying the two.

> Desperate as we Christians are to stem the tide of immorality and degeneracy, we must not pretend that it is simply *qua* [as] Christians that we man the barricades. It is an insult to paganism to suggest that it is only by virtue of our Christian conscience that we are offended by the collapse of morality and public decency. It is not just St. Paul, St. Augustine, John Bunyan, or John Wesley who would be horrified at what we have come to acquiesce in the way of legalized embryonicide and pornography. Surely Virgil and Seneca, Plato and Plotinus would be horrified too.[7]

So the death of Christendom (which extended into the West the concerns of classical civilization) tempts evangelicals in at least two ways.

First, they are prone to confuse the recovery of civilized behavior as a distinctively Christian crusade and to attach all of the rhetoric and emotion of defending the kingdom of God to the imperative, but lesser task, of driving out the barbarians. Second, they prosecute this crusade (which they identify as spiritual) using political means. In the first error, the spiritual is reduced to the cultural; in the second, the cultural is reduced to the political.

Following this two-stage transformation, distinctively Christian principles and duties are in danger of being compromised or confused with legitimate but secular concerns; theology is reduced to morality, and then morality is reduced to ideology. The advance of the barbarians, whether they be in abortion clinics, university English departments, or multinational corporations, incites great passion and defensiveness. But Christians must remain clear about who the enemy is, what the cause is, and which weapons are appropriate to which battles. Without such clarity, the church will certainly degenerate into a moral rearmament society and nothing more. That is just what theological liberalism did to many of the mainline churches. It would be a horrible irony if the moral passion of evangelicals led them to the same end.

Therefore, the "better way" we are to pursue in this situation is to recover the art of theologically informed discernment—not just for the "ivory tower" theologians but for the average Christian; to recognize the difference between the kingdom of God and the kingdoms of this world; and yet to accept our role in both without turning one into the other. There is nothing wrong with Christians getting involved in politics, especially in a democracy. In fact, Christians ought to be interested in every aspect of life, just as is God Himself. And yet, such involvement in culture, important as it is, is not the building of Christ's kingdom. By standing beside our Lord as He builds His kingdom, we can be assured that no film, no policy, no ideology, indeed, not even the gates of hell, shall stand in the way of our Sovereign's triumph.

NOTES

1. NAE press release issued from the Carol Stream, Illinois, office, September 28, 1988.
2. Charles Krauthammer, "The Temptation of Martin Scorsese," *Washington Post,* August 19, 1988, p. A23.
3. Addison H. Leitch, *Winds of Doctrine: The Theology of Barth, Brunner, Bonhoeffer, Bultmann, Niebuhr, Tillich* (Westwood, N.J.: Revell, 1966), p. 30.
4. Peter J. Leithart, "The 'Mabelized' Church," *First Things,* May 1991, p. 10.
5. Ibid.
6. Harry Blamires, *Where Do We Stand? An Examination of the Christian's Position in the Modern World* (Ann Arbor, Mich.: Servant, 1980), p. 17.
7. Ibid., p. 19.

PART 2
POWER EVANGELISM

This is what each of you keeps on saying to his friend or relative: "What is the Lord's answer?" or "What has the Lord spoken?" But you must not mention "the oracle of the Lord" again, because every man's own word becomes his oracle and so you distort the words of the living God, the Lord Almighty, our God.

Jeremiah 23:35-36

POWER EVANGELISM

3

In Search of Spiritual Power

John H. Armstrong

Having been marginalized by the society whose respect it once commanded, evangelicalism has demonstrated its unwillingness to take defeat lying down. With impressive, grand-scale enterprises, the movement adopted an aggressive posture characterized by such spirited words as "crusade" (or the latest Latin American derivative, *conquistas,* "conquests"), "campaign," and other battle terms.

The particular manifestation of power we intend to explore in this section is the quest for what is called "power evangelism." Although there appears to be a general rise in mysticism even within evangelical spirituality, one specific movement that will serve as an example of this larger phenomenon is the remarkably successful signs and wonders enterprise. If the reader is looking for a general critique of the charismatic movement or the usual rehearsal of anti-charismatic rhetoric, he or she will not find it in this section (or, for that matter, in this volume). We are concerned not with the question of whether God can be or even is still a God of miracles (for on that we are all agreed that He can be and He is). Rather, the signs and wonders movement represents a deeper challenge.

JOHN H. ARMSTRONG is an ordained Baptist clergyman and the founder and director of Reformation and Revival Ministries, Carol Stream, Illinois.

THE THIRD WAVE

What exactly is meant by the designation "Third Wave"? This descriptive terminology was first used by C. Peter Wagner, a professor of missions at Fuller School of World Mission in Pasadena and a supporter of the Vineyard movement, as the title of a book published in 1988, *The Third Wave of the Holy Spirit.*[1] According to Wagner, the First Wave was the rise of modern Pentecostalism in the early decades of this century. The Second Wave referred to the charismatic movement of the 1960s, which touched virtually every non-Pentecostal mainline group. The Third Wave, which Wagner believes began in the late 1970s, is making a distinctive contribution among the more dispensational and Reformed evangelical groups that historically have rejected "second blessing" emphasis, thus resisting at least theologically the first two waves.

The emphasis of the Third Wave is upon "signs and wonders," understood as (1) miraculous, or "power," healings; (2) deliverance from demons and demonic powers; and (3) "words of knowledge" that come as immediate revelations of God's mind and heart for the believer and the gathered church; the capacity to utter "words of knowledge' is generally believed to be the gift of prophecy.

The distinctive teachings of the Third Wave movement center around (1) a new perspective on what is called "worldviews"; (2) the presence of the future, or the ministry of God's kingdom, in the present age, not just in a future-only kingdom; and (3) "power evangelism," evangelism accompanied by dramatic manifestations of miraculous healings and prophetic utterances.

As Clark Pinnock puts it in the foreword to Charles Kraft's book, *Christianity with Power,* the Third Wave of power ministries "requires that we decide which camp (pro- or anti-Pentecostal) we belong to"[2] David Barrett, a respected researcher, writing in the *Dictionary of Pentecostal and Charismatic Movements,* estimates that 20 million believers worldwide could be counted as fitting into this Third Wave pattern.[3] For this reason alone, we should try to understand the appeal—and the potential pitfalls—of Third Wave approaches.

THE VINEYARD MOVEMENT

The Vineyard movement is closely associated with the Third Wave. In the North American context the rise of the Vineyard can be traced to the friendship of two men associated with Fuller Theological Seminary, C. Peter Wagner, already mentioned, John Wimber, the founding pastor of the Anaheim Vineyard, and Ken Gulliksen, the pastor of the churches from which the Vineyard took its name.

C. Peter Wagner came to Fuller Theological Seminary in 1971 as an understudy to the late Donald A. McGavran, the founder of the missions program at the seminary and a specialist in church growth.[4] Prior to coming to Fuller, Wagner had been a missionary to Bolivia, serving in several capacities with the South American Mission and Andes Evangelical Mission (now SIM International).

Wagner had been opposed to Pentecostalism, but his research for a book on the rapid growth of the Pentecostal church in Latin America led him to the conclusion that Pentecostalism was "the driving force in much of church growth in the Third World."[5] The church at large, Wagner argued, should adopt Pentecostalism's methods and patterns.

John Wimber came to Christ in 1963.[6] He studied sociology and religion at Azusa Pacific University, a Bible college associated with the Yearly Meeting of Friends Churches, a conservative Quaker Association, and in 1970 joined the staff of the Friends church in Yorba Linda, California. The church grew, but the period was a difficult one for Wimber, for although he was a dispensationalist, believing that charismatic gifts had ceased, he was encountering what he believed to be miraculous healings. Leaving the pastoral ministry, in 1975 he joined Wagner in the pioneering work of the Charles E. Fuller Evangelistic Association.

Wimber's wife, however, continued to be active in the Yorba Linda congregation as well as in a small worship group formed by members of that church. In 1978 the new group began meeting as a separate church, Calvary Chapel of Yorba Linda. That year Wimber left the Fuller Evangelistic Association and became the full-time pastor of the new church. As the congregation grew, Wimber continued to lead it more and more into the phenomena of the charistmatic movement. On Mother's Day 1981, following a testimony, the youth of the church were asked to come forward, and the result was the beginning of what is now called "power evangelism." Young people began to shake, speak in tongues, and fall to the floor.

From that point the congregation, now numbering seven hundred, grew remarkably. By May 1982 the name was changed to "the Vineyard" in order to identify with Ken Gulliksen and his existing seven Vineyard churches. By September 1983 the Vineyard had relocated to Anaheim. The denomination claims five hundred churches formally connected throughout the United States, Canada, South Africa, Australia, New Zealand, Sweden, Germany, Ireland, and Great Britain, with many more informally adopting Vineyard-style approaches. The parent church in Anaheim numbers six thousand.

Wimber continued his association with Fuller Theological Seminary while also serving the Vineyard. He introduced a lecture, "Signs, Wonders, and Church Growth," in 1981, and, with Wagner, introduced in 1982 the controversial course "MC510: The Miraculous and Church Growth," featuring laboratory (i.e., hands-on) training in signs and wonders. During one session, Wagner volunteered for healing from high blood pressure. In the book *Power Encounters,* edited by Kevin Springer, Wagner reports what happened then: "I dimly heard John saying to the class, 'The Holy Spirit is on him. Can you see the Holy Spirit on him?' . . . In a few days I went to the doctor and he was surprised to see my blood pressure so low. . . . He took me off the medication gradually, and in a few months I was taking none.'"[7] During this period Springer also worked with Wimber on *Power Evangelism*[8] and *Power Healing.*[9] "Power" was in the air, with such defenses as Christian psychologist John White's *When the Spirit Comes with Power.*[10] Wagner even called together a conference at the seminary in an effort to get Christian leaders to bind the various demons (including the demon of homelessness, the demon of sickness, and the demon of the Bermuda Triangle). After a good deal of controversy, the seminary decided to cancel the course, but out of this experience John Wimber and Peter Wagner forged a friendship that would only be improved by the addition of other essential relationships, that of Paul Cain and the Kansas City Prophets.

The Kansas City Prophets are a group of evangelistic speakers, believed also to be prophets, associated with the Kansas City Fellowship, a large church in Kansas City established in October 1984 by Mike Bickle, who previously had had a highly successful ministry in St. Louis.[11] Paul Cain became associated with the Bickle ministry in 1987[12] following many years of independent ministry. He is considered, along with Bickle, John Paul Jackson, Bob Jones (not the Bob Jones of the university by that name), and several others, to be one of those prophets, perhaps even the most prominent.[13]

Wimber first met Bickle 1985; in October 1988 Wimber invited Bickle to accompany him on a tour of Great Britain.[14] In May 1990 the Kansas City Fellowship formally joined the Vineyard Fellowship.[15]

From its inception the Kansas group has had a controversial ministry. Its principal thrust centers on "power encounters" that move in the realm of the prophetic. Michael Maudlin, in the *Christianity Today* issue featuring the Kansas City ministry, wrote:

> For instance, some prophetic ministers have tried to establish revelations or doctrines that were not grounded in scripture (such as the idea that eating beef was necessary for discerning demons). That practice is now forbidden. All KCF and Vineyard leaders stress that the prophetic movement is immature and apt to make mistakes (*except for, they stress, Paul Cain*). While they believe that many of their prophets are extremely gifted, they also recognize that few have had biblical and theological training.[16] (italics added)

The Vineyard has sought to respond to its critics by bringing the Kansas City prophet John Paul Jackson to the Vineyard headquarters in Anaheim for closer supervision. Nevertheless, the leadership does not even flinch when interviewed, for instance, by the *Los Angeles Times,* about Jackson's claims to be gifted with the ability to smell God (apparently He smells like roses) and the devil (he carries a sulfur odor).[17] Wimber and Jack Deere, the former professor at Dallas Theological Seminary, "admit the whole thing is *'weird.'* . . . But weird doesn't necessarily mean *untrue,"* says Deere.[18]

The mother of Paul Cain was dying of cancer at age forty-four when an angel allegedly informed her that she would not only be healed herself, but would give birth to a unique boy whom she was to name Paul, after the apostle. His mother lived another sixty years and Paul himself began receiving angelic visits at age eight. A high point of Cain's testimony is his claim that Jesus materialized in his (that is, Cain's) Lincoln automobile during the 1950s to inform him that He was jealous of the prophet's fiancée and to command him to remain single and celibate for the rest of his life.[19]

Cain was also an associate of the healer-evangelist William Branham, who received revelations from an angel, too. Among those revelations were the following: the doctrine of the Trinity is "a doctrine of demons"; Eve's sin involved sexual relations with the serpent, but the "seed of God" were Branham's followers, otherwise known as "the Bride" or "the New Breed" (popular designations in the "Latter Rain" version of Pentecostalism).[20] Furthermore, Branham proclaimed himself the angel of Revelation 3:14 and 10:7, eventually baptizing people into his own name and leading others to do the same. Branham prophesied that by 1977 all denominations would be subsumed under the World Council of Churches, which would be under the control of the Roman Catholic Church. Among those who acknowledge his influence on their ministries are Jack Coe, A. A. Allen, T. L. Osborne, Oral Roberts, Kenneth Hagin, and Benny Hinn; the latter two claim he was a prophet. So does Paul Cain.

But why mention Branham? Isn't that simply guilt by association, trying to place Branham and Cain side by side simply because the latter was the evangelist's associate? Yes, it would be guilt by association, were it not for the fact that Cain refuses to distance himself *completely* from Branham. In an interview conducted by Kevin Springer[21] a question regarding this matter was asked of Cain:

> You have been quoted from a taped talk as saying, "William Branham was the greatest prophet in the 20th century." How could this be true if he denied the historic, orthodox view of the trinity . . . and if he taught the so-called "Serpent's Seed" theory of original sin? . . . How could he teach such serious error and have a genuine gift?

Cain responded that such errors were "such a small part of his presentation that it just swept by everyone, until it became his pet theology" and then turned attention to Branham's character, which was not the issue in question: "No one ever challenged his [Branham's] Christ-like character." Affirming that he had indeed said that Branham was "the greatest prophet of the 20th century," Cain nevertheless insisted that that was due not to Branham's doctrines but to "his gifting in the word of knowledge." After all (and notice the pragmatism here that so often resists genuine criticism), "during that time thousands came to a saving knowledge of Christ in his meetings." How one comes to a saving knowledge of Christ from such distorted messages one can only guess. One need only compare Cain's guarded endorsement of Branham to the doctrines and practices of that evangelist's ministry outlined in the *Dictionary of Pentecostal and Charismatic Movements,* an academic work compiled by thoughtful Pentecostals and charismatics.

Although the Vineyard acknowledges that the movement is in its growing stages and is, therefore, liable to error from time to time, that caveat does not seem to extend to Cain himself, as Maudlin noted in his interviews (cf. above). I once heard Mike Bickel say that we all miss sometimes, "except for Paul Cain. He hits the target all the time." That is maintained even though vague predictions of every immoral Christian's being purged from the "new breed . . . before the nineteen-eighties are out"[22] and of revival breaking out "in Great Britain in October 1990"[23] have gone unfulfilled.

THE MESSAGE OF POWER EVANGELISM

In *Power Evangelism* Wimber writes: "Encounters with demons have become a common experience for me. Missionary Alan Tippett calls these events *power encounters,* the clashing of the kingdom of God with the kingdom of Satan. These conflicts, these clashes, may occur anywhere, anytime. The expulsion of demons is most dramatic, though power encounters are far from limited only to those where Satan takes the form of the demonic."[24]

Power encounters are public events, showdowns between the forces of light and the forces of darkness. Much as was Elijah in 1 Kings 18 when he confronted the prophets of Baal, we today are engaged in similar acts of high drama. Kevin Springer actually refers to the incident in 1 Kings as an ancient "shoot-out at the OK Corral."[25]

However, as one listens to the tapes, attends the conferences, and reads the materials, the following points seem to form the basic substance of the power evangelism movement's message:

1. *The signs and wonders present in Jesus' ministry are to be regarded as power encounters and as normative.* Wimber calls signs and wonders "the calling cards of the kingdom"[26] and writes in reference to the inauguration and the consummation of the kingdom of God: "This explains the twofold pattern of Christ's ministry, repeated wherever he went: first, proclamation, then demonstration. First he preached repentance and the good news of the kingdom of God. Then he cast out demons, healed the sick, raised the dead—which proves he was the presence of the kingdom, the Anointed One."[27] That pattern thus establishes the ministry of every believer since that time:

> There is no difference between the *words* and *works* of Jesus. The *works* have exactly the same message as the *words*. The message and words concentrated on the announcement of the kingdom of God. The miracles and works show us what the kingdom is like. . . . The *words* and the *works* of Jesus both center on the Kingdom of God. They are a unity. They both *show* and *tell* what the Kingdom is. (Italics in original.)[28]

Thus, for evangelism to be accompanied with power, simple proclamation of the good news is not enough. The Christian must be able both to show and to tell in order to engage in power evangelism. "Our lives should read the same way."[29]

2. *Power encounters often produce bizarre spectacles.* That might be taken as a given, but it is an essential aspect of Vineyard teaching and experience. "Around the world among Christians of various theological persuasions," writes John White, are "reports of great weeping or laughter, shaking, extreme terror, visions, falling (or what is sometimes called 'being slain in the Spirit'), being 'drunk with the Spirit' and other revival experiences."[30] In fact, Wagner reports an incident in which unbelievers merely passing the stadium in Latin America where power evangelist Carlos Annacondia, a Latin

American evangelist of considerable following, was preaching were slain in the Spirit.

Mike Flynn, an Episcopal minister who embraced the Vineyard movement, reports the following experience:

> When I went up to the altar rail for Communion, something unbidden, unexpected, and alarming happened when the priest put the bread in my hand. Suddenly something like electricity began happening in me. . . . As he touched the cup to my lips, the whole business climaxed: I felt as though a Vesuvius of sorts was spewing straight out of the top of my head; I was certain that I was emitting a brilliant white light and that everybody was gawking at me; and my insides were riot with that electrical sensation.[31]

After the initial experience faded, Flynn repeated the event at the altar rail. After only six months that second dramatic experience also dissipated. Only after a woman prayed for his healing of memories did Mike have relief, though it didn't happen all at once. Here is how Flynn explains it:

> But a couple of weeks later, a woman came into my office, sat down, and explained her serious marriage problems, stemming from spouse abuse. She was in need of the healing of damaged emotions. After a brief argument in my head with God, I agreed to pray for her. But I realized with a shock that I hadn't the slightest concept of how to do it. I had been practicing Christ's presence visually, seeing Jesus on a throne wherever I went. So I looked at Jesus. He got off his throne, knelt down beside the woman, put his arm around her shoulders, and with his left hand reached right into where it shrank until it evaporated. Then he reached into his own heart again and took out a glob of white jello which he carefully inserted into the woman's heart where the darkness had been. Finally he turned to me and said, "Do that." I felt rather foolish, but I described out loud in prayer what I had seen Jesus do, and the woman was rather gloriously and immediately healed.[32]

Flynn has now himself taught for the Vineyard, including a seminar entitled, "Calling Down the Holy Spirit." He says, "After teaching for a couple hours, it was time to call Him down."[33]

3. *The Western church needs to shift to a worldview more conducive to the supernatural.* The Vineyard movement urges a major paradigm shift from rationalism to a more Eastern worldview. Wimber develops this point in *Power Evangelism:*

> All that I have said about worldviews points toward one conclusion: Christians' worldviews affect their theology. If Christians have a worldview that is affected by Western materialism, they will probably deny signs and wonders are for today. Though they may use a theological rationale, the real issue is that it upsets their worldview. In contrast to this, a second group of Christians have a worldview that is affected by Western rationalism; they might acknowledge signs and wonders, but consign them to the irrational. These people seek signs and wonders for the thrill of the experience, as an end in itself. They do not understand the purpose of signs and wonders: to demonstrate the kingdom of God.[34]

Wimber concludes: "So God uses our experiences to show us more fully what he teaches in Scripture, many times toppling or altering elements of our theology and worldview."[35]

Charles Kraft, missions professor at Fuller Seminary, also urges this paradigm shift and is a major proponent of Third Wave thinking among professional missiologists. Kraft defines a "worldview" as "the central systematization of conceptions of reality to which members of their culture assent (largely unconsciously) and from which stems their value systems."[36] The proponents of power evangelism insist that the Western worldview of rationalism and materialism have so prejudiced men and women against the supernatural that this bias must be abandoned. How do we respond to this observation?

First, we must agree that the modern West is indeed strongly influenced by secularism and, as a result, tends to reject the supernatural. Many today will reject our Lord's miracles, including His resurrection, simply because "those things don't happen"—they violate their secular worldview.

Nonetheless, two objections ought to be noted here. First, as a result of decades of secularism and agnosticism about spiritual realities, modern culture is rapidly moving into hyper-spirituality, with the rise of metaphysical cults, the occult, and the New Age movement. Westerners do indeed still want the supernatural, especially if it will bring power into their lives so that they can enjoy a better lifestyle.

Beyond this, the culture appears to be moving even more rapidly into pure superstition, as some reputable scientists, philosophers, and artists of all types express an open hostility to rational thought and move progressively toward a blending of magic and science.[37] As several major works have pointed out in recent years, the American mind is closing itself to rational thought. Are we not, in reality, experiencing a secular paradigm shift from a modern Western worldview to an Eastern model already? Is it possible that the advocates of power evangelism are merely themselves being swept into a secular worldview?

A second objection, however, has to do with Wimber's assertion that "though [Christians who deny the Third Wave] may use a theological rationale, the real issue is that it upsets their worldview."[38] That may be true of Christians who are alive today, but how could it apply to the generations of believers before the advent of Western rationalism and materialism? The church Fathers, who came almost entirely from the East, believed that the apostolic gifts had ceased. That they so believed can be seen in the controversy over Montanism (from a convert named Montanus), a prophetic movement that appeared at about A.D. 172. The Montanists, whom some Third Wave advocates claim as precursors,[39] caused a great disturbance over their assertion that they had recovered the gifts of prophecy, tongues, and healing. At the heart of their prophetic life was the prediction that Jesus would return within their lifetimes to their hometown of Phrygia. Needless to say, the ancient church condemned Montanism. In A.D. 230 the validity of Montanist baptism was rejected by the Synod of Iconium. Since much of the church leadership of that time was in the East, and since the reaction took place thirteen centuries before the Enlightenment, how does Wimber account for the church's rejection of such phenomena? Similarly, Augustine during this same period condemned Montanism, and he was an African Christian who believed in and experienced the supernatural without any reservations.

The phenomena Third Wave proponents hold forth as normative for believers today (including shaking, falling down, jumping up and down in place, heavy breathing)[40] were not even normative (or, for that matter, even practiced in isolated cases) in the apostolic church. Though such movements have appeared from time to time throughout church history, the church itself, Eastern and Western, has never adopted what is today being repackaged as "power evangelism." That does not prove that power evangelism is wrong, but it does demonstrate that the historic witness of Christians throughout the centuries, with the exception of small and sporadic sects, has consistently condemned such movements without any influence from modern scientific rationalism.

John Wimber holds that "Western Christians must undergo a shift in perception to become involved in a Signs and Wonders ministry, a shift toward a worldview that makes room for God's miraculous intervention."[41] But where are the disclaimers assuring us that this position does not mean the embrace of a pantheistic worldview? After all, the Eastern worldview is more influenced by non-Christian religious mysticism than by a mere openness to the involvement of a personal, omnipotent God. In *The Universe Next Door*, James Sire writes, "The swing to Eastern thought is, therefore, a retreat from Western thought. . . . With its anti-rationalism, its syncretism, its quietism, its lack of technology, its uncomplicated lifestyle and its radically different religious framework, the East is extremely attractive."[42] Sire is writing about the attractiveness this shift has for secular society. He does not have the Vineyard in mind, nor am I suggesting that he should. The only point we need to make here is this: The paradigm shift from a Western to an Eastern worldview, advocated by leaders of the Third Wave, may be one more case of the church following the culture, all the while thinking it (the church) is being original.

I am not suggesting that the Vineyard movement or the Third Wave is part of an end-times New Age conspiracy. If I were, then what you will read in Kim Riddlebarger's chapter of this volume would appear rather contradictory. Nevertheless, there does appear to be an uncritical adoption of some aspects of Eastern mysticism, which in some ways are more a part of popular culture and entertainment today than is scientific rationalism. The New Age movement is famous for trying to blend technology and spirituality, or as Ferguson calls it, "science and magic." Techniques abound for harnessing the force of power in the universe. Matter is not real, but spirit is. By employing certain principles, one can manage the force of spiritual power and channel it effectively wherever it is needed. Again, no one is suggesting that John Wimber or other "power evangelists" endorse this high-tech mysticism. Nevertheless, the recurring images of the testimonies (electricity, a Jell-O-like substance applied for the healing of memories, and so on) appear to borrow more from popular science fiction than from Scripture.

A tendency toward spiritual technology, though subtle, is apparent in the Vineyard movement. For instance, Wimber says concerning his healing practices: "At the same time I'm gathering information with my five senses I'm sending up my antenna into the cosmic reality."[43] Is this what our Lord and his apostles did when they engaged in healing? This leads us into the fourth major feature of the Third Wave's emphasis, the nature of spiritual technology.

4. *Healing and prophecy are learned skills.* Spiritual technology must be created to harness the power, and this sort of imagery is often employed, rendering a picture of God as more of a power source, impersonal force, or dispenser, than as a sovereign, personal deity.

Wimber writes:

So, shortly after I saw my first healing, I asked myself, "Is it possible to develop a model for healing from which large numbers of Christians may be trained to heal the sick?" I thought the answer was yes and became committed to developing that model. Jesus used the show, tell, deploy, and supervise method of training. . . . Throughout the process, I developed teaching to explain the theology and methodology of divine healing. . . . After testing and adapting this model for several years in my congregation and at a course I helped teach at a local seminary, I developed a healing seminar in which people are trained to pray for the sick. Over the past few years thousands of Christians from Protestant, Catholic, and Orthodox traditions have been trained through these seminars, which are now conducted by me and about twenty of my associates.[44]

Says Wimber, "Emphasis on doctrinal knowledge and character development is good; this other dimension of Christian growth adds much more. This was a difficult lesson for me to learn, which explains why nothing happened for many months."[45] To his credit, Peter Wagner insists, "There is no secret formula, ritual, or procedure, which when used correctly, makes the healing, and we cannot write the script" for God.[46] And yet, amazingly, only a few pages later Wagner offers "a five step process" to be followed in obtaining the miracle of healing. (Wimber also uses this formula in chapters 11 and 12 of *Power Healing*.) This procedure is taught in Vineyard seminars, defended in the vast literature, and practiced in major conferences and in after-meetings. Peter Wagner states,

> At this point (i.e. in the process of the healing procedure) you also decide whether to use oil. I carry a vial of oil—which has been consecrated for healing—in my pocket at all times. Sometimes I anoint the person with it, depending on how I feel God is leading during the prayer selection phase. Some use holy water. Some use consecrated salt. Some use the sacrament of holy communion. Others use none of the above, but depend on prayer alone. So many people I respect do it so many different ways that I hesitate to recommend any one of the above over the others. I find oil is best for me.[47]

In the fourth stage of this five-stage process, "Sometimes there is a fluttering of eyelids or a kind of aura that surrounds the person. Sometimes there are other manifestations."[48] Such a statement, of course, goes beyond the question of whether the gifts are still in use in our day, for even if they are, surely nothing like the phenomena Wimber mentions appears in all of Scripture. Where in Scripture does one find such a sophisticated technology for miracles, complete with auras to let the person know when something is happening?

In other cases the indicator is not an aura but a change in the color of the power evangelist's hands. Bob Jones, one of the Kansas City Prophets mentioned earlier, gives us an example:

> I was over there with Jim awhile ago. My hands turned blue, and then they turned purple. And when that happens that means

you've got some incense that's gone up. You've got some interces-
sion that's gone up that Papa's saying yes to. . . . When you've got
this kind of anointing some of you are already entering that secret
place of the Most High. You're already bowing down to that altar
of incense. Your tears are falling on those coals and they're coming up before Papa. Papa's saying, "Come with more. Believe for
more." Because when my hands turn purple it means you're getting through to Royalty; you're getting through to the top. It's yea
and amen, and that's what He's calling you into: that holy place of
divine health. The Holy of Holies which your children are called to
enter in can crash that threshold. It's called the place of divine
health. . . . That's what the children are entering into: they'll have
the Spirit without measure, they'll walk through walls; they'll be
translated—everything that was ever in the Scripture.[49]

But these things, of course, must be learned. One advances
in spiritual technology; it doesn't come all at once. Like the faith
healers critiqued in *The Agony of Deceit,* Peter Wagner appears to be
embarrassed by the petition in the Lord's Prayer, "Thy will be done."
That is a "passive approach," Wagner argues. "The active approach
does seem to release more healing power."[50] Notice, anything Wagner might say in terms of cautioning us against making healing the
result of a formula or ritual is ruled out by such statements as these.
The whole movement is rife with what Grant Wacker, in *The Reformed Journal,* called "run-away pragmatism."[51] "One can scarcely
tell where pragmatism ends and manipulation begins," Wacker
writes.[52] In fact, when Wagner commends the crusade ministry of
Carlos Annacondia, he reasons,

What is Carlos Annacondia doing that other urban evangelists do
not do? Annacondia has a great deal in common with crusade
evangelism, . . . [but] I believe the major difference is Carlos Annacondia's intentional, premeditated, high-energy approach to
spiritual warfare. A permanent fixture of Annacondia's crusade is
one of the most sophisticated and massive deliverance ministries
anywhere. . . . With a high-volume, high-energy, prolonged challenge, he taunts the spirits until they manifest in one way or another. To the uninitiated the scenario might appear to be total
confusion, but to the experienced member of Annacondia's thirty-

one crusade ministry teams it is just another evening of power encounters. . . . So great is the spiritual power that unsuspecting
pedestrians passing by the meeting have been known to fall down
under the power of the Holy Spirit.[53]

Notice the merging of pragmatism and spiritual technology.
What sets Annacondia apart is a "high-energy approach"; his is "one
of the most sophisticated and massive deliverance ministries anywhere" with "a high volume, high-energy, prolonged challenge" to
demons. And this only makes sense to the "initiated." None of Annacondia's apparent success is credited to the gospel or even to God
Himself in this appraisal.

As with all the movements we are analyzing in this book, the
signs and wonders movement appears to place doctrine in the back-
seat, downplaying the importance of a well-defined understanding
of biblical content in comparison to experience.[54] When that happens, openness to the Spirit (which we always need in every age) de-
generates into superstition and magic. Wimber states that the two
most important miracles for impressing unbelievers are "falling in
the power of the Spirit and filling teeth."[55] "On a fairly regular basis," Wimber states, "decayed teeth are filled and new teeth grow
where there were none before."[56] As I mentioned earlier, the power
prophets even "smell God" and when those seeking healing come to
them the walls in their offices dissolve as they see visions of the person's past.[57] Clouds with dollar signs appear over the heads of people
in an auditorium, indicating financial problems. Advanced courses
in healing are offered, as though it were training in the magical arts.

Where are the courses the disciples took in order to learn the
skills necessary to fill teeth, lengthen legs, smell God, and discern
clouds with dollar signs? Evangelism in the New Testament does not
appear to be a skill to be learned, but a message to be known and
proclaimed clearly, in the power of the Holy Spirit, through weak
human vessels (1 Corinthians 1:18–2:5).

One wonders how far these practices are from the medieval
superstition against which the Reformation was launched. In fact,
Wimber has actually defended the practice of employing medieval
relics in healing: "In the Catholic church for over a 1,200-year period people were healed as a result of touching the relics of the saints.

We Protestants have difficulty with that . . . but we healer's shouldn't, because there's nothing theologically out of line with that."[58]

Wimber adds a few experiences of his own. For instance, his experience with demons taught him that "there are many demons that don't have a body." (Of course, demons are spirits and none possesses a body.) "Having a body (for a demon) is like having a car. They want to have a car so they can get around. If they don't have a body, they're a second-class demon. They're not first-class. I'm not kidding you. That's the way it works, and to them, having a body is a big deal."[59]

What makes this Third Wave of Pentecostal experience more attractive to mainstream conservative evangelicals than the previous two? Its attractiveness may lie in the fact that there is a more low-key, middle-class cast to it. Nevertheless, there is little doubt that the Vineyard movement goes far beyond the teaching and practice of the mainstream charismatic movement within evangelical circles. I am not anticharismatic, but every Christian—charismatic or not—ought to be concerned by the issues the Vineyard movement raises. Those issues represent not merely one more round of charismatic versus anticharismatic rhetoric but have to do with a different debate altogether, one related to but far beyond the issue of supernatural gifts in contemporary Christian experience.

POWER EVANGELISM AND SCRIPTURE

In printed notes distributed at a Vineyard Conference in Australia in 1990, Jack Deere (the former Dallas Seminary professor and for some time a member of the staff at the parent church in Anaheim) wrote the following:

> In order to fulfill God's highest purpose for our lives we must be able to hear His voice both in the written word and in the Word freshly spoken from heaven. . . . Satan understands the strategic importance of Christians hearing God's voice so he has launched various attacks against us in this area. . . . Ultimately this doctrine (the sufficiency of Scripture) is demonic even though Christian theologians have been used to perfect it.[60]

It must be said in John Wimber's favor that the Kansas City Prophets were disciplined because they were adding new doctrines to Scripture. Vineyard leaders affirm the inerrancy and authority of the written Scriptures in print and in person, Wimber's *Power Points*[61] offering a clear example. Furthermore, in personal correspondence and private cordial conversation Jack Deere has assured me that he does not deny the classical doctrine of the sufficiency of Scripture. Nevertheless, he has stated what appears to be a *practical* denial in more than one place.[62] Though Wimber wants us to take his word for it that he is consistently evangelical, one has to wonder when he says, "I identify myself as a 'conservative evangelical' in my theology. I identify myself as something other than that in my practice."[63]

It is in the practice of its theology where the movement creates, I think, its greatest confusion on the matter of the sufficiency of Scripture. Mark Thompson highlights what I too observed in the conference I attended:

> At one point this separation between theology and practice became open conflict. On Wednesday evening, John Wimber emphasized his commitment to the Reformation principle of the indissoluble connection between the Word of God and the Spirit of God. "I believe in that connection," he said, "I'm committed to it." But in this meeting, as in the others, his own practice repudiated his words. Every General Meeting during the week had two distinct components, the message and the "ministry." The Bible was opened (if not correctly used) during the message time, but it was "the direct communication of God through the Spirit" that was characteristic of the ministry time. Often (and Paul Cain made this explicit in his last talk of the Conference) the message time appeared to be little more than an obligatory prelude to what we really wanted to get into, namely the "ministry time."[64]

Wimber relates, "I have talked with many evangelical theologians who have undergone significant changes in their theology because of an experience."[65] While we ought not to discount the role our experiences play in making us more aware of passages we had ignored or in responding to passages we have recently understood, shifts in one's theology ought to be motivated by a change of mind that has come about after careful reflection on the meaning of Scripture. Our experiences are never sufficient in overturning theological convictions we claim to have derived from the text itself.

Very often, our experience is unreliable. For instance, we *feel* sometimes as though God has abandoned us, that we are beyond God's forgiveness. But we know better, not because we have had a counter-experience, but because we believe what the Bible tells us: "Jesus loves me, this I know, for the Bible tells me so," as the children's song goes. If we put experience before Scripture, there is no reason we should not return to medieval superstition, such as the relics of saints.[66]

Donald Lewis, a professor at Regent College in Vancouver, Canada, wrote about his experience at a Vineyard conference several years ago. He reports that Wimber said, "At some point critical thinking must be laid aside." To that comment Lewis replied in the following manner:

> Wimber several times equated critical thinking with unbelief, and his apparent inability to distinguish the two is most disturbing. At one point he (Wimber) asked: "When are we going to see a generation who doesn't try to understand this book (the Bible), but just believes it?" In effect, this is saying, "When are we going to see a generation that believes my interpretation of this book without question?" This strongly anti-intellectual strain which shows through in Wimber is typical of 19th century American Revivalism and is just the sort of thing that Evangelicalism has been trying to live down in the 20th century. It disparages God's gracious gift of our mind and reflects ill on a Creator who chose to endow us with the ability to think critically.[67]

If we cannot think critically, logically, or rationally and arrive at our conclusions on the basis of objective facts rather than subjective experiences, the authority of Scripture is effectively undermined, regardless of how firmly one insists he or she maintains it.

POWER EVANGELISM AND THE GOSPEL

Although it is a matter of great debate whether the evangel proclaimed by the first Protestant evangelicals during the Reformation was (and is) the genuine biblical message, the assertion that the gospel as defined by the great confessions of the Reformation is the *evangelical* message (i.e., the belief of classical Protestantism) is beyond dispute. Justification by grace alone through faith alone, the sufficiency of Scripture and the ordinances of baptism and communion, and God's freedom and sovereignty in salvation have all been key motifs in the preaching of the gospel in the history of evangelicalism. In our own day, of course, doctrine in general takes a back seat to experience, pragmatism, comfort, and so on, and the sharp focus on those distinctives has largely been lost, even within evangelical circles.

Power evangelism is no exception, even though Wimber himself claims to be a "conservative evangelical" in theology. According to a former ministerial associate of the Vineyard, "during a Vineyard pastors' conference, he went so far as to 'apologize' to the Catholic church on behalf of all Protestants."[68] Of course, there are things for which Protestants ought to apologize, but standing up for the essence of the gospel is not one of those things. Nevertheless, Wimber stated in a seminar on church planting that "the pope, . . . by the way, is very responsive to the charismatic movement and is himself a born-again evangelical. If you read any of his texts concerning salvation, you'd know he is preaching the gospel as clear as anybody is preaching it in the world today."[69] This assertion of the possibility that a Christian leader who is bound by his office and his creed to regard anyone who believes in justification by grace through faith alone as "eternally lost" (cf. The Canons of the Council of Trent) may be "preaching the gospel as clear[ly] as anybody is preaching it in the world today" surely says more about the confusion of Protestant preaching than the faithfulness of the pope to the gospel. And if John Wimber thinks the pope is preaching the gospel so clearly, ought one not to seriously question Wimber's understanding of the gospel?

One of the most significant things I noticed while reading Wimber's *Power Evangelism* was his failure to offer any definitions of the evangel (i.e., the gospel message). Center stage are healings, words of knowledge, phenomena of the Spirit's presence—all things Wimber believes will bring people to faith. One searches in vain for exposition of the content of the gospel itself. If "power evangelism" is something other than the proclamation of the truth of the gospel of God's grace, then is it not something more, by definition? Concerns such as these have been expressed by John Woodhouse:

> In John Wimber's theology, signs are understood to have power which surpasses the power of the gospel. . . . Evangelism which has the gospel, but not signs and wonders is not "power evangelism." True, Wimber admits that he "would not deny" that the gospel has intrinsic power. And no doubt, if asked, he would affirm it, but it does not have a central place in his theology. The keys given to the church are "spiritual insights and authority," not the gospel. "In order to enter the warfare, we must correctly understand power and authority in the kingdom," which is something other than the gospel. What people need is something over and above the gospel. . . .
>
> Wimber says many people who make decisions for Christ "do not encounter God's power, and thus frequently do not move on to a mature faith. . . . There is something inadequate about their conversion experience."[70]

I am not claiming that Wimber and his associates are denying the essential articles of the gospel. Nevertheless, when the focus is on the unusual phenomena of signs and wonders rather than on the rational content of the gospel itself, confusion as to the main features of that message is bound to arise.

With a shift in emphasis from the need for grace to the need for power, the gospel takes on a completely different shape. Donald Lewis notices this danger:

> A second theological difficulty is Wimber's radical Arminianism. He seems to have little or no appreciation for the doctrine of the fall and speaks of his ministry in terms of "restoring the Edenic state." Has he any place for an ongoing struggle with the old nature in the life of a Christian, which the New Testament teaches the believer to expect? Will such a view not lead to disillusionment

(when the promised state is not obtained) or to a refusal to face reality by denying one's own experience of temptation and sin? Relating to this strong emphasis on man's ability is Wimber's view of God's inability. Wimber insists that God often does not get His way in this world, that God's will is regularly thwarted. Here we may question his doctrine of God.[71]

At this point, however, Lewis cites the concern expressed by his colleague at Regent, J. I. Packer, who has engaged in fair-minded dialogue with John Wimber and Vineyard leaders:

My God is not frustrated by any failure on man's part (as Wimber suggests). I think that this is the Bible's view of God: He is a sovereign God; He does whatever He pleases. . . . God works out all things according to His own will (Eph. 1:11). God does whatever He pleases (Ps. 135). And if you are going to lose sight of that aspect of the matter, well then, your doctrine of God is out of shape.[72]

Others have attended Vineyard conferences hoping to find clear references to the cross, at least in evangelistic services, but in the midst of all the displays of power such references did not occur. Writes one observer, "I was left wondering what faith people would have been converted to that night."[73]

Vineyard leaders and writers go to great lengths to make the point that non-Christians often are healed, slain in the Spirit, and converted without any knowledge of the gospel. Anecdotes abound in which unbelievers came to faith without any communication of the Person and work of Christ (cf. John White's *When the Spirit Comes with Power,* Kevin Springer's *Power Encounters*). If the gospel is so essential and the power only half of the story, why is the latter center stage and the former self-consciously ignored in order to underscore the unusual and supernatural nature of the conversion?

A further note must be added to this discussion of power evangelism and the gospel. In the first two waves of the charismatic movement, the Wesleyan-Holiness emphasis on a two-stage experience was prominent. First-class, Spirit-filled Christians not only were regenerated, they were also baptized in the Spirit by a subsequent crisis experience. Although the Third Wave wants to downplay (in some cases, deny altogether) this classical Pentecostal position, its leaders cannot escape this conclusion. For instance, Wimber insists that "power encounters authenticate conversion experiences in a way that mere intellectual assents do not. This gives new Christians confidence about their conversion, a solid foundation for the rest of their lives."[74] This is clearly not the classical evangelical position, which argued that the full definition of saving faith is knowledge, assent, and *trust,* not knowledge, assent, and *power encounters.* Obviously, "mere intellectual assents" cannot provide the solid foundation for the Christian life, since that is not saving faith. The Reformers challenged the Roman Catholic Church on that very point. Trust was necessary in addition to knowledge and assent.

But by replacing that third element of trust with power encounters, Wimber, perhaps unintentionally, creates the classical Pentecostal caste system. In other words, those who have had the power experience enjoy "confidence about their conversion, a solid foundation for the rest of their lives." But the rest, evidently, must live without such confidence, since "power encounters authenticate conversion experiences." For evangelicals historically, and for those of us who would maintain the biblical doctrine of saving faith today, that simply will not do. Every Christian is given confidence and a solid foundation, not because of what he or she has experienced, but because of what (or better yet, whom) he or she has believed and trusted. We are urged to "fix our eyes on Jesus, the author and perfecter of our faith" (Hebrews 12:2), not on our own experiences, no matter how spectacular they might be.

ENCOURAGING ELEMENTS

One hopeful product of this renewal movement is seen in its stress on placing no limits on God's power and freedom (albeit, within the Arminian framework Lewis described). We live in an age in which masses of men and women deny the supernatural intervention of God in human history, and the Vineyard movement reminds us of our responsibility to expect remarkable and even unusual and unexpected phenomena when the Spirit is at work. No Christian should be afraid of that, for we worship the Holy Spirit as well as the Father and the Son.

Out of the Vineyard's stress on not placing limits on God's power and freedom flows an intense desire to worship God in a meaningful and positive way. I have sensed in my dialogue with Vineyard people a real hunger to meet God and to worship Him as the living, powerful God of Scripture. Simple, but sometimes quite moving and scriptural, praise music also is a product of that desire. We use some of these Vineyard songs in my own congregation.

Further, there is a positive stress on *koinonia,* or fellowship. In our highly technocratic age we crave relational ministries, and far too often the church has responded with very impersonal programs.

The passion I have noticed among Vineyard people for the lost is also encouraging. Greater zeal for perishing sinners is desperately needed in our evangelical churches. In both personal interaction and in public meetings, I saw a genuine desire to reach out to non-Christians.

Emphasis on the presence of the kingdom of God, "now but not yet," is yet another encouraging aspect of the Vineyard's emphasis. Much of eschatology today has led either to defeatism on the one hand or triumphalistic political maneuvering on the other. The balanced perspective, seen most clearly in the writings of the late George Eldon Ladd, is, in my estimation, a welcome change. One does not have to agree with the Vineyard's view of signs and wonders in order to appreciate Ladd's major New Testament contributions to this whole area (especially since Ladd himself was not an advocate of pentecostal experiences).

Nevertheless, the critique still stands:

1. Fascination with power is replacing serious interest in the actual content of the gospel.
2. Pragmatism rather than doctrinal consensus appears to drive this movement, like so much of evangelicalism generally.
3. Personal experiences often replace biblical exposition and exegetical defenses. Although many of the Vineyard people I met were zealous, that fervor was rarely combined with a serious grasp of such biblical essentials as justification by

grace through faith, repentance, and so on. Nor were such doctrinal discussions featured in the meetings I attended or in the materials I have read from the movement itself.

4. The anecdotal character of the movement runs the risk of justifying superstition on the basis of unsubstantiated reports, either from the past or from the present.

5. The call for a shift from a Western to an Eastern worldview appears to be based on a superficial understanding of church history and the historic rationale for the church's (both East and West) rejection of such movements.

Edward Gross, professor of missions at Biblical Seminary in Pennsylvania, expressed the ambivalence I feel in offering a critique of John Wimber and this movement:

> In my opinion, John Wimber represents the best of evangelistic concerns united with some of the worst current theological beliefs. Although mixture of truth and error is extremely dangerous, we are not warranted to hastily defame Wimber as some self-serving magician. There are tremendous weaknesses in his position, but insincerity, greed, and willful deception are not among them. Our position is never strengthened by unfairly representing those with whom we disagree.[75]

Nevertheless, when we begin to see the power of the gospel replaced with a gospel of power, we would do well to heed the warning of that great evangelist, Charles Spurgeon:

> Do you not know . . . what God's estimate of the gospel is? Do you not know that it has been the chief subject of His thoughts and acts from all eternity? He looks on it as the grandest of all His works.[76]

So must we.

NOTES

1. C. Peter Wagner, *The Third Wave of the Holy Spirit* (Ann Arbor, Mich.: Servant, 1988).

2. Charles H. Kraft, *Christianity with Power: Your Worldview and Your Experience of the Supernatural* (Ann Arbor, Mich.: Vine, Servant, 1989), p. vii.

3. C. Peter Wagner, quoting David Barrett, in Stanley M. Burgess and Gary McGee, eds., *Dictionary of Pentecostal and Charismatic Movements* (Grand Rapids: Zondervan, 1988), s.v. "Third Wave," pp. 843-44.

4. C. B. McGee, in Burgess and McGee, eds., *Dictionary of Pentecostal and Evangelical Movements,* s.v. "Charles Peter Wagner."

5. C. Peter Wagner, *What Are We Missing?* [formerly titled *Look Out! The Pentecostals Are Coming*] (Carol Stream, Ill.: Creation House, 1973).

6. C. Peter Wagner, in Burgess and McGee, eds., *Dictionary of Pentecostal and Evangelical Movements,* s.v. "John Wimber."

7. Kevin Springer, ed., *Power Encounters* (San Francisco: Harper & Row, 1988), pp. 51-52.

8. John Wimber and Kevin Springer, *Power Evangelism* (San Francisco: Harper & Row, 1986).

9. John Wimber and Kevin Springer, *Power Healing* (San Francisco: Harper & Row, 1987).

10. John White, *When the Sprit Comes with Power* (Downers Grove, Ill.: InterVarsity, 1988).

11. David Pytches, *Some Say It Thundered: A Personal Encounter with the Kansas City Prophets* (Nashville: Oliver Nelson, 1991), pp. 54-68.

12. Ibid., pp. 130-33.

13. Ibid., p. 104.

14. Ibid., p. 135.

15. Ibid., p. 147.

16. Michael Maudlin, "Seers in the Heartland: Hot on the Trail of the Kansas City Prophets," *Christianity Today*, January 14, 1991, p. 21.

17. Roy Rivenburg, "A Question of Faith," *Los Angeles Times* (Orange County edition), January 28, 1992, sec. E, p. 1.

18. Ibid.

19. The story is recorded in several places, including Michael Maudlin, "Seers in the Heartland: Hot on the Trail of the Kansas City Prophets," *Christianity Today*, January 14, 1991; and Kevin Springer, "Paul Cain: A New Breed of Man," *Equipping the Saints*, Fall 1989, pp. 11-13.

20. See *Dictionary of Pentecostal and Charismatic Movements*, s.v. "Third Wave."

21. Springer, "Paul Cain: A New Breed of Man," *Equipping the Saints*, Fall 1990, p. 9.

22. Terri Sullivant, "Paul Cain's Ministry," *The Grace City Report*, special ed., Fall 1989, p. 5.

23. Springer, "Paul Cain: A New Breed of Man," *Equipping the Saints*, Fall 1990, p. 9. An advertisement prominently displayed on the back cover offered Cain's prophecy that revival would break out in Great Britain in October 1990 and that the Vineyard would have representatives from Britain address the upcoming Anaheim conference to tell about it. This revival has not yet taken place.

24. Wimber and Springer, *Power Evangelism*, p. 16.

25. Springer, ed., *Power Encounters*, p. xiv.

26. Wimber and Springer, *Power Evangelism*, p. 109.

27. Ibid., p. 6.

28. John Wimber, "The Words and Works of Jesus: Is the Message the Same or Different?" *First Fruits*, May-June 1986, p. 6.

29. Wimber and Springer, *Power Evangelism*, p. 23.

30. White, *When the Spirit Comes with Power*, pp. 17-18.

31. Springer, ed., *Power Encounters*, pp. 139-40.

32. Ibid., pp. 142-43.

33. Ibid., p. 145.

34. Wimber and Springer, *Power Evangelism*, p. 89.

35. Ibid.

36. Charles H. Kraft, *Christianity and Culture* (Maryknoll, N.Y.: Orbis, 1977), p. 53.

37. See Marilyn Ferguson, *The Aquarian Conspiracy* (New York: St. Martin's, 1987).

38. Wimber and Springer, *Power Evangelism*, p. 89.

39. Ibid., pp. 157-74.

40. Wimber and Springer, *Power Healing*, pp. 215-23.

41. Wimber and Springer, *Power Evangelism*, p. 82.

42. James W. Sire, *The Universe Next Door* (Downers Grove, Ill.: InterVaristy, 1976), pp. 130ff.

43. John Wimber, Healing Seminar Series (3 audiotapes, 1981); published in John Goodwin, "Testing the Fruit of the Vineyard," *Media Spotlight* (1990), p. 32. Goodwin, a former associate of Wimber's, writes a revealing critique of the Vineyard.

44. Wimber and Springer, *Power Healing*, pp. 169-70.

45. Wimber and Springer, *Power Evangelism*, p. 44.

46. C. Peter Wagner, *How to Have a Healing Ministry Without Making Your Church Sick!* (Ventura, Calif.: Regal, 1989), p. 228.

47. Ibid.

48. Ibid., p. 228.

49. Bob Jones, "Visions and Revelations"; audiotape, 1989.

50. Wagner, *How to have a Healing Ministry Without Making Your Church Sick!*, p. 229.

51. Grant Wacker, "Wimber and Wonders—What About Miracles Today?" *The Reformed Journal* 37 (April 1987), p. 18.

52. Ibid.

53. C. Peter Wagner, "Spiritual Power and Urban Evangelism: Dynamic Lessons from Argentina," research article on file with CURE.

54. John Wimber, "Healing: An Introduction," audiotape no. 5 (Placentia, Calif.: Vineyard Ministries International, 1985).

55. Wagner, *The Third Wave of the Holy Spirit*, p. 96.

56. Ibid.

57. Roy Rivenburg, "A Question of Faith," *Los Angeles Times* (Orange County edition), January 28, 1992, sec. E., p. 1.

58. John Wimber, Church Planting Seminar (3 audiotapes, 1981); cited by John Goodwin in *Media Spotlight* (1990), p. 24. Goodwin was a ministerial associate of Wimber's for eight years.

59. John Wimber, Healing Seminar Series (3 audiotapes, 1981; audiotape no. 2); cited in Goodwin, *Media Spotlight*, p. 26.

60. "John Wimber: Friend or Foe?" reprint from *The Briefing* (Sydney, Australia: St. Matthias Press, 1990), p. 18. Article by Mark Thompson, "Spiritual Warfare, II."

61. John Wimber and Kevin Springer, *Power Points* (San Francisco: Harper & Row, 1991), chapters 6-9.

62. John MacArthur, Jr., *Charismatic Chaos* (Grand Rapids: Zondervan, 1991), p. 135, cites Jack Deere, "God's Power for Today's Church," audiotape 1 (Nashville: Belmont Church, n.d.).

63. "John Wimber: Friend or Foe?," p. 19.

64. Ibid., pp. 20-21.

65. Wimber and Springer, *Power Evangelism*, p. 88.

66. Wimber, Church Planting Seminar (3 audiotapes, 1981); cited by John Goodwin in "Testing the Fruit of the Vineyard," *Media Spotlight* (1990), p. 4.

67. Donald M. Lewis, "Assessing the Wimber Phenomenon," Vancouver: Regent College, 1985, p. 1.

68. *Media Spotlight* (1990), p. 24.

69. Wimber, Church Planting Seminar (3 audiotapes, 1981), audiotape no. 2; cited by John Goodwin in "Testing the Fruit of the Vineyard," *Media Spotlight* (1990).

70. John Woodhouse, Paul Barrett, and John Reid, *Signs and Wonders and Evangelicals: A Response to the Teaching of John Wimber,* ed. Robert Doyle (Homebush West, Australia: Lancer Books, 1987), pp. 37-39.

71. Donald M. Lewis, "An Historian's Assessment," in James R. Coggins and Paul Hiebert, eds., *Wonders and the Word* (Hillsboro, Kans.: Kindred, 1989), p. 58. This chapter is a revision of "Assessing the Wimber Phenomenon" (see note 64 above).

72. Ibid.

73. Woodhouse, *Signs and Wonders and Evangelicals*, p. 20.

74. Wimber, *Power Evangelism*, p. 48.

75. Edward N. Gross, *Miracles, Demons, and Spiritual Warfare* (Grand Rapids: Baker, 1990), p. 12.

76. Charles H. Spurgeon, *The Metropolitan Tabernacle Pulpit* 48 (Pasadena, Tex.): 536.

4

The Purpose of Signs and Wonders in the New Testament

D. A. Carson

INTRODUCTION

Until three decades or so ago, most Christians in the West who emphasized the importance of healing and miracles developed their understanding of the Bible out of the grid of classic Pentecostalism. Spirit-baptism normally follows conversion; God's will is that we be healed; God's power in healing (and in other displays) can be called forth by faith; a want of healing typically signals a want of faith.

Over against this understanding of Scripture, two groups of evangelicals staunchly insisted that the age of miracles (including "tongues") is forever past. The stricter dispensationalists ruled miracles out of court on the ground that God's current administration of His sovereign reign has left such phenomena behind in an earlier era. Many other evangelicals, not least those in the Reformed tradition, though unpersuaded by dispensationalism, nevertheless came to the same conclusion. They did so by agreeing with Warfield, who argued that signs and wonders are tightly tied in the Bible to the purpose of attesting those of God's servants who exercised peculiar

---

D. A. CARSON is research professor of New Testament at Trinity Evangelical Divinity School in Deerfield, Illinois.

ministries in the sweep of redemptive history. Since all the public redemptive acts are behind us (except for the second advent), we should beware of counterfeit claims to miracles in our day.[1]

Many evangelicals who could not accept the arguments of cessationism were nevertheless able to keep Pentecostalists at arm's length because they were convinced that the undergirding "second blessing" theology was exegetically wrong and pastorally divisive. Worse, the pastoral practice that allowed suffering people to writhe in self-inflicted guilt because they did not have the faith to be healed was unconscionable.

Enter John Wimber and the Vineyard movement.[2] Wimber disavows "second blessing" theology and insists that not everyone will be healed. The basic structure of his theology reflects an eschatological vision that most evangelicals happily espouse. The kingdom of God has dawned and is at war with the kingdom of Satan. Although the final victory awaits the consummation, the decisive victory was achieved by Christ Himself. The demonstration of the kingdom's coming lies in the clash between the kingdom of God and the kingdom of Satan, and this clash includes displays of signs and wonders. Although signs and wonders in the New Testament frequently attest who Jesus is or who the apostles are, they cannot be limited to a role of *mere* attestation: they are displays of kingdom power.

Since the kingdom has dawned and is operating, Wimber argues, we should expect signs and wonders as surely as we expect conversions. In Wimber's predominant usage, signs and wonders include exorcism, healing the sick, and words of knowledge. They not only serve to confirm the Christian's faith, but they are *necessary* manifestations of the kingdom's presence and advance. That does not mean that Wimber thinks a miracle should take place every time someone is converted, or in every instance where there is evangelism, but that in the sweep of our evangelism signs and wonders *must* find a place or the gospel we present is defective, robbed of its power. Signs and wonders have an apologetic function in evangelism.[3]

There is a growing literature criticizing and defending the Vineyard movement, much of it fairly partisan. In addition, there are numerous treatments of the nature of prophecy and revelation, obviously relevant to the topic at hand. My purpose, however, is much more constrained. Against the backdrop of the present controversy, I shall survey the purpose of signs and wonders in the New Testament, with some necessary references to the Old Testament. The brevity of the chapter ensures that this will be nothing more than a hasty glance over the whole. Although a thick volume might easily be devoted to the subject, the virtue in the present procedure is the same as that achieved by examining the Rockies from a high altitude airplane: you find it somewhat easier to maintain a sense of proportion than when you spend a lot of time on the ground hunting for particular kinds of rock. However sketchy the survey, I shall end with some theological and pastoral observations.

A SURVEY OF THE BIBLICAL MATERIAL

To organize and limit this section, I have shaped the material into an apostolic number of points.

1. At the purely linguistic level, "signs and wonders" is not a particularly apt way to designate the Vineyard movement. Most of the events that the Bible designates as "signs and wonders" are miraculous, redemptive-historical acts of God. In the Old Testament, the events surrounding the Exodus take pride of place (Exodus 7:3; cf. 3:20; 8:23; 10:1, 2; 11:9, 10; 15:11; Numbers 14:22; Deuteronomy 4:34; 6:22; 7:19; 26:8; 29:3; Joshua 3:5; 24:17). Later generations of Israelites could testify, "[God] sent his signs and wonders into your midst, O Egypt, against Pharaoh and all his servants" (Psalm 135:9; cf. Nehemiah 9:10; Psalm 105:27; Jeremiah 32:21). Stephen, steeped in the Scriptures, refers to the Exodus events the same way: "[God] led them out of Egypt and did wonders and miraculous signs in Egypt, at the Red Sea and for forty years in the desert" (Acts 7:36).

No other event in the Old Testament attracts this array of witnesses speaking of signs and/or wonders. One theme comes close, namely, threatened judgment on the people of Israel. After God describes the wretched curses that will befall His people if they do not obey, He adds this summary: "They [the curses] will be a sign and a wonder to you and your descendants forever" (Deuteronomy 28:46). In the context of the Pentateuch, that is a way of saying that the "signs and wonders" that effected Israel's deliverance were simultaneously terrible judgments on Egypt—and those same judgments would be turned against the covenant community if they did not obey. Jeremiah 32:20 picks up the same usage; Daniel 4:2-3; 6:27 extends the threat to eschatological dimensions (the latter in connection with the rescue of Daniel from the lions' den).[4]

With this controlling Old Testament background, the New Testament application of the expression "signs and wonders" to Jesus' ministry, especially at Pentecost (Acts 2:19 [referring to Joel 2:30], 22), suggests that at least some Christians saw the coming of Jesus as a major redemptive-historical appointment, on a par with the Exodus (and, I would argue on other grounds, its "fulfillment"), combining in the one event great salvation and great judgment.[5]

Of course, many miracles in the Bible are not specifically referred to as "signs and wonders." I shall say more about some of them below. But at the purely *linguistic* level, "signs and wonders" cannot easily be made to align with the kinds of phenomena that interest Wimber.

2. When "signs and wonders" refers to God's major redemptive-historical appointments, what function do such references have in the texts where they are found? One of their major purposes is to call the people of God back to those foundation events, to encourage them to remember God's saving acts in history, to discern their significance, and to pass on that information to the next generation.

> In the future, when your son asks you, "What is the meaning of the stipulations, decrees and laws the Lord our God has commanded you?" tell him: "We were slaves of Pharaoh in Egypt, but the Lord brought us out of Egypt with a mighty hand. Before our eyes the Lord sent miraculous signs and wonders—great and terrible—upon Egypt and Pharaoh and his whole household. But he brought us out from there to bring us in and give us the land that he promised on oath to our forefathers. The Lord commanded us to obey all these decrees and to fear the Lord our God, so that we might always prosper and be kept alive, as is the case today." (Deuteronomy 6:20-24)

Unbelief in Israel is nothing other than the reprehensible forgetting of all the wonders God performed at the Exodus (Psalms 78:11-12; 106:7); by contrast, the psalmists extol God by calling to mind the redemptive deeds of the Lord (e.g., Psalms 77:11, 15; 105:5).

A similar strand can be found in the New Testament. In the fourth gospel, Jesus' miracles are often referred to as "signs." The climax of the gospel is reached when, after the resurrection, the evangelist tells us: "Jesus did many other miraculous signs in the presence of his disciples, which are not recorded in this book. But these are written that you may believe that Jesus is the Christ, the Son of God, and that by believing you may have life in his name" (John 20:30-31). In others words, John's readers are called to reflect on the signs that he reports, to think through the *sign*ificance of those redemptive events, especially Jesus' resurrection, and thereby believe. The mandate to believe here rests on John's reports of God's past redemptive-historical signs, not on testimonies of present on-going ones.

3. The significance of signs deserves a little more elaboration. The New Testament writers treat Jesus' miracles in a rich diversity of ways and see in them a plethora of purposes and achievements. In John, many if not all of the "signs" (which in John always refer to what we would label the miraculous) are not mere displays of power but are symbol-laden events rich in meaning for those with eyes to see. John teases out some of those lessons by linking some signs with discourses that unpack them, or with surrounding events that elucidate their meaning. The feeding of the five thousand precipitates the "bread of life" discourse. Part of the significance of that sign, therefore, is that Jesus not only provides bread but is Himself the "bread of life," apart from which men and women remain in death (John 6). The raising of Lazarus is placed in conjunction with one of the great "I am" claims of Jesus: "I am the resurrection and the life" (John 11). More examples could be adduced. The point is that one of the purposes of Jesus' "signs" stretches far beyond display of raw power and personal attestation: they frequently serve as acted parables, pregnant acts of power, suggestive signs.

4. For the sake of completeness, it should be mentioned that not all biblical "signs" or even "wonders" are miraculous.[6] Several prophets performed ordinary but symbol-laden actions that were called "signs" (e.g., Ezekiel 12:1-11; 24:15-27), or in one case "a sign and wonder" (Isaiah 20:3, KJV; NIV, "a sign and portent"). Isaiah designates himself and the children the Lord has given him as "signs and symbols ["signs and . . . wonders," KJV] in Israel from the Lord Almighty" (Isaiah 8:18, NIV).[7] There is no similar use of "signs" in the New Testament (though the "signs of the times" in Matthew 16:3 are probably not restrictively miraculous).

On the other hand, there is a conceptual parallel in the New Testament that is worth pondering. The *charismata* include not only such "miraculous" gifts as healing and prophecy, but also such "nonmiraculous" gifts as helping and administration—and even marriage and celibacy (1 Corinthians 7:7). Of course, this observation does not itself address substantive issues in the modern so-called charismatic movement; it does remind us, however, that if we adopt *biblical* terminology, it is exceedingly difficult to think of any Christian as "noncharismatic" if all of us have received *charismata* ("grace-gifts") from God.

5. Not all signs and wonders (I now use the expression as a general category, roughly on a par with "miracles," not merely at the linguistic level) receive positive reviews in Scripture. There are at least four differentiable dangers:

a. Signs and wonders can be performed quite outside the heritage of the God of the Bible. The Egyptian magicians could match Moses miracle for miracle for quite a while (Exodus 7:8– 8:18). Paul predicts, "The coming of the lawless one will be in accordance with the work of Satan displayed in all kinds of counterfeit miracles, signs and wonders, and in every sort of evil that deceives those who are perishing" (2 Thessalonians 2:9-10). The second beast in Revelation 13 "performed great and miraculous signs, even causing fire to come down from heaven to earth in full view of men" (v. 13).

Perhaps in some cases these are nothing more than disgusting tricks, like the nasty little sleights of hand practiced by many who lead séances. But there can be little doubt that the Bible presents many of these signs and wonders as genuinely miraculous, in the sense that what takes place is entirely at odds with the the normal ordering of things. In the worst case they are demonic. In one of the most perceptive analyses of Wimber, Alan Cole, who has served Christ in several different cultures, writes:

> None of these signs are new to me (healings, visions, tongues, exorcisms). But the trouble is that I have seen *every one of them* (yes, tongues too) in non-Christian religions, and outwardly, there was no difference in the signs, except that one was done in the name of Jesus and the other was not. Of course, if the person was also responding to the Gospel, there was a real and lasting change in life. That is why I cannot get excited about healings in themselves, and why I can reverently understand how Jesus used them sparingly, and retreated when the crowds became too great.[8]

More than fifteen thousand people a year claim healing at Lourdes. Testimonies of healing are reported in every issue of the *Christian Science Sentinel.* Pakistani Muslims claim that one of their revered saints, Baba Farid, has healed people with incurable diseases and traveled great distances in an instant. Thousands of Hindus claim healing each year at the temple dedicated to Venkateswara in Tirupathi. Some Buddhist sects provide yet another set of reports of healing.

None of this demands that we conclude that genuine miracles have ceased or that all miracles ostensibly performed in a Christian context are necessarily counterfeit or even demonic. It is simply to insist that because both in Scripture and in Christian experience miracles can occur both in the context of biblical religion and outside it, it is unwise to make too much hang on them, especially if the gospel is left behind. More strongly put, it is always perilous to equate the supernatural with the divine.

There remain three further dangers that are perhaps more relevant to contemporary Western Christianity.

b. Signs and wonders performed within the believing community can have deceptive force. That was true in ancient Israel.

If a prophet, or one who foretells by dreams, appears among you and announces to you a miraculous sign or wonder, and if the sign or wonder of which he has spoken takes place, and he says, "Let us follow other gods" (gods you have not known) "and let us worship them," you must not listen to the words of that prophet or dreamer. The Lord your God is testing you to find out whether you love him with all your heart and with all your soul. It is the Lord your God you must follow, and him you must revere. Keep his commands and obey him; serve him and hold fast to him. That prophet or dreamer must be put to death, because he preached rebellion against the Lord your God, who brought you out of Egypt and redeemed you from the land of slavery; he has tried to turn you from the way the Lord your God commanded you to follow. (Deuteronomy 13:1-5)

Observe that the text does not question the reality of those signs and wonders. Nor does it assign them to the work of the devil. At one level, God Himself is behind them: "The Lord your God is testing you to find out whether you love him with all your heart and with all your soul"! More than likely these false prophets sometimes announced the false god they championed as Yahweh, the Lord—as Hananiah does in Jeremiah 28. Not every bit of idolatry introduces a god with another name; indeed, a false prophet within the believing community is pernicious precisely because, like Hananiah, he or she appeals to Yahweh's name and says that Yahweh has spoken even when Yahweh has not spoken.

The test that Moses introduces in Deuteronomy 13 is illuminating. It turns not on the reality of the miracle or the accuracy of the false prophet's prediction, but on whether the prophet has the effect of drawing people away from the God who performed some redemptive-historical act. In Moses' day, that was the Exodus; in ours, it is the cross and resurrection. If the people of Israel are being drawn to a god they have not known as the God who brought them out of Egypt and redeemed them from the land of slavery, the prophet is false.

The contemporary application is pretty clear. The question is not first of all whether the miracles reported by the Vineyard movement are real (though that is an important question), nor even whether people are drawn to renewed love for "Jesus." There are, after all, many Jesuses around: the Mormon Jesus, the Jehovah's Witness Jesus, the Muslim Jesus, the classic liberal Jesus, and so forth. The question, rather, is whether the movement draws men and women to renewed love for the Jesus of God's great, redemptive-historical act, the Jesus of the cross and resurrection. That is an issue of extraordinary importance; I shall return to it again. For the moment it is only necessary to remind ourselves that Jesus could warn against the efforts of false Christs and false prophets who by performing signs and wonders would "deceive the elect—if that were possible" (Mark 13:22). The language suggests they are extraordinarily deceptive and come within a whisker of this end. That means it will take more than usual discernment to see what is askew; and our generation of believers is not noteworthy for discernment.

c. The third danger connected with signs and wonders in the Scripture, a danger not always distinguishable from the second, is the corruption of motives that is so often connected with pursuit of them. The four gospels preserve many instances where people demanded a sign from Jesus and He roundly denounced them for it, sometimes dismissing them as "a wicked and adulterous generation" (Matthew 12:38-45.; cf. 16:1-4; Mark 8:11-12; Luke 11:16, 29). One can understand why: the frequent demands for signs was in danger of reducing Jesus to the level of a clever magician, able to perform tricks on demand. The result would be a domesticated Jesus; Jesus would have to "buy" faith and allegiance by a constant flow of miracles done on demand. Such a demand is wicked and adulterous: it makes human beings the center of the universe and reduces God to the level of someone who exists to serve us. He may capture human allegiance if He performs adequately, but at no point is He the unqualified Sovereign to whom we must give an account, and who alone can save us. In the worst case, a Simon Magus insists that he himself must have the wonderful power to confer the Spirit and His gifts (Acts 8), as if the Spirit is so easily tamed or is so easily purchased.

In two reports (Matthew 12:39-40; Luke 11:29-32) Jesus says the only sign that will be given those who demand signs is the sign of the prophet Jonah, which turns out, in the context, to be a portent of His own resurrection. In other words, Jesus wants faith to be firmly based on His own death and resurrection.

It is important not to infer too much from this evidence. As we shall see, signs can have a legitimate subsidiary role in establishing faith. But the uncritical quest for signs is easily corrupted by impure motives. And in any case there is ample evidence that Jesus Himself drives those who hunger for signs back to His resurrection.

d. The final danger connected with signs is hypocrisy. Of course hypocrisy finds a home in many forms of religious observance; I here mention its home in signs and wonders simply because that is the topic of this essay. Jesus says, "Not everyone who says to me, 'Lord, Lord,' will enter the kingdom of heaven, but only he who does the will of my Father who is in heaven. Many will say to me on that day, 'Lord, Lord, did we not prophesy in your name, and in your name drive out demons and perform many miracles?' Then I will tell them plainly, 'I never knew you. Away from me, you evildoers!'" (Matthew 7:21-23). Their exorcisms, prophecies, and miracles are all performed in Jesus' name. Jesus Himself does not bother to question their reality. It is quite possible that those who ask these questions of Jesus on the last day honestly think they *ought* to be admitted to the kingdom (just as the "goats" are surprised by their fate in Matthew 25:41-45). But they are turned away, unrecognized by Jesus, because however "powerful" they may be in the realm of the miraculous, they do not display the marks of obedience: they do not do what Jesus says, they do not produce good fruit (cf. 7:20).

Once again, the wrong inference must not be drawn. The point is not that signs and wonders are inevitably bad but that they are never of first importance. One thinks of the flow of the argument in 1 Corinthians 12-14: various *charismata* may be distributed to members of Christ's Body, the church, but the "most excellent way [not "gift"!]" required of all believers is the way of love. Similarly here: the critical test for who is and who is not a genuine follower of Jesus is obedience, not displays of power. And some displays of power, even some done in Jesus' name, are proof of nothing at all.

6. Even within the ministry of Jesus, healings and exorcisms are clearly placed in a subsidiary role to Jesus' teaching and preaching.[9] When Jesus' intention is stated or His initiative described, almost always His teaching and preaching are in view, not His healings (e.g. Mark 1:14-15, 21, 35-39; 2:2, 13; 3:14, 22-23; 4:1; 6:1-2, 34; 7:14;

8:31, 34; 9:30-31; 10:1; 12:1, 35). By contrast, apart from one or two summary statements (e.g., Matthew 4:23), when Jesus heals individuals or casts out demons from them, either the initiative is with the sufferer (e.g., Matthew 8:3-4; 9:20-22, 27-31; 17:14-18; Mark 1:23-26; Luke 7:1-10; John 4:46-54—including the initiative of the sufferer's friends, Matthew 9:27-31; 12:22; Mark 1:30-31, 32-34; 6:55-56), or Jesus may take some initiative with an individual after His purpose for being there is established on some other basis. For instance, in the case of the crippled woman of Luke 13:10-13, "Jesus was *teaching* in one of the synagogues, and a woman was there. . . . *When Jesus saw her, he called her forward*" (cf. also Matthew 12:9-13; John 5).

Not for a moment is this to suggest that Jesus did not see His healings and exorcisms as part of His messianic work: we shall return to this theme again (see Matthew 8:16-17; 11:5-6). It is simply to point out that there is no record of Jesus going somewhere in order to hold a healing meeting, or of Jesus issuing a general invitation to be healed, or of Jesus offering generalized prayers for healing. Where Jesus does undertake to heal an individual, the procedure is never prefaced by some generalizing announcement (there is no "I have a word from the Lord: there is someone here with back pain, and God wants to heal you"), and the result is never ambiguous.

7. On the other hand, signs and wonders do have an attesting function in Jesus' ministry. At one level, that is not unlike the attesting function of signs and wonders in the life of, say, Joshua (3:7; 4:14). But in most cases there are additional overtones connected with Jesus' role as the promised Messiah.

For instance, when John the Baptist sends envoys to question Jesus' credentials, Jesus responds with a summary of His ministry: "Go back and report to John what you hear and see: The blind receive sight, the lame walk, those who have leprosy are cured, the deaf hear, the dead are raised, and the good news is preached to the poor. Blessed is the man who does not fall away on account of me" (Matthew 11:4-6). The important point to observe is that Jesus frames this summary as a fulfillment of messianic prophecy (Isaiah 35:5-6; 61:1-2): His miracles attest that He is the one who would bring in the new order promised in the Scriptures. What Jesus purposely leaves out of each of the passages He here quotes from Isaiah is the note of judgment, "the day of vengeance of our God" (Isaiah 61:2); He does not include the words "he will come with vengeance; with divine retribution he will come to save you" (Isaiah 35:4) in his allusion. Probably that was what was troubling the Baptist: John had preached that the One whose sandals he was unworthy to loosen would not only baptize His people in the Holy Spirit but would thoroughly clear His threshing floor and burn up the chaff with unquenchable fire (Matthew 3:11-12). Jesus is saying, in effect, that the dawning of the kingdom in His own ministry is introducing the long-awaited blessings of the messianic age, even though the judgments are delayed. Meanwhile, John, having started well, is encouraged not to draw back now: "Blessed is the man who does not fall away on account of me" (Matthew 11:6).

Again, on the day of Pentecost, Peter describes Jesus in these terms: "Jesus of Nazareth was a man *accredited by God to you by miracles, wonders and signs,* which God did among you through him, as you yourselves know" (Acts 2:22, italics added).

Still, even in these and other passages, at least two things must be borne in mind. The person being accredited is Jesus, God's own Son, the unique Redeemer. In this case, at least, it is improper to think of the potential of signs and wonders to command faith without also thinking of where the faith is to be placed. Of course, that means we shall need to explore just how far some similar role is assigned to signs and wonders performed by others, but that is a subject to be treated further on.

Second, although Acts 2:22 insists Jesus was accredited by God to Peter's hearers by miracles, wonders, and signs, the fact of the matter is that those hearers did not become believers until Pentecost and the gift of the Spirit. In other words, Peter appeals to the signs and wonders to establish the unique redemptive-historical gift from heaven bound up in the Person and work of Jesus Messiah; all his preaching turns on this point. Even so, the miracles themselves did not command faith, not even in the ministry of Jesus.

John's gospel puts some of these tensions in proportion. In one and the same book, several perspectives on signs and wonders are brought together. On the one hand, Jesus' signs display His glory, at least to His disciples (John 2:11). On the other hand, Jesus' initial response to a man who cries for help is the firm reproach "Unless you people see miraculous signs and wonders . . . you will never believe" (4:48). The religious leaders are convinced that Jesus is actually performing miracles whose reality they cannot deny, but that does not foster faith: rather, it fuels their rejection and anger and nurtures their plot to corrupt justice and have Him executed (e.g., 11:47-57). Precisely because they will not believe Jesus' words and do not perceive that He does what His Father does, Jesus begs them at the very least to reconsider His miracles: "Do not believe me unless I do what my Father does. But if I do it, even though you do not believe me, believe the miracles, that you may learn and understand that the Father is in me, and I in the Father" (10:37-38). Here, too, the appeal is to learn from the signs and wonders Jesus performs exactly who Jesus Himself is. From the way Jesus phrases Himself, we conclude that He sees such faith as of inferior quality, but certainly better than unbelief. And in any case His appeal is futile: His hearers do not believe. Elsewhere, some do believe because they see Jesus' works (e.g., 11:45), though not all faith triggered by Jesus' signs proves valid: some of it is spurious (2:23-25; cf. 8:30-31). The narrative of the last of the twelve to believe in Jesus' resurrection is revealing. Thomas comes to believe in Jesus' resurrection precisely because Jesus graciously proffers the hard evidence of the miraculous that satisfies His doubting apostle. But the same relatively negative valuation is given: better than the kind of faith that insists on seeing Jesus' signs first hand is the faith that rests on the reports of the unique signs of Jesus (20:29-31).

8. I turn now to the postresurrection period. Once again it proves helpful to begin at the purely linguistic level. It is rather startling to observe that "signs and wonders" (or some minor variation) as a *linguistic category* is almost exclusively restricted to the apostles. I have argued that "signs and wonders" are heavily tied in the Old Testament to the major events surrounding the redemptive-historical event of the Exodus, and that the category is quickly applied to Jesus in the New Testament. After reporting that Peter on the day of Pentecost proclaims that God has once again performed "wonders" and "signs" through His Son Jesus (Acts 2:19, 22), Luke immediately summarizes the results of that first Christian sermon:

"Everyone was filled with awe, and many wonders and miraculous signs *were done by the apostles"* (Acts 2:43, italics added). The same point is repeated in Acts 5:12. Signs and wonders are attributed to Paul and Barnabas in Acts 14:3; 15:12. Considering Luke's consistent usage, the "signs and wonders" for which the church prays in Acts 4:29-30 are most plausibly understood to be miracles that the apostles would perform. In Acts, the only other individuals who are said to perform "signs and wonders" are Stephen (Acts 6:8) and Philip (8:13), who at least are closely associated with the apostles. Paul himself refers to the "signs and miracles" or "[marks of] an apostle" that he performed (Romans 15:19; 2 Corinthians 12:11-12). Although some take Hebrews 2:3-4 another way, the most natural reading is that the "signs, wonders and various miracles" by which God testified to the gospel were performed by those who first heard the word (i.e., the apostles) and who then passed the message on.

Once again it is vital not to draw the wrong conclusion from this evidence. It cannot be made to support the conclusion that miraculous signs and wonders have ceased altogether. But a substantial linkage can be made between "signs and wonders," taken as a linguistic entity, and the two major events of redemptive history, namely, the Exodus and the coming of Jesus Messiah. In this light the activity of the apostles is part and parcel of the Christ-revelation.

Something of this vision is retained in the prologue to the epistle to the Hebrews. In the past, the writer tells us, God spoke to the fathers *"through the prophets* at many times and in various ways, but in these last days he has spoken to us *by his Son"* (1:1-2, italics added). This Son-revelation is thus a step beyond the older revelation. The writings of the first witnesses, the writings of the apostles and apostolic men, are thus not seen as further revelations beyond the Son-revelation but as inscripturating the Son-revelation, rounding it out as it were. This Son-revelation is climactic: it has taken place in the "last days." Thus the apostles and other New Testament writers must be viewed as something more than proto-Christians, models of what all other Christians should enjoy and experience: in some respects they are *uniquely* tied to the climactic, once-for-all Christ-revelation. At certain levels, of course, they function as models for Christians in every generation. What is remarkable, however, is that the "signs and wonders" terminology is forcefully linked to the central redemptive-historical focus and embraces not only Jesus and His death and resurrection but the first articulation of that truth in the apostolic circle that was peculiarly accredited to that ministry.

Lest I be misunderstood, I must repeat: this does not mean Warfield was entirely right in arguing that the age of miracles ended with the apostles. We have still not considered such miracles as, say, the gifts of healing mentioned in 1 Corinthians 12. But at the purely linguistic level, "signs and wonders" in both the Old and New Testaments seems to enjoy primarily a narrow focus and is therefore a misleading label to apply to the Vineyard movement and its phenomena. The problem is more than one of labeling: by using the expression so freely, the Vineyard movement frequently applies to itself Scriptures and principles that a more sober reading refuses to warrant.

9. If, then, against New Testament usage, we apply the expression "signs and wonders" to all Christian expressions of the more spectacular *charismata,* or of miracles generally, can we discern other functions of signs and wonders in the New Testament? There are, I think, primarily two kinds of passages to consider.[10]

a. First, there are the passages where Jesus authorizes either the twelve (Matthew 10:8; Luke 9:1-2) or the seventy-two (Luke 10:9) to heal the sick (or, in the former passages, to heal the sick, raise the dead, and cast out demons). On the one hand, it will not do to limit the applicability of the command to the twelve, since the seventy-two receive a similar commission. On the other hand, it will not do to cite Matthew 28:20, "teaching them to obey *everything* I have commanded you," as if that authorizes the automatic applicability of those passages to all believers: after all, the same commissions to the twelve and the seventy-two also included prohibitions against going to the Gentiles or the Samaritans, and commands to take no bag for the journey, and so forth. The historical particularities of these trainee missions must be thought through; their theological significance must be quietly and thoroughly studied before glib proof texts are cited.

Without embarking on a full-scale exegesis of the passages, I would be inclined to say at least these things. First, there is an important sense in which the first disciples' ministry, even before the cross, was an extension of Jesus' ministry and a prefiguring of the in-breaking kingdom. This, too, was part of the Son-revelation. Second, although the application of the text to all Christians is fraught with difficulties (unless we want to apply *everything* in these chapters to all Christians and are prepared to deny that there was *nothing* special reserved for the first followers of Jesus), there is nothing to suggest that it would be impossible for *any* other believers, after the resurrection, to be gifted in similar ways. Third, it is imprudent to miss, in one of the three passages, the remarkable conclusion to the mission. When the disciples return with joy exclaiming, "Lord, even the demons submit to us in your name" (Luke 10:17), Jesus not only reminds them of what authority has been confided to them (vv.18-19) but warns, "However, do not rejoice that the spirits submit to you, but rejoice that your names are written in heaven" (v. 20). In other words, far more important, and far more justly a cause of joy than any miracle I might perform, is God's elective knowledge of me as one of His own people. And that, surely, is the rightful heritage of all the people of God.

b. Second, there are passages that speak of gifts of healing (such as the crucial discussion of *charismata* in 1 Corinthians 12-14) or that casually assume that more miracles were taking place among first-century believers than those performed by the apostolic band and a few others (e.g., Galatians 3:5; James 5:13-16). These, I think, serve as the death-knell to the strong form of the Warfield thesis. There is no sufficient evidence for supposing that all genuine miracles came to an end at the close of the apostolic age. Doubtless Wimber and others have been helpful in reminding some Christians of that fact.

Nevertheless, it is important to remember that all of these passages that assume the presence of miraculous gifts outside apostolic ranks focus, without exception, not on the justification of miracles but on their purpose or limitation or control in some way. For example, 1 Corinthians 12 insists that not all Christians have the same gifts, that believers with gifts not greatly respected should be greatly honored in the church, that the gifts should edify the church, and much more along the same lines.[11] Galatians 3:5 drives its readers back to the apostolic gospel; James 5:13-16 focuses on personal holiness. In all of these passages, the driving concern lies deeper than the presence or absence of miracles (though their presence is assumed); in no passage are readers berated because they have been insufficiently concerned with gifts of healing and exorcisms.

10. When we examine the notion of power in Paul, we find it centrally tied to neither evangelism nor healing, but to perseverance, faith, hope, love, spiritual stamina, endurance under trial, and growing conformity to Jesus Christ. That is easily confirmed not only by word studies of "power" and related terms but by careful and meditative study of Romans 8:31-39; 1 Corinthians 1-4; 2 Corinthians 10-13; Ephesians 3:14-21; and many other passages. A thorough study of Paul's prayers similarly discloses where the heart of his concern for his readers is.

11. Another way to approach this question is to study all that the New Testament has to say about the Holy Spirit. It is surely correct to say that under the New Covenant there is a tremendous emphasis on the gift of the Spirit, poured out on all children of the covenant without exception, in fulfillment of Old Testament promises. In one sense, this is the age of the Spirit; if someone does not have the Spirit of God, he or she does not belong to God.

But having said that, the biblical material rapidly becomes so rich (and sometimes disputed) that it becomes difficult to say much more without embarking on a much longer chapter than this one. Two comments must suffice.

First, the tendency in some literature (both scholarly and popular) is to fence off the Spirit from some phenomena. Some Christians have argued, for instance, that the only unique ministry of the Spirit under the New Covenant is His work in unifying believers into one body. A few minutes with a concordance should disabuse students of that conviction. At a more academic level, many scholars have argued that in Luke-Acts the Holy Spirit is the Spirit of prophecy, whereas Luke thinks of healings and exorcisms and the like as the fruit of *dynamis* ("power"), not the Spirit. This thesis has recently been ably rebutted by Turner.[12]

Second, the burden of the associations with the Spirit in Paul is not on miracles but on sanctification, ethics, revelation, transformation of character, the mediation of all that God provides for His people under the New Covenant. Although the theme deserves extensive exploration, it cannot be probed here.

12. Finally, the purpose of signs and wonders in the New Testament could be usefully explored by examining minutely many important passages and classifying the results. For example, one might argue that signs and wonders, in the larger sense, demonstrate Jesus' mercy and compassion in Matthew 9:35-36; 14:14; 20:34; Mark 1:41; they serve to establish the preeminence of faith, both inside and outside Israel (Luke 7:1-10); and so on. But most of those purposes could easily be made to slip under the points already made.

Two passages, however, deserve a little extended comment:

a. *Matthew 11:2-15.* We have already thought through vv. 4-6, where Jesus answers the Baptist's doubts by referring to his own ministry in terms of two passages from Isaiah. Jesus then turns to the crowds and speaks to them about John. As John bore witness to Jesus, so Jesus now bears witness to John—though as we shall see, it is witness of a special type.

In brief, Jesus asks a number of rhetorical questions regarding the expectations of the crowds when they went to see John in the desert. The final question leads Jesus to affirm that John the Baptist was a prophet (11:7-9)—indeed, "more than a prophet." How so? The Baptist is more than a prophet, Jesus insists, because John not only spoke the Word of God, but was someone of whom the Word of God spoke. Jesus cites Malachi 3:1: John is the one of whom the prophet Malachi said, "I will send my messenger ahead of you, who will prepare your way before you" (Matthew 11:10).[13] That is what makes John the Baptist more than a prophet. In fact, Jesus does not hesitate to offer this staggering evaluation of John: "Among those born of women there has not risen anyone greater than John the Baptist; yet he who is least in the kingdom of heaven is greater than he" (11:11).

The second part of the verse shows that Jesus means John is the greatest born of woman *up to that time.* From the time of the kingdom onward, John is outstripped in greatness by the least in the kingdom. Still, the first part of the verse must have raised a few eyebrows in the first century. It means that in the evaluation of Jesus John the Baptist is greater than Moses, greater than King David, greater than Isaiah or Jeremiah, greater than Solomon. Why?

Bearing in mind the quotation from Malachi, the only possible answer is that John the Baptist is the greatest because to him was given the task and privilege of pointing Jesus out more clearly than all before him. True, on Jesus' reading of the Old Testament, Moses, David, Isaiah, Jeremiah, and Solomon had all pointed to Jesus in one fashion or another, but John pointed out just who Jesus was in time, on the plane of history, before his peers. That is what made him the greatest person born of woman to that point in history. The brief assessment reported by the fourth evangelist is pertinent: "Then Jesus went back across the Jordan to the place where John had been baptizing in the early days. Here he stayed and many people came to him. They said, '*Though John never performed a miraculous sign* [italics mine], all that John said about this man was true.' And in that place many believed in Jesus" (John 10:40-42). This means, of course, that although it is true to speak of Jesus' witness to John, it is a peculiar witness indeed: He is in fact using John to point afresh to Himself. The Baptist's entire greatness turned on the clarity of his witness (owing to his position in redemptive-history) to Jesus.

And then Jesus adds that "he who is least in the kingdom of heaven is greater than he" (Matthew 11:11). For the comparison to be meaningful, the categories of "greatness" must be the same as those that applied to John the Baptist. The least in the kingdom are greater than John because even the least in the kingdom can point Jesus out more clearly and with greater depth than could the Baptist. All of us live this side of the cross and resurrection; none of us is slow to affirm that Jesus is simultaneously the conquering king and the suffering servant, the Davidic king and the priest in the order of Melchizedek, the sovereign Lord and the bleeding sacrifice, the crucified Messiah and the resurrected Savior.

That is what establishes the Christian's greatness: to us has been given the indescribably great privilege of bearing witness to Jesus' Person and work. It does not depend on performing miracles, as

John the Baptist's greatness did not depend on performing miracles (John 10:40-42): it depends on the privilege of knowing God in Christ Jesus, this side of the cross and resurrection, this side of the dawning of the promised kingdom.[14]

Anticharismatics must not milk this exegesis for more than it is worth. There is no warrant for concluding that the children of the kingdom *must not* perform signs and wonders (in the generic sense) in their witness to who Jesus is, on the ground that John the Baptist *did not.* What is entirely clear, however, is that greatness in Jesus' mind is not tied in any way to the performance of miracles. The greatest person born of woman until the dawning of the kingdom performed no miracles but pointed Jesus out more immediately than all before him. The least in the kingdom is still greater than he, for the obvious analogous reason: he or she can point Him out with even greater clarity because of the fuller revelation we have in the New Testament. That is tremendously humbling; it is staggeringly Christ-centered; it establishes that proclamation of the truth about Jesus (i.e., the gospel) is fundamental to our significance.

b. *John 14:12.* What about "greater things"? In the farewell discourse Jesus says, "I tell you the truth, anyone who has faith in me will do what I have been doing. He will do *even greater things than these* [italics added], because I am going to the Father" (John 14:12). The passage has become a more or less standard proof text not only in many traditionally charismatic circles but also for many in the Vineyard.

Before summarizing what the text means, it is worth mentioning what it *can't* mean. First, it cannot simply mean *more* works: the church will do more things than Jesus did. There are perfectly good ways to say that sort of thing in Greek, and John did not choose any of them. Second, it cannot mean *more spectacular* works or the like—though some such meaning seems to be assumed by many Vineyard people. We must remember that Jesus walked on water, raised the dead (in Lazarus's case, after he had been dead four days), fed five thousand from a lunch, and turned water into wine. I know of no one in the Vineyard, or anywhere else, for that matter, who claims, with any sort of public attestation at all, that he is performing *more spectacular* miracles than these. I know no person who is matching them; I know no group that is collectively matching them. In fact, it is difficult to imagine what kinds of miracles could possibly be classed as more spectacular than these.

Interpretative clues to the meaning of the passage are provided by the context. First, the verse before verse 12 must not be ignored: "Believe me when I say that I am in the Father and the Father is in me; or at least believe on the evidence of the miracles [lit., "works," which in John include miracles] themselves" (14:11).[15] In this context, the "greater things" (v. 12) that believers will perform surely derive their relative greatness from the fact that they are performed after the cross and resurrection for which Jesus is at this point preparing His followers. Both Jesus' words and His deeds were somewhat veiled during the days of His flesh, as the previous verses make clear. Even His closest disciples misunderstood much of what He was saying and doing. But in the wake of Jesus' glorification and the descent of the Spirit (themes that dominate chaps. 14-17), the words and deeds of Jesus' followers, empowered by the Spirit of truth, the *Paraclete,* will take on a clarity, and thus a "greatness," that *necessarily* eluded some of Jesus' words and deeds in the period before the cross. The words and signs of Jesus *could not* be as effective before the cross as they become after, when they are reported, in the wake of Jesus' exaltation and His gift of the Spirit. In the same way, Jesus' followers perform "greater things" (the expression is ambiguous enough to include more than miracles), precisely because they belong to the period of greater clarity, of less ambiguous witness to Jesus. In short, the argument is not unlike what we discover in Matthew 11.

Second, this interpretation is confirmed by the causal clause at the end of the verse. When Jesus says His followers will do greater things than what He is doing "because I am going to the Father," He cannot possibly be understood to mean that they will somehow have greater scope for their wonderful efforts because He will have faded from the scene and abandoned the stage to them. Rather, their works are classed as greater precisely *because* Jesus is going to the Father—a category in the fourth gospel that embraces His death, resurrection, and exaltation. They *belong* to that postexaltation period.

Third, there is an important parallel in 5:20: "For the Father loves the Son and shows him all he does. Yes, to your amazement he

109

will show him even *greater things than these"* (exactly the same Greek expression as here). The context of 5:20 shows that the "greater things" the Father will show the Son, and that the Son will manifest to His followers, are displays of resurrection and judgment (5:17, 24-26). And this life-giving power of the Son turns on His death, resurrection, and exaltation—what John calls His "glorification."

In short, the greater things that believers do include all their words and works empowered by the Spirit and performed this side of the Son's exaltation. They are greater precisely because they bear witness most tellingly to who Jesus is (note the witness theme throughout this gospel, not least in these chapters, e.g., 15:26-27). Doubtless they may include miracles, but there is not a scrap of evidence to restrict those "greater things" to miracles, and certainly not to miracles that are judged more spectacular than those of the Lord Jesus.

SOME THEOLOGICAL AND PASTORAL REFLECTIONS

Assessing the Vineyard movement. The subject of this chapter deserves more detailed work than these few pages can provide. Still, I dare to hope that for some it will provide something of a foil both to the works of strict cessationists and to the writings of Wimber and others who tend to focus on relatively few themes and passages, richly sweetened by many personal and moving anecdotes. To strengthen this hope, I offer the following reflections:

1. Few movements in the history of the church have been entirely good or entirely bad. To expect all the leaders of the Vineyard movement to be only heroes or villains is naive. The evidence of other, somewhat similar movements in the history of the church tends in the same direction. In the sixth century, St. Gregory describes a preacher from Bourges who drew large numbers through his healing ministry. Before him, Montanus gathered large numbers through his emphasis on the Spirit; a century and a half after St. Gregory, Aldebert, an itinerant preacher described by St. Boniface, claimed to effect many cures, and certainly gathered many people. In the days of Whitefield and Wesley, the French Prophets believed

they were led by the Spirit in ways not experienced by most Christians. Many others have claimed that the kingdom has come in its fullness in the locus of their ministries. The results have almost always been mixed. In some cases the theology was decidedly aberrant (e.g., Montanus); in other cases, nothing essential was denied, but the balance of Scripture was decidedly skewed. Sometimes some part of the church experienced a measure of genuine renewal; in other cases, the renewal so quickly led into forms of sheer subjectivism that the movement, at first popular, became isolated, self-righteous, totally dependent on authoritarian gurus. But the point to be observed is that few movements in the history of the church have been entirely unequivocal in their effects, and so we need to be cautious, humble, even-handed, and patient in our attempts to be discerning. This is all the more urgent if we are in danger of becoming a merely reactionary movement—a movement constantly reacting *against* whatever is going on—and likely to fall under the same limitations that befall most movements, becoming decidedly mixed in our self-identity and effect.

2. Although some people in the Vineyard movement justify their emphasis on healing by saying that at least the movement prays for the sick, whereas mainstream evangelicalism fails to do so, that has not by and large been my experience. Doubtless there are some evangelicals who never ask for healing, and, if they pray for the sick at all, pray exclusively for perseverance and stamina and the like. But far more, at least in North America, focus a large percentage of their public praying on the sick. I have been to countless prayer meetings where 70 or 80 per cent of the prayers have canvassed the illnesses of sundry friends and relatives, in each case petitioning the Almighty for healing.

The distinction of the Vineyard movement does not lie in its prayers for the sick but in its insistence that signs and wonders *must* be part of normal Christianity. That means frequent claims of healing must be present, or the movement loses its raison d'être. In my observation, that has badly skewed the objectivity of the reporting. Remarkable healings may take place both within and outside the Vineyard (and other related) movements. I suspect they take place more frequently in mainstream evangelicalism than some think, and considerably less frequently within the Vineyard than some think.

Meanwhile, by making not only prayers for the sick but an expectation that a certain percentage of them must be cured miraculously a central plank in the movement's raison d'être, the Vineyard has (doubtless unwittingly) spawned something of a reaction in some branches of mainline evangelicalism. For example, some Christians have become more timid in their prayers for the sick, simply because they do not want to be identified with the Vineyard.

In all such tussles, the most important thing we can do to breed maturity is to turn again and again to the Scriptures, and try to take the measure of our ministry from this lodestar.

3. The Vineyard is to be commended for disavowing a systematic two-tier form of Christianity, based on a second-blessing theology in which only some Christians enjoy some sort of inside track with the Spirit (however expressed). In practice, however, the Vineyard displays more of the inner ring syndrome than its formal theology justifies. Endless testimonies are of the "before-I-entered-the-Vineyard-and-after-I-entered-the-Vineyard" variety. There are no prizes for guessing which side is more spiritual, powerful, effective, godly, and so forth.

This goes beyond the normal Christian testimony about the changes that take place when the individual meets Christ. So many of these testimonies deal with self-perceived improvements effected by connection with the Vineyard. The result is a practical two-tier system of spirituality after all.

I have no doubt that many thousands of people have been genuinely helped by the movement. They may have been oppressed by the feeling of desperate unreality that afflicts so many mainstream evangelical churches. They may have been drawn to the excellent times of corporate praise that characterize some Vineyard churches.

Yet the fact remains that the Vineyard not only fosters an inner ring syndrome that caters (however unwittingly) to spiritual arrogance and tends toward divisiveness, but it does so on the basis of a certain perception of the nature of spirituality. There are, of course, many different visions of that in which spirituality consists.

Some speak of the spirituality of sacrament, others of the spirituality of nature, still others of the spirituality of worship. Central to the Reformed tradition is the spirituality of Word—a vision that desperately needs recapturing and rearticulating in our day, as it is so frequently misconceived as nothing more than rational exegesis. So far as I can see, the vision of spirituality in the Vineyard movement might be dubbed a spirituality of power, whether in ostensible miracle or in frequent and private divine disclosure. To assess this vision fairly would take us too far afield, but the least that must be said is that this focus on power caters to the infatuation with triumphalism so disturbingly endemic to modern Western culture. There is so little perception that God's power is perfected in weakness, that we triumph as we endure—and frequently that we conquer as we suffer. There is so little call to self-denial, to the way of the cross.

4. More generally, on the basis of the biblical evidence the Vineyard movement seems to have focused on the relatively peripheral (namely, the kinds of phenomena found in 1 Corinthians 12-14 and some other passages), called them "signs and wonders," and elevated them to a place of central importance. Because signs and wonders (at least in the generic sense) are part of the biblical heritage, there is no wisdom in despising them and some danger in doing so. But to elevate them to what is central is to lose the central, or at least to send it into eclipse.

Undoubtedly one of the models of freeing people in the New Testament is healing. But the modern propensity to speak of virtually every act of transformation as a "healing" tends to squeeze out other models—freeing people from the slavery of sin, forgiving debts, bringing them into new birth and life, and much more. Above all, these models are all tied in the New Testament to the cross. It is virtually impossible to imagine a Vineyard preacher saying, with Paul, "I resolved to know nothing while I was with you except Jesus Christ and him crucified" (1 Corinthians 2:2). Indeed, in scores of their public meetings, where checks have been made as to the place given the cross in hymns, songs, prayers, and preaching, this element, so foundational to New Testament Christianity, scarcely registers on the scale of what is important—even though no one would overtly disown its importance.

That is extremely troubling. It may be that the movement will restore some of the biblical balance. That is eminently to be longed for.

5. There can be little doubt that the Vineyard leaders believe they are bringing genuine integration back into Christian life. The West is so rationalistic, so enslaved by the prevailing scientism, that it leaves no place for the power of God. We have tended to restrict God to the other-worldly and leave normal life to the domain of science, to the power of natural processes with their tight circles of cause and effect. This bias needs to be broken down, and the Vineyard movement at its best helps to accomplish this task.

Nevertheless, the way it does so may actually serve the opposition. In any deeply biblical view of God's work, the rain falls at God's command, however much His commands may be thought sufficiently regular that the science of meteorology is possible. Not a sparrow falls from the heavens without His sanction. The stars "come out" at night at His command; through His Son, God upholds all things by His powerful word (Hebrews 1:3). When God performs what we call a miracle, it is not as if He is doing something for a change. Rather, He is doing something extraordinary.

But this means that if the power of God is praised primarily in what is perceived to be extraordinary, there is a strong tendency to view God as *not* operating in the "ordinary." If God heals by a miracle, *He* heals; if He heals through "natural" processes, then maybe it is not God who is doing it. This leads to enormous pressure to dramatize the mundane, to claim miraculous intervention when no one else can detect a miracle—even where other Christians, more subdued, do detect the power of God. In short, this vision of reality is in constant danger of reverting to the God-of-the-gaps theory; it is in constant danger of reinforcing secularism.[16]

Not long ago, a couple committed to the Vineyard movement were visited by a chap who complained, over dinner, that he was suffering from fairly constant headaches. As the couple tell the story, the woman felt impelled (a word from the Lord?) to ask if their visitor had had his eyes tested. He confessed that he hadn't. That week he followed their advice, discovered he needed spectacles, and his headaches disappeared. In mainstream evangelicalism, this development would be construed, at the lowest level, as "common sense"; the more reflective would say that this community wisdom is also under the sovereign sway of God, and thank Him for it, remembering that He gives gifts of wisdom (including "common" sense!) to His people. But because of their Vineyard connection, the couple in question felt compelled to analyze what happened as divine intervention, the immediate impress of the Spirit on a human mind, a prophecy, and display it as evidence, even justification, for their theological outlook. But this represents not only the triumph of triteness, it reflects a profoundly secular worldview broken up by moments of divine intervention. That is sad; it may also be dangerous.

6. Although Wimber and others acknowledge the existence of the biblical passages that warn against false signs and wonders, and sometimes erect some useful tests to distinguish between the true and the false, they have not adequately probed the different *kinds* of falseness. The choice, as we have seen, is not always between the divine and the demonic. There can be genuine signs and wonders pursued by thoroughly corrupt motives; there can be signs and wonders designed to test our faithfulness. Above all, biblical warnings against the *deceptiveness* of some signs and wonders must be taken more seriously.

Among the tests to be applied (certainly not an exhaustive list) are these:

(a) Do these displays of power give glory to God or to people (cf. John 7:18; 8:50; 17:4)? This test should not be applied only to the formulas used but to the reality of what actually happens in the meetings. It is a particularly difficult test to apply fairly in North America, where a cultural bias toward rugged individualism tends to exalt leaders to a dangerous degree.

(b) Do those involved display the fruit of the Spirit (Galatians 5:22-25)? Do they walk in the way of love (1 Corinthians 13)? The genuine power of God ultimately transforms us into the likeness of Jesus Christ.

(c) Do those involved in these displays of power cheerfully submit to the lordship of Christ (James 2:14-19; 1 John 2:3-5; 5:3)? This, too, is not a question of profession but of performance, not simply a question of orthodoxy but of obedience (Matthew 7:21-23).

(d) Do these displays of power edify others and foster the unity of the church (1 Corinthians 12-14)? This test must not be applied simplistically: divisions sometimes occur for valid reasons. Still, the drift of a movement in this regard is important, since the New Testament holds the unity of the church in high regard. The projection of an image of spiritual superiority, of an inner ring, is potentially destructive of both love and sound doctrine.

Other tests could be added. Are the leaders genuinely accountable? Do they prove self-correcting as they grow in maturity, or are they largely impervious to advice (except, perhaps, from a coterie of camp followers)? But perhaps it will be sufficient to add one more:

(e) Do these displays of power drive people to the Jesus of the gospel, to Jesus crucified, risen, exalted? Or is the Jesus who is praised another Jesus, one largely detached from the gospel? Do people in the movement expect men and women to be transformed by the message of the cross or by powerful signs? Meditate long on 1 Corinthians 1:18–2:5. How do the public meetings of the movement display the commitments of the leaders in this regard?

7. Finally, it is vital to recognize that the long-term blessing or corrosive influence wielded by any Christian movement turns in no small degree on its ability or inability to integrate its dominant features with other streams of Christian thought. In other words, it must strive for biblical balance and proportion, or it will degenerate into yet another eccentricity, possibly even a heterodoxy. When Jesus castigates some Pharisees in His day, He does not belittle their scrupulous commitment to apply the tithing laws even to the herbs

grown in the garden; rather, He tears a strip off them for scrupulously observing the tithing laws while ignoring the far weightier matters of justice, mercy, and faithfulness (Matthew 23:23-24).

Consider the Corinthians. They were so obsessed with the blessings and gifts they had received in Christ that they overlooked the blunt fact that Christianity has a "not yet" as well as an "already." They left nothing for the new heaven and the new earth; they thought they had it all already (see especially 1 Corinthians 4:8-13).[17] The result was that they had few categories for future hope, laid no emphasis on death to self-interest and self-fulfillment (it is impossible to imagine a Corinthian delighting in Mark 8:34-38), and could not defend themselves against the *deceptive* sins of their culture. It was not that they went around overtly *denying* the complementary truths of the faith; rather, they ignored them so successfully that those truths played no governing part in their values and conduct. To what extent are similar things true of the Vineyard movement?

Even though this problem is largely one of balance and proportion, it is not incidental. We may gratefully concur with the Vineyard movement that genuine signs and wonders (in the generic sense) *sometimes* in the New Testament become occasional causes of belief, and that they may do so today as well. But on the evidence of Scripture, it is doubtful this theme is anywhere near as central as some think. Occasional causes of faith include any number of personal experiences: personal tragedies, a kind deed performed by a friend, a good argument, a deep friendship, a sudden bereavement, some Christian music, an exorcism. But biblical evangelism is not substandard when any one of these phenomena is lacking—and it is not substandard when no genuine sign or wonder is performed. Serious imbalance in this area is in danger of distorting the gospel itself.

We may probe further into this problem of proportion and ask if the emphasis on signs and wonders in the Vineyard makes it difficult to articulate and teach a theology of suffering, a theology of faithfulness, a theology of perseverance, a theology of the Word of God, a theology of the cross, a theology of the regenerating power of the Holy Spirit—all of which are far more central to biblical thought, and far more important to Christian maturity, than the power of signs and wonders to serve as an occasional cause of faith.

NOTES

1. B. B. Warfield, *Counterfeit Miracles* (London: Banner of Truth, 1972 [orig. 1918]).
2. It must be said that many charismatic groups today espouse a structure of thought not very different from that of Wimber, if perhaps less articulate or less published. For example, many of the house churches in Britain, with no connection with Wimber, applaud much of his theology. In this essay it is convenient to use the Vineyard movement as a foil because of its high visibility and numerous publications.
3. The two most important books articulating this theological structure are John Wimber and Kevin Springer, *Power Evangelism* (San Francisco: Harper & Row, 1986); idem., *Power Healing* (San Francisco: Harper & Row, 1987). Wimber's views have changed slightly over the years, but I think he would own the summary I have just presented.
4. On other, minor uses of the expression in the Old Testament, see the discussion below.
5. I am indebted to an unpublished paper by John Woodhouse, "Signs and Wonders and Evangelical Ministry," produced for EFAC (The Evangelical Movement in the Anglican Communion), for first prompting me to reflect on this concatenation.
6. Definition of "miracle" is surprisingly difficult. In a theistic universe, everything that takes place is in some sense God's deed. But we may think of God normally doing things in regular ways, entirely in accordance with the nature of the universe He has Himself created, thus making modern science possible; and we may think of God occasionally doing something in an extraordinary way, out of step with the nature of the universe that He has Himself established. We should not think of a miracle as something that occurs when God intervenes to do something for a change (it being tacitly understood that ordinarily He does little); rather we should think of a miracle as what takes place when God does something highly unusual.
7. In the singular and without any connection with "wonder," "sign" in the Old Testament covers a considerably wider range of phenomena. But the full classification of uses need not be presented here.
8. *The Southern Cross* (April 1987), p. 13 (italics his).
9. I here summarize some of the argument presented more fully in my book *How Long, O Lord?* (Grand Rapids: Baker, 1990), pp. 125-26.
10. I do not here examine demonization and exorcism, as that would push the chapter's limits out of bounds.
11. I have discussed these matters at length in *Showing the Spirit* (Grand Rapids: Baker, 1987).
12. Max Turner, "The Spirit and the Power of Jesus' Miracles in the Lucan Conception," *NovT* 33 (1991), pp. 124-52.
13. The Interpretation of this verse is disputed. In my view it means that if the "messenger" is John the Baptist, the "me" is Jesus, identified in Malachi as Yahweh, yet at the same time the "messenger of the covenant."
14. It is probably worth adding that the passage does not establish ranking within the kingdom, as if it were saying that the best witness to Jesus is the greatest person.
15. See the comments above on this verse's only close parallel, namely, 10:38.
16. Cf. the thoughtful essay by Paul G. Hiebert, "Healing and the Kingdom," in James R. Coggins and Paul G. Hiebert, eds., *Wonders and the Word* (Winnipeg: Kindred, 1989), pp. 109-52
17. Cf. A. C. Thiselton, "Realized Eschatology at Corinth," *New Testament Studies* 24 (1978), pp. 510-26.

5

A Better Way:
The Power of the Word and Spirit

James M. Boice

W e live in such a mindlessly pluralistic society that it is thought uncouth if not wickedly immoral to suggest that some religions may be better than others or, even worse, that some religions may be wrong. But some are wrong. In fact, all are wrong that do not call us to faith in Jesus Christ. And not only that. There are ways of doing even the true religion wrongly.

That is what Paul is talking about in Romans 10, where he writes, "The righteousness that is by faith says: 'Do not say in your heart, "Who will ascend into heaven?"' (that is, to bring Christ down) 'or "Who will descend into the deep?"' (that is, to bring Christ up from the dead). But what does it say? 'The word is near you; it is in your mouth and in your heart,' that is, the word of faith we are proclaiming: That if you confess with your mouth, 'Jesus is Lord,' and believe in your heart that God raised him from the dead, you will be saved" (vv. 6-9), and later on, "Faith comes from hearing the message, and the message is heard through the word of Christ" (v. 17).

WHAT MOSES SAID

One wrong way of doing religion is by proclaiming signs and wonders rather than the *message* through which, as Paul states,

JAMES M. BOICE is pastor of Tenth Presbyterian Church and was the chairman of the International Council on Biblical Inerrancy.

faith comes to us. In the passage just cited, Paul introduces the appeal to ascending or descending a mystical ladder as a way in which the religion of faith does *not* speak.

The apostle explains this by reference to Deuteronomy 30:12-14, and by understanding Moses' purpose in that statement we will better grasp Paul's reiteration of it here.

Moses is addressing the people, assuring them that God will bless the nation if the people obey His commands and decrees. "What I am commanding you today is not too difficult for you or beyond your reach. It is not up in heaven, so that you have to ask, 'Who will ascend into heaven to get it and proclaim it to us so we may obey it?' Nor is it beyond the sea, so that you have to ask, 'Who will cross the sea to get it and proclaim it to us so we may obey it?' No, the word is very near you; it is in your mouth and in your heart so you may obey it."

Moses' point was that Israel had the Word of God, the law, and that the law was all they needed. They were not to seek an additional revelation but were to busy themselves with obeying what they had.

That is the passage Paul quotes, but he throws in an additional twist, explaining Moses' reference to ascending into heaven by adding "that is, to bring Christ down," and his reference to going beyond the sea (or descending into the abyss) by explaining "that is, to bring Christ up from the dead." To most people those explanations do not do much to explain the Deuteronomy text and even confuse Paul's point, but these additional explanations are crucial. This is a case in which a basic, original meaning is declared to contain additional meanings, each of which has bearing on Paul's point. What, then, is the meaning in Paul's additions?

The first point: *Israel did not need an additional word from God.* That is the literal meaning of the words in Deuteronomy, and although Paul adds specifically Christian interpretations to them, that meaning alone is true both for Israel in the Old Testament and for the Christian community. As far as Israel is concerned, the people did not need an additional word from God, because, as Paul teaches elsewhere, the law (i.e., Old Testament) itself contained announcements of the gospel and was sufficient in itself to lead to saving faith. That was the point of Romans 4, where Paul demonstrated that the doctrine of justification by faith was known to Abraham and David and that what they knew had saving power for them.

As far as Christians are concerned, the same meaning holds. For neither do Christians need an additional word from God. They have what they need already, and it is the gospel message being proclaimed by the apostles: "That if you confess with your mouth, 'Jesus is Lord,' and believe in your heart that God raised him from the dead, you will be saved" (v. 9). The meaning of this confession is explained by the full biblical revelation.

The second point: *Israel did not need to do something in order to bring the Messiah to them.* That is the unique sense of what Moses said to the people. For we notice that he did not speak merely of waiting for a new word from heaven or from beyond the sea, but rather of "ascending" into heaven or "crossing" the sea to get it.

In his short but valuable book on Romans 9-11, the Danish professor of New Testament Johannes Munck argues from rabbinical texts that "the Jews held that it would require an effort to bring the Messiah down from heaven. Israel must repent before the Messianic era can begin."[1] The Jews wanted to *do* something to earn their salvation. They wanted to ascend, descend, or cross something to get it. Yet even before the Messiah came they were not expected to do anything, only to believe God's word and look forward to Him in faith, even as Abraham, David, and the other Old Testament believers did. This "faith alone" is proclaimed by the patriarchs, but it is even more apparent as revelation unfolds in the New Testament. The Messiah has come and has died for sin. There is, therefore, no need to ascend into heaven to bring Him down to us. Again, there is no need to descend into the world of the dead to bring Him back. He has been resurrected. All that is needed is to believe on Him.

The third point: *Neither Israel then nor Christians today are to seek for a religion of signs.* It is because of this meaning that I have referred to Paul's statement as a confrontation with the "religion of signs." That is part of this passage because, as nearly every commentator points out, the expressions about ascending into heaven to bring Christ down and descending into the abyss to bring Christ up are proverbial expressions for what is clearly impossible.[2] If someone could produce Christ or His power on demand, bringing

Him down from above or up from below, that person would be a miracle worker. But, as Christ is seated firmly on His heavenly throne, we are not to look for that any more than we are to look for an additional revelation.

Yet that is exactly what the "signs and wonders" movement is trying to do. In addition to seeking out new revelations from God, explained as being "open to the Spirit," the signs and wonders movement is trying to do evangelism, not by the power of the Spirit of God working through the Word of God, but by miraculous displays designed to attract the attention of unbelievers and impress people the evangelist is seeking to convert to faith in Christ.

THE VINEYARD MOVEMENT

The most visible manifestations of this movement in our day are the Vineyard churches associated with the name of John Wimber, founder and pastor of the original Vineyard Christian Fellowship of Pasadena, California. This church started in his home in 1977 but has now grown to more than two hundred congregations scattered throughout the English-speaking world.

For a short time Wimber taught as an adjunct professor at the School of World Mission at Fuller Theological Seminary, which he refers to often to establish credibility. The course was called MC:510, "The Miraculous and Church Growth." From the material of this course he produced a book, actually written by Kevin Springer, called *Power Evangelism*. That was followed by another, called *Power Healing*.[3] Those books contain endorsements by such evangelical leaders as C. Peter Wagner of the School of World Mission, Michael Green of Regent College, and popular evangelical authors Richard J. Foster and John White. The endorsements show that John Wimber's views are not to be taken lightly.

Spiritual warfare. The starting point of Wimber's theology is that Christians are involved in a spiritual battle against the devil and demonic forces. That is because the kingdom of God has come into the world as a result of Jesus' coming but is opposed by Satan's kingdom. Christians are Jesus' soldiers in this conflict, and they have been given authority to oppose Satan and cast him out. Wimber calls clashes between the kingdom of God, represented by Christians, and the kingdom of Satan "power encounters." They are tests of strength: Who is stronger? Who will win?

Surely any Christian who recalls the statement of Paul in Ephesians 6 will recognize the reality of spiritual warfare. However, we will also remember that Ephesians 6 does not promote miracle-working as the way to do battle against Satan but instead admonishes us to be clothed with Christ's righteousness and to be armed with "the sword of the Spirit, which is the Word of God" (v. 17). The Spirit's weapon, therefore, is not additional revelation, nor "power encounters," but the written text of Holy Scripture. We are constantly reminded that the way to defend ourselves against Satan's onslaught is not by miracles but by the effective proclamation and teaching of Scripture.

Power evangelism. It follows from the first point, according to Wimber, that the way to do evangelism is by miraculous demonstrations of the superior power of God, which he calls "signs and wonders." Those "signs and wonders" involve such activities as exorcism, healing the sick, and receiving and acting upon special personal revelations from God about what another individual has done, or is thinking, facts otherwise unknown to the evangelist. Wimber calls these revelations "words of knowledge."

Wimber distinguishes at this point between what he is recommending and what he calls "programmatic evangelism." Programmatic evangelism is traditional evangelism. It is "message-oriented" and appeals to "rational arguments." It "attempts to reach the minds and hearts of people without the aid of charismatic gifts." It is evangelism, but because its goal is "decisions for Christ" instead of making disciples, the people reached by it "do not move on to a mature faith. . . . There is something inadequate about their conversion experience."[4]

By contrast, "power evangelism" is dependent upon the moment by moment leading of the Holy Spirit and by His revelation of what is going on in the lives of other people. "In power evangelism key obstacles—an adulterous affair, bitterness, a physical ailment, demon possession—are exposed and overcome, striking deeply into the hearts of people. This frees new believers from major obstacles so that they may experience future spiritual growth. Further, power encounters authenticate conversion experiences in a way that mere intellectual assents do not. This gives new Christians confidence about their conversions, a solid foundation for the rest of their lives."[5]

In short, the best and most effective evangelism, growth in the Christian life, and lasting assurance of salvation are attained by miracles, according to Wimber and his associates.

We can agree that much of traditional Christianity is weak in our day, including its evangelism. It often is a religion of assent rather than a deeply-rooted faith that produces heart-felt repentance. It is frequently formal and even dull. In large sections of the church very little evangelism takes place.

Further, we can be open to the claim that God can and does perform miracles. There is a difference of opinion on this point among evangelicals, and we ought to be very careful to maintain a certain liberty of conviction in the matter of spiritual gifts. In fact, D. A. Carson, who also contributed to this section, argues that the New Testament gifts are not restricted to the apostolic age.

Princeton theologian Benjamin B. Warfield is usually understood as restricting them to the apostolic age. In his classic study of the alleged miraculous events in church history, *Counterfeit Miracles,*[6] Warfield exposes many bogus claims of miracles from the patristic age to the twentieth century. But although Warfield began from the perspective that miracles were given by God to authenticate the office of the apostles and ceased with them and their immediate successors (those upon whom they laid their hands and passed on their gift), he nevertheless believed, as do Christians everywhere, that God answers prayer and sometimes heals and does other humanly inexplicable things in answer to prayer. "We believe in a wonder-working God," he wrote, "but not in a wonder-working church."[7]

Where we all come together is on the centrality of the gospel message and the error of seeking a gospel of miracles.

SIGNS AND WONDERS IN THE BIBLE

As D. A. Carson pointed out in his essay in this book, we ought to go directly to Scripture—not to find out what the apostles did and merely reduplicate them, but to discover what the *purpose* for signs and wonders was in the first place.

In 1987 John Wimber paid a much-publicized visit to Australia, in response to which pastors in the Evangelical Fellowship in the Anglican Communion (the EFAC of Sydney) prepared a helpful study of Wimber's teaching, which they distributed to their parishes by way of pastoral guidance. The book was titled *Signs and Wonders and Evangelicals: A Response to the Teaching of John Wimber.* Written by professors Paul Barnett, Robert Doyle, and John Woodhouse, and also by the Bishop of South Sydney, John Reid,[8] the book surveys the ways "signs and wonders" are referred to in the Bible. In that book Woodhouse lists four helpful categories.

1. *Signs accompanying the historical redemptive acts of God.* This is the most common use of the term "signs and wonders," and it is localized at two points of the biblical revelation: the deliverance of the people of Israel from Egypt and the earthly ministry of Jesus Christ.

In the first category are such texts as Exodus 7:3 ("I will harden Pharaoh's heart, and though I multiply my miraculous signs and wonders in Egypt, he will not listen to you"); Deuteronomy 26:8 ("The Lord brought us out of Egypt with a mighty hand and an outstretched arm, with great terror and with miraculous signs and wonders"); and Acts 7:36 ("He led them out of Egypt and did wonders and miraculous signs in Egypt, at the Red Sea and for forty years in the desert"). There are also texts that state that God will unleash the same judgment signs against Israel if the people depart from God and do not repent of their sin (cf. Deuteronomy 28:45, 46). In the second category are such texts as Acts 2:19, which quotes Joel 2:30 ("I will show wonders in the heaven above and signs on the earth below") and Acts 2:22 ("Jesus of Nazareth was a man accredited by God to you by miracles, wonders and signs, which God did among you through him").

This comparison suggests that the signs accompanying the redemptive work of Jesus parallel the signs accompanying the redemption of Israel from Egypt. But here is the important thing: neither the Old Testament signs nor the New Testament signs are put forward as examples of corresponding contemporary miracles but as redemptive events that are the work of faith to remember.

John Woodhouse writes, "Faith involves remembering the signs and wonders by which God redeemed his people. . . . Unbelief is precisely a failure to remember those wonders. . . . A consequence of this is the fact that a desire for further signs and wonders is sinful and unbelieving."[9]

That is exactly what Jesus told the Pharisees. He said:

A wicked and adulterous generation asks for a miraculous sign! But none will be given it except the sign of the prophet Jonah. For as Jonah was three days and three nights in the belly of a huge fish, so the Son of Man will be three days and three nights in the heart of the earth. The men of Nineveh will stand up at the judgment with this generation and condemn it; for they repented at the preaching of Jonah, and now one greater than Jonah is here. The Queen of the South will rise at the judgment with this generation and condemn it; for she came from the ends of the earth to listen to Solomon's wisdom, and now one greater than Solomon is here. (Matthew 12:39-42)

Jonah did no miracles in Nineveh, yet Nineveh repented. Solomon did no miracles in Israel, yet the Queen of the South came to hear him speak. So the Jews' demand that Jesus give them a sign was actually an evasion. Their real problem was that they did not like what He was teaching. However, just as the *preaching* of Jonah reached the people of Nineveh and the *wisdom* of Solomon reached the Queen of the South, so the word of the gospel is the means by which God reaches and saves sinners today. As Jesus announced of Himself, "One greater than Jonah . . . and now one greater than Solomon is here."

We might also note that signs do not in themselves create faith in the hearts of observers and can even harden hearts, as was the case with Pharaoh. In other words, even so spectacular signs as the plagues against Egypt and the miracles of Christ do not in themselves promote faith. Why? Because the power of God that saves sinners is *not seen* in any contemporary miracle, but only in the death of Christ on the cross.

That is why Paul told the Corinthians, "Jews demand miraculous signs and Greeks look for wisdom, but we preach Christ crucified: a stumbling block to Jews and foolishness to Gentiles, but to those whom God has called, both Jews and Greeks, Christ the power of God and the wisdom of God" (1 Corinthians 1:22-24).

2. *Deceptive signs and wonders.* This is the second category Woodhouse offers. John Wimber does not talk about this second class of miracles, but it too is a prominent strain in the Bible. For example, in Deuteronomy the people are warned against prophets who do signs and wonders yet proclaim other gods. "You must not listen to the words of that prophet or dreamer. The Lord your God is testing you to find out whether you love him with all your heart and with all your soul" (Deuteronomy 13:3). In the same way, Jesus warned against "false Christs and false prophets [who] will appear and perform great signs and miracles to deceive even the elect—if that were possible" (Matthew 24:24). In Revelation 13 we have a culmination of these utterly deceptive miracles in the signs of "the beast" who serves Satan and Antichrist.

I am not suggesting by this strain of evidence that John Wimber and his followers do miracles by satanic power. I am actually inclined to think that they are not real miracles at all but are only self-induced "mind cures" for relatively innocuous and unverifiable ailments, but that is not my point. My point is that miracles alone prove nothing. They may be false and deceptive as well as true and instructive, and we are never told that they are God's means for converting unbelievers or that we should seek to perform them.

3. *"Signs" done by God's prophets.* There are a few scattered "signs" performed by God's prophets, but these are not usually what we would call miracles. They are usually only symbolic or significant things or actions (cf. Isaiah 8:18; 20:3; Ezek. 12:1-11; 24:15-27).

4. *The signs of the apostles.* The final category of biblical signs consists of those miracles performed by the apostles, the effect of which was to authenticate their unique office and ministry. They are referred to in such texts as Acts 2:43 ("Everyone was filled with awe, and many wonders and miraculous signs were done by the apostles"); Acts 5:12 ("The apostles performed many miraculous signs and wonders among the people"); and 2 Corinthians 12:12 ("The things that mark an apostle—signs, wonders and miracles— were done among you with great perseverance").

Those are the miracles that mean so much to the Vineyard congregations. But in their rush to take them over into the present time and perpetuate them, the pastors of the movement make a fundamental error of interpretation. One great principle of hermeneutics (the science of Bible interpretation) is that narrative events are to be interpreted by didactic or teaching events rather than the other way around. In other words, that something has happened once or even more than once does not mean that it is to be taken as normative for us. For instance, we do not repeat annual crossings of the Red Sea. Such miraculous events are redemptive events and are not presented as normative for Christian experience. They are to be *remembered*, not *repeated*. What is normative is to be determined by the New Testament's explicit teaching, and, as we have seen, the New Testament does not teach that evangelism is to be done by cultivating miracles.

The bottom line of this investigation is that signs and wonders are not to replace the focus of the gospel on Christ and Him crucified, as Paul criticized the Jews for having done.

FROM THE SUBLIME TO THE RIDICULOUS

When we turn from a gospel with its feet firmly rooted in the soil of ancient Palestine, where miraculous and redemptive events took place in history, to a signs and wonders gospel, the motif is no longer sin's guilt, power, and presence versus the justification, liberation, and glorification that God promises in His word.

Let me reiterate that I believe in miracles. I believe that God answers prayer in healing the sick. I believe that there is such a thing as demon possession and exorcisms, particularly in areas of the world saturated with paganism, such as those targeted by pioneer missionaries. But if I believed that casting out demons and performing healings was the way to do evangelism, what would I do? Either I would go around looking for a lot of demons to cast out, or I would begin to interpret demonism to include a lot of other things I encountered.

It is this second approach that describes Wimber's activity in my estimation. It is true that he writes about what seems to be genuine demon possession, people who are taken over by other personalities, speak in other voices, fall down and thrash about, and spew out obscenities and hatred, particularly against Jesus Christ.[10] But those accounts quickly slide over into descriptions of demonization and exorcism of a very different order, descriptions involving "demons" of bondage, temptation, fear, pain, and even physical ailments like itching.[11] In fact, Wimber explains that he prefers the word "demonized" rather than "demon possession" for the purpose of including those phenomena.[12]

But that trivializes and cheapens the reality of spiritual warfare. It reduces the seriousness of our war with the heavenly rulers to the silly. One well-known evangelical missions school even held a conference for the purpose of binding the demons of the Bermuda Triangle, and the spirits of homelessness, alcoholism, and so on. When perfectly natural explanations are available, why should we discredit the genuinely supernatural by turning to superstition?

Again, the signs and wonders movement shifts from the sublime to the ridiculous. It cheapens and overshadows the gospel. It cheapens it because it reduces its promises to shrinking goiters, straightening backs, and lengthening legs, all of which are described at length in *Power Healing.* Those alleged wonders are next to nothing in comparison to the message of God's redeeming work in Jesus Christ or the true miracle of the new birth, which the preaching of the gospel, accompanied by the power of the Holy Spirit, produces in human lives. In fact, one of the striking things about Wimber's books, especially *Power Evangelism,* is that the message of the gospel is virtually unmentioned. There is much about miracles, but we are never told what Jesus accomplished on the cross or by His resurrection. That is a surprising omission for a book on evangelism: an evangelism without an evangel.

Indeed, if we are to take Wimber's illustrative material literally, it would seem that it is possible to become converted without hearing the gospel at all. "Wait a minute," I hear someone saying. "Now you're really jumping to conclusions. Who among the Vineyard leaders would say it's possible to be converted without hearing the gospel at all?" John Wimber: "One day a group of our young people approached a stranger in a parking lot. Soon they were praying over him, and he fell to the ground. By the time he got up, *the stranger was converted.* He is now a member of our church."[13]

Whatever happened to Romans 10: "If you confess with your mouth, 'Jesus is Lord,' and believe in your heart that God raised him from the dead, you will be saved" (v. 9)?

The signs and wonders movement also cheapens suffering. Suffering has various causes, some arising within ourselves. But there is suffering that is given to Christians by God that is intended for their growth and His own glory. Such were Job's trials, the suffering of the man who had been born blind, the thorn in Paul's flesh, and the various hurts, disappointments, and forms of physical anguish endured by countless numbers of God's people today—anguish that the Bible assures "produces character" (Romans 5). Miracle-seeking not only replaces gospel-seeing, it undermines character-seeking by eliminating the mundane hassles and frustrations of the normal Christian life. The religion of signs reduces all those to unnecessary affliction and further burdens us with lacking faith if the demon of suffering cannot be quickly cast out. That is a cruel burden to lay on God's people.

It is more. "It is," writes Woodhouse, "a version of Christianity in which the gospel is not sufficiently powerful to produce mature Christian faith, the Scriptures are not sufficiently revealing for the life of faithful obedience to God, the finished work of Christ is not sufficiently relevant for effective evangelism, and the hope of Christ's coming is not sufficiently comforting for those who are suffering."[14]

The Bible declares that the saints overcame Satan "by the blood of the Lamb and by the word of their testimony" (Revelation 12:11), not by *power evangelism.*

THE BETTER WAY

If there is to be reformation and revival in the church today, all of us—charismatic and noncharismatic—will have to regain our confidence in the power of God's Word to change lives. Here the words of the aged apostle Paul to his young co-worker Timothy speak strongly: "People will be lovers of themselves, lovers of money, boastful, proud, abusive, disobedient to their parents, ungrateful, unholy, without love, unforgiving, slanderous, without self-control, not lovers of the good, treacherous, rash, conceited, lovers of pleasure rather than lovers of God" (2 Timothy 3:2-4). Although those verses describe every society to some degree, they seem especially appropriate to our own time and place. But here is the tragic thing:

immediately after those two verses Paul adds, "having a form of godliness but denying its power" (v. 5). That means that it is not the culture at large about which Paul is speaking but the church. It is those who have "a form of godliness" who are like that.

We might say at this point, "If days as terrible as those are coming, days in which we are to have not only a dying society but a moribund church as well, certainly Paul is going to find something new and astonishingly effective to offer Timothy to see him through such times. Surely a secret weapon will be introduced to Timothy for our use.

"Perhaps he will offer him a new revelation, some new truth that no one has seen or known before.

"Perhaps he will suggest a new evangelistic methodology.

"Perhaps he will urge him to cultivate the gift of tongues or learn certain rules of healing and demonic confrontation."

Paul does nothing of the sort. Instead of those things, Paul says, "But as for you, continue in what you have learned and become convinced of . . . ."

And what is that?

Answer: "the holy Scriptures, which are able to make you wise for salvation through faith in Christ."

And why is that the answer?

It is because "all Scripture is God-breathed and is useful for teaching, rebuking, correcting and training in righteousness" (vv. 14-16).

That is why Jesus said, "The words I have spoken to you are spirit and they are life" (John 6:63). It is why Jesus prayed, "Sanctify them by the truth; your word is truth" (John 17:17). It is why the author of Hebrews declared, "The word of God is living and active. Sharper than any double-edged sword, it penetrates even to dividing soul and spirit, joints and marrow; it judges the thoughts and attitudes of the heart" (Hebrews 4:12). It is why the apostle Peter wrote, "For you have been born again, not of perishable seed"—and we know how perishable are the seeds of those who lose interest when the show is over—"but of imperishable, through the living and enduring word of God" (1 Peter 1:23).

It is why God said through the prophet Isaiah,

As the rain and the snow
   come down from heaven,
and do not return to it
   without watering the earth
and making it bud and flourish,
   so that it yields seed for the sower and bread for the eater,
so is my word that goes out from my mouth:
   It will not return to me empty,
but will accomplish what I desire
   and achieve the purpose for which I sent it. (Isaiah 55:10-11)

It is why the apostles, who were able to perform miracles, nevertheless were sent into the world to be "witnesses" (Acts 1:8) and "teachers" (Matthew 28:20). And it is why even Jesus, when urged to return to Capernaum to perform miracles there as He had done before, replied, "Let us go somewhere else—to the nearby villages—so I can preach there also. That is why I have come" (Mark 1:38). The next chapter tells us that a few days later, when He did in fact return to Capernaum, "he preached the word to them" (Mark 2:2).

Robert L. Saucy summarizes these and other important texts by writing, "Only as we expose ourselves to the Word and allow the illuminating work of the Spirit to lift the veil from our eyes do we find faith in the living Word. Only as we gaze on the truth of the Word, which is finally the Person of the Savior, and allow the Spirit to glorify him before us, will we commit ourselves to him. Since God uses the Word to incite faith, its use in evangelistic efforts is absolutely imperative."[15]

HOW TO DO EVANGELISM

That brings us back to Paul's point in Romans 10, our starting point. It is a straightforward presentation of the gospel of faith in Christ's Person and finished work, accompanied by the power of Christ through His Spirit, that makes the presentation effective. How does true faith speak? Paul answers in verses 8 and 9. "'The word is near you; it is in your mouth and in your heart,' that is, the word of faith we are proclaiming: That if you confess with your mouth, 'Jesus is Lord,' and believe in your heart that God raised him from the dead, you will be saved."

That is the right way to do evangelism.

Why?

First, *because it is focused on Jesus and His work alone.* Verse 4 taught that Christ is "the end of the law so that there may be righteousness for everyone who believes." In other words, Christ is everything. It is the same here. For the message that is near us, in our mouths and hearts, is Jesus Christ, and the confession of faith through which we are saved is that "Jesus is Lord" and that God raised Him from the dead. Those are not simplistic doctrines; they involve a great amount of biblical theology. But they are about the Savior exclusively. Christianity *is* Jesus Christ. Therefore, anything that detracts from Him or His work, even so-called miracles done in His name, is misleading and potentially harmful.

Our Lord's words to those who pretended to represent Him and to perform miracles in His name should be a warning to all of us: "Many will say to me on that day, 'Lord, Lord, did we not prophesy in your name, and in your name drive out demons and perform many miracles?' Then I will tell them plainly, 'I never knew you. Away from me, you evildoers!'" (Matthew 7:22-23).

Of the Holy Spirit, Jesus Himself taught, "When the Counselor comes, whom I will send to you from the Father, the Spirit of truth who goes out from the Father, he will testify about me" (John 15:26). And again, "He will bring glory to me by taking from what is mine and making it known to you" (John 16:14). If it is true that the work of the Holy Spirit is to glorify Christ, which is what these passages declare, then whenever Jesus is truly glorified, there the Holy Spirit is at work; and whenever glory is being given to anyone or anything else, to a miracle worker or even to the Holy Spirit Himself, we can be sure that there the Holy Spirit is not working and that another spirit is involved.

Second, *because it calls for faith on the part of those who are hearing the gospel.* We are not saved either by good works or miracles, but that does not mean that salvation is somehow extraneous to us in the sense that it happens mechanically. On the contrary, it is as intimate, personal, and life-transforming as anything could possibly be. It finds us as dead men and women, under God's curse, and it changes us into spiritually regenerated people who now live under God's protective love and blessing. It is through faith that we are justified, and that is what Paul has been teaching all along. In spite of what is claimed, the working of miracles detracts from faith because it focuses attention, not on Christ, but on the miracle worker and because, in many cases, the miracle works independently of an individual's knowledge of the gospel, assent to it, or trust in its promises.

Third, *because the teaching of the Word of God accompanied by the power of the Spirit of God is effective.* "Faith comes from hearing the message, and the message is heard through the word of Christ" (v. 17).

The world does not understand this divine working, but it is nevertheless true that the most important thing happening in the world at any given time is the preaching of the gospel. For there the Spirit of God is at work. Those who do not have faith in the Word of God do not preach it. They find other sources of power, even very noble substitutes. But those who do have that proper faith in the Word of God teach it, and it is by that means that men and women are truly delivered from the bondage of sin and the power of Satan and are set free spiritually.

I do not hesitate to say that the weaknesses of today's church, for all its numerical and financial strength, can be traced precisely to its failure to trust and, consequently, its failure also to preach and teach the Scriptures.

GOD'S POWER TODAY

Several years ago I had the task of finding a person to write a foreword to a small booklet, *Freedom and Authority,* written by J. I. Packer, which the International Council on Biblical Inerrancy produced as part of its ten-year program to "elucidate, vindicate and apply the doctrine of biblical inerrancy as an essential element for the authority of Scripture and a necessity for the health of the church." At once I thought of Charles W. Colson because of his years in government and his work with Prison Fellowship. I thought he could put the case for a link between freedom and authority well.

Colson agreed to write the foreword, but what I got back was not what I expected. It was better. Colson told how, when he had first heard of the International Council on Biblical Inerrancy, he thought that its cause did not concern him. He was dealing with "practical" issues, not "ivory tower theology." But he said that he changed his mind when he saw the effects of a high and low view of Scripture on the front lines of spiritual warfare in the prisons.

He wrote:

> Experiences in the past two years have profoundly altered my thinking. The authority and truth of Scripture is not an obscure issue reserved for the private debate and entertainment of theologians; it is relevant, indeed critical, for every serious Christian—layman, pastor, and theologian alike.
>
> My convictions have come, not from studies in Ivory Tower academia, but from life in what may be termed the front-line trenches, behind prison walls where Christians grapple in hand-to-hand combat with the prince of darkness. In our prison fellowships, where the Bible is proclaimed as God's holy and inerrant revelation, believers grow and discipleship deepens. Christians live their faith with power. Where the Bible is not so proclaimed (or where Christianity is presumed to rest on subjective experience alone or contentless fellowship) faith withers and dies. Christianity without biblical fidelity is merely another passing fad in an age of passing fads. In my opinion, the issue is that clear-cut.[16]

This kind of religion is not calculated to stroke the fallen, Adamic ego, and it is not spectacular as the world considers spectacle. It will not win the attention of the world like jumping unharmed from the pinnacle of the Temple or casting out demons or predicting the future or healing the sick. But it is God's true religion. And what is most important, it is the teaching God honors in accomplishing the most important miracle of all, namely, the regeneration of those "dead in trespasses and sins" (Ephesians 2:1), so that one who was formerly condemned to eternal judgment is adopted into God's very own household of faith.

NOTES

1. Johannes Munck, *Christ and Israel: An Interpretation of Romans 9-11*, trans. Krister Stendahl (Philadelphia: Fortress, 1967), p. 87.

2. See, for instance, Leon Morris, *The Epistle to the Romans* (Grand Rapids: Eerdmans; and Leicester, England: Inter-Varsity, 1988), p. 383 n. 31. Morris notes that they are used this way in the Talmud.

3. John Wimber with Kevin Springer, *Power Evangelism* (San Francisco: Harper & Row, 1986), and *Power Healing* (San Francisco: Harper & Row, 1987).

4. Wimber, *Power Evangelism*, pp. 45-46.

5. Ibid., p. 48.

6. Benjamin B. Warfield, *Counterfeit Miracles* (Carlisle, Pa.: Banner of Truth, 1986). Original edition, 1918.

7. Warfield, *Counterfeit Miracles*, p. 58.

8. John Woodhouse, Paul Barnett, and John Reid, *Signs and Wonders and Evangelicals: A Response to the Teaching of John Wimber*, ed. Robert Doyle (Homebush West, Australia: Lancer Books, 1987).

9. Robert Doyle in *Signs and Wonders and Evangelicals*, pp. 21-23.

10. Wimber, *Power Healing*, pp. 97-98, 113-14.

11. Ibid., pp. 106-9, 182, 232.

12. Ibid., p. 109.

13. Wimber, *Power Evangelism*, p. 26.

14. Robert Doyle in *Signs and Wonders*, pp. 34-35.

15. Robert L. Saucy, *The Bible: Breathed from God* (Wheaton, Ill.: Victor Books/Scripture Press, 1978), p. 117.

16. Charles W. Colson, "Foreword," in J. I. Packer, *Freedom and Authority* (Oakland, Calif.: International Council on Biblical Inerrancy, 1981), p. 3.

PART 3
POWER GROWTH

*My people have committed two sins: They have for-
saken me, the spring of living water, and have dug
their own cisterns, broken cisterns that cannot hold
water.*

Jeremiah 2:13

*We do not use deception, nor do we distort the word
of God. On the contrary, by setting forth the truth
plainly we commend ourselves to everyone's conscience in the sight of God. And even if our gospel is
veiled, it is veiled to those who are perishing.
. . . For we do not preach ourselves, but Jesus Christ
as Lord. . . . But we have this treasure in jars of clay
to show that this all-surpassing power is from God
and not from us.*

2 Corinthians 4:2-7

POWER GROWTH

6

Is the Church Growth Movement Really Working?

Bill Hull

To ask the question, "Is the church growth movement really working?" is, of course, to appeal to pragmatism as the ultimate test of whether a particular avenue is worth pursuing. At least, that is the case in American culture, where the question, "Will it work?" often replaces concern for the truth. It is not my concern in this chapter to cover the question of pragmatism, however, but rather to direct our thinking in a different course. Even if pragmatic concerns *were* the ultimate test, by those standards is the church growth movement a success? Regretfully, I must answer no.

I say "regretfully" because I am not against the church growth movement. In fact, I have been a part of that effort for many years and continue to assist churches in the strategies for growth. However, what I have observed in some quarters has caused me great concern. Obviously there are some useful aspects: "common sense" advice concerning the way churches present themselves to their community; improving leadership qualities and communication; giving a more professional polish to church bulletins; providing insights into interesting options in outreach programs.

And yet, the evangelical church seems to have become like the child with a new toy. As churches and pastors expect a more

---

BILL HULL is the director of church ministries for the Evangelical Free Church of America (EFCA).

clever gadgetry from the marketing wizards, the latter are encouraged to become increasingly creative until the *methods* eventually bury the *message* in obscurity. For that reason, church growth should not be a primer for building effective churches; it has a sociological base, it is data-driven, and it worships at the altar of pragmatism. It esteems that which works above all and defines success in worldly and short-sighted terms. It offers models that cannot be reproduced and leaders who cannot be imitated. The principles of modern business are revered more than doctrine; the latter, in fact, often being perceived as a detriment or at least a distraction to church growth. Yet churches are supposed to be driven by scriptural teachings, not by the latest marketing surveys or consumer trends.

In short, theology before sociology, please.

But again, beyond the criticism of pragmatism's replacing theology, my argument in this chapter will be that even on the level of pragmatism, the church growth movement has made more promises than it can deliver. I would argue that the church growth principles are overrated in their effect.

One must not "lionize" or "demonize" the movement, as there are many church growth principles that are clearly useful, practical guides. Rather, it is the excess that must be criticized, particularly when those excesses are becoming characteristic of the movement itself.

THE FIGURES DON'T ADD UP

The church growth movement does not produce lasting results, a point that has been recognized within the church growth movement. Though unwilling to concede that there was "anything intrinsically wrong" with the church growth principles they had developed, one prominent church growth advocate was quoted in an article in *Christianity Today* as acknowledging that "somehow they don't work."[1]

That same leader also pointed out that during the 1980s the percentage of American adults attending church remained almost the same (about 45 percent), whereas Protestant church membership actually declined. That squares with research done by George

Barna, George Gallup, and James Hunter. In fact, in his widely read work *Evangelicalism: The Coming Generation,*[2] Hunter demonstrates a *decline* in real numbers of evangelicals during the past twenty-five years. Research by my colleague Bob Gilliam shows the average evangelical church in the United States introduces 1.7 people to Christ per year per 100 who attend worship. A church with 200 worshiping adults, then, would introduce a fraction over 3 people annually.

George Barna tells us that we are only replacing the dead, that the evangelical body is not growing. Churches are growing by the rearranging of the saints. Evangelicals are simply playing "musical churches," moving around to more exciting, larger churches. The megachurch's feeder system is the smaller church and disgruntled believers who have quit their churches. What is going to happen when that feeder system dries up? What we are *not* doing is penetrating our world for Christ. Real evangelism, real discipleship, real outreach is simply not taking place on any serious level, as the cold facts plainly demonstrate.

The founder of the Fuller Institute of Church Growth, the late Donald McGavran, had a dream to help churches "make disciples of all nations" (Matthew 28:19), to seek the lost and find them. That would be the source of church growth. But church growth has not happened, and instead of church growth principles *replacing* evangelism, they have merely succeeded at *undermining* it by placing success in the hands of technicians instead of the believing community as it discharges its duties of bearing witness to the gospel.

If this is the case, how have we arrived at this state of affairs, and what can be done about it?

THE LIMITATIONS OF CHURCH GROWTH

The church growth movement has served an important purpose simply by helping church leaders face the need for practical changes in very simple, but important, external matters. Their research has aided churches in understanding where our contemporary culture stands with regard to faith and has helped us gain an important perspective on the dominant perceptions or misperceptions of the church, which we perhaps unwittingly perpetuate. They have insisted on church renewal and measurable results. The real dangers lie not in the intention but in the unfocused application of the findings. Evangelicals were shocked in the earlier part of this century when mainline liberal denominations began to adopt the policy that "the world sets the church's agenda." Now, evangelicals themselves appear to be more comfortable with the idea.

Now for some specific dangers.

It is seductive. Peter Berger writes: "He who sups with the devil of modernity must have a long spoon." Os Guinness warns that the two most powerful cultural forces that have been accepted uncritically by the church are the managerial and therapeutic movements. The danger is to address church renewal through managerial technique. In this scenario, the pastor uncritically shapes his role based on the new wave of leadership technique. Or he uses support groups and "felt needs" as a primary means of evangelism. Before long, like any corporate executive, the pastor becomes the slave to the marketplace; he has to tell the consumers what they want to hear if he wants to keep his job and secure results. A "user-friendly" church, if by that we mean catering to the cultural and selfish goals of contemporary fashion, is an unfaithful church. There may be a lot of people in the seats, but have they been confronted with the serious issues raised by the gospel (sin and grace) and the calls to discipleship?

The gospel is confrontational in its very nature. Any presentation of the gospel that does not present a challenge to the unbeliever to radically change his or her thinking and attitudes toward God and His saving work in Christ is not the same gospel preached in the pages of the New Testament! Today, people can be happy, healthy members of evangelical churches without ever having to face a God who is anything more than a "buddy," a Savior who is anything more than an example, and a Holy Spirit who is anything more than a power source. And that can happen without faith, without repentance, indeed, without conversion.

The problem is, we are often driven by sound motives. We really do want to reach a community that is becoming increasingly secular and hardened to the gospel, and sometimes we even wonder ourselves whether the gospel itself is enough to do the job: is it *really* "the power of God unto salvation"? So, like Paul's countrymen who failed to accept the gospel, the zeal of many runs ahead of their knowledge (see Romans 10:2). In desperation, gimmicks and simple solutions appear so promising—and therein lies the seduction. We have forgotten that God is sovereign and that Christ is the one building His church.

The need to reach out to a hurting world, and the need to use tools invented by the world in order to do so, cannot be denied. The trouble comes when we employ those tools uncritically, without careful biblical scrutiny. The more the church *accommodates* to culture, the more it becomes secularized itself and, therefore, incapable of offering solutions as a hand *outside* a ruined culture, reaching into the pit to pull the captives to freedom. A secularized church cannot *make* disciples because it is not itself a faithful servant of its risen King.

But what accounts for this seduction? What attracts leaders to church growth seminars? Although there is the danger of overstating the case, I must confess as an "insider" that the subliminal message of seminars entitled "Breaking the 200, 400, or 800 Barrier" is less than novel, regardless of the motive. The reasons for numerical bottle-necks are presented as structural, and the solutions are as well. The perilous dual message is that secondary issues (structural) are primary and primary issues (doctrinal) are secondary. Therefore, a spiritual ill can be cured by a structural remedy. A second message is that success is measured by size. Therefore, failure is "small"; success is "large." The research shows that by those standards, most church leaders are failures.

I must confess that my motive for attending a conference and learning about a new method was to meet my ego needs. My church was stagnant, and I needed help. Hoping that I would meet upon some new, revolutionary method or quick fix, I learned that many of the other pastors who were there came looking for the same thing. The eager rush of evangelical pastors to working models led by luminaries has become a major attraction. Of course, I'm speaking of "soft data" in this instance, since it is impossible to research motives. Nevertheless, my own insights, and those of my colleagues, lead me to believe that the church growth movement is both encouraging and benefiting from a success syndrome that has turned many pastors into secular executives.

A further attraction to the ego is the parade of role models. In a weight-lifting contest the contestants emerge from a back room with glinting muscle structure that is at the same time stunning and grotesque. As they lift the weights above their heads, awestruck crowds cheer and wiry teens return home determined to work out every day until they can perform the same feats. But eventually most kids burn out on the idea and return to their normal routine, resigned to the idea that they will never be quite as awesome as the heros they have by now forgotten. The same is true of many pastors who attend these seminars. Evangelical luminaries have done and and can do incredible feats. They tell their stunning stories and then deliver an exhortation to the conferees, "You can do it too!" That is, of course, not true for most of the people there. The fact is, the success of a particular pastor is often due to personal charisma, rare leadership, and creative genius that cannot be duplicated by others.

If one combines the power of the flesh to be successful with the message that more bodies, bucks, and buildings equals success, then the seduction is complete and the pastor is set up for the fall. Culture joins hands with the ego's craving for recognition, power, and achievement by painting the pastor into the corner that only by breaking through numerical barriers will his church be valid and pleasing to God. The most seductive part of it all is that this is never said by church growth leaders; in fact, they would probably abhor the idea. And yet, it is the unspoken message that is most powerfully communicated through the faculty, the curriculum, and the seminars.

The fact is that 90 percent of churches in America have two hundred or fewer worshipers, and judging by current indicators that will not change significantly in the next decade. It will not change for reasons other than those addressed by the church growth movement, which can only serve secularization if it is placed at the apex of solutions.

It is based on growing models. Starting with principles, not models, is the key to building leaders. Therefore, it is the key to meaningful church growth as well. If you want short-term results and a dependent future, encourage leaders to rely on models. If you desire long-term results and a continual stream of working models emerging from those principles, start building a philosophy of ministry.

Too often, we let the "experts" do our thinking for us. We do this in many areas of life: politicians, therapists, personal financial counselors, and so on, until we eventually have nothing left to work out for ourselves. But pastors and church leaders *must* think for themselves about their philosophy of ministry, and this is an outgrowth of one's theology. The mad rush to "successful working models" is the new evangelical holy grail of pragmatism. Never mind that my preaching might be shallow and redundant, or that the music doesn't reflect much thought and effort—there must be a quicker, easier way to the big church like so-and-so has down the street!

We are in danger of having an entire generation of pastors committed to clever programming instead of Scripture. That, of course, will not happen with any official declarations; in fact, those who engage in this idolatry of method will not even really think they are doing so. Still, the simple proclamation of God's Word and care of souls will take a back seat in church life to programs and strategies that have more in common with big business than with Christ's kingdom. We must not create a new generation of pastors who are dependent on a few charismatic creators, pastors who zigzag all over the cultural landscape trying to copy the successful.

THE LIMITS OF WORKING MODELS

There are, of course, dangers of working models, but even in cases where dangers are minimal, there are limits in terms of the success. Let me suggest some reasons that is so.

You can't transfer context. Sometimes I have a pastor call or write (the braver ones confront me in person!): "Bill, it didn't work for me. I tried your stuff, my board resisted, and my congregation didn't respond." Every one of the disappointed leaders made the same mistake: they took my working model and attempted to impose it on their system. Working models almost always fail when they are plopped down in a different context.

That is why I repeatedly warn all interested parties, *"You must write your own principled script."* We will offer practical tips and some helpful advice, but the local church leadership must decide how to contextualize the information. Common mistakes are usually errors in people skills; pastors often fail to lay the proper groundwork with the leadership before going public. The only way it can work long term is for the leadership to be convinced that the new direction is biblically sound *and* methodologically sound. We often think that theology and methodology are separate and that we can have a sound theology while employing any methods we deem most promising. But methodology is never independent of a philosophy of ministry. Those, for instance, whose sound theology tells them that God does the saving cannot resort to methods that make it appear as though the preacher does. Those who believe that unbelievers can only respond to God by a gift of His grace will not act as though it all depended on clever marketing techniques. What is your theology? And from that, what is your philosophy of ministry?

Often, eager leaders confuse methods and practices that are culturally accepted in the creator's context but not in theirs. Take, for instance, the "user-friendly," "seeker-sensitive" worship service. User-friendly in San Francisco may not be user-friendly in Ping Pong, Minnesota. Such issues as leadership training, streamlining of committees, reduction of services, changing of the target audience on Sunday morning are relative and contextual and must not be confused with absolute and universal issues of theology and philosophy of ministry.

You can't transfer personality and gifts. The distressing truth about contemporary pastoral role models is that in large part they cannot be reproduced. The men who are presented at conferences as worth listening to are charismatic, highly gifted servants, and I wish them well; but they are uniquely gifted in their natural talents. Their personality and gifts cannot be folded up, placed in a box with wrapping paper, and sent home for the price of registration.

Much of the content of conference presentations by evangelical luminaries results in the presenters' impressing the crowd. Pastors in smaller, unadorned churches, with less personal charisma and fewer rhetorical, gifts dream, "If only I were like this person!" Of course, that is not to discount lessons we may learn from their experience, but the fact is, such encouragement as "Look what I did! And you can do it, too!" is ego-centered and unrealistic. The danger, therefore, is *impersonation* instead of *imitation.* We are all familiar with the embarrassment we feel for an Elvis impersonator: *Get a life!* we say to ourselves. The ecclesiastical equivalent is the less-equipped pastor who impersonates a successful pastor or tries to duplicate his high-tech entertainment with his average resources.

But what are we to imitate in others? Paul encouraged the immature Corinthians, "Follow my example, as I follow the example of Christ" (1 Corinthians 11:1), and earlier in that epistle he used Timothy as an example of what he meant by imitation. "He will remind you of my way of life in Christ Jesus, which agrees with what I teach everywhere in every church" (1 Corinthians 4:17). Paul passed on a set of principles that were to be taught in every church; he was not passing on personality or personal gifts but an example of sound teaching and godliness. I wonder how many pastors would turn out for a church growth seminar on sound teaching and godliness these days. Imitating, or impersonating, other people for other reasons seems to be a greater attraction. Timothy's instructions from Paul are not terribly striking for their cleverness. (Paul went to great pains in trying to explain to the Corinthians why his simple gospel of Christ and Him crucified was not inferior to the charisma and rhetorical skill of the "super-apostles," as he called them.) The apostle merely commanded Timothy, "The things you have heard me say in the presence of many witnesses entrust to reliable men who will also be qualified to teach others" (2 Timothy 2:2).

If we are going to teach church leaders responsibly, it must be with a theology and philosophy of ministry first, and methods and working models second. It must be with a set of principles for leadership and outreach, people development and evangelism, such as that espoused by Paul for the corporate church in Ephesians 4:11-16.

You can't transfer spirituality. An often forgotten factor in church growth and renewal is the spiritual character of the creative personality. It is superficial to consider the highly gifted only "flash and dash." I have been pleasantly surprised by the commitment of many charismatic and highly gifted pastors to basic spiritual discipline and godliness. Some of them have arrived at their "success" through years of learning the hard way—after struggling, persevering, and rethinking things.

The personal life of the creative/entrepreneur pastor will eventually reveal itself. Popularity will erode human veneer. The pressures that come with success will drive the true nature of a person to the surface. That may require years as culture slowly eats away at one's biblically based perspective, leaving behind essentials for the esoterics. The tragic fall of many evangelical leaders can be attributed to their leaving behind their fundamental doctrinal convictions and simple devotion that brought them success in the first place. Nevertheless, many gifted pastors and leaders have remained faithful; we must never confuse giftedness or creativity with deviance.

The danger for church leaders looking to benefit from working models is that they can so easily neglect the importance of spiritual character in the process. God uses people who honor Him and serve Him rather than bringing themselves recognition. They are not to build *their* church, but *Christ's* church. And yet, so often, Christ does not even come up in these discussions. More time and energy is often spent on the orthodoxy of the latest business trends or marketing techniques than on the criteria laid out for us in Scripture for the definition of the church's mission.

But again, godliness and growth come through our own personal life's tapestry of suffering, joy, sorrow, perseverance, tragedy, transformation, and pain. Each of us is being shaped into Christ's image through completely different circumstances, and there is no "working model" for sanctification other than Christ Himself. We cannot imitate or impersonate what God is doing in someone else's life. Just as we cannot send the pastor home with a neatly wrapped box of charisma and gifts, so we cannot with the price of registration send the pastor home with a box of Christian character.

CALL THE PLAYS THE PLAYERS CAN RUN

Good coaches know their talent. John Wooden is considered among the best coaches ever to lead a college basketball team. In the early sixties Wooden's teams were small and quick. In 1964 they won the national championships with no player taller than 6-feet, 5-inches. During the late sixties and early seventies, his teams were built around agile giants Lew Alcindor (Kareem Abdul-Jabbar) and Bill Walton. In 1975 Wooden won his tenth championship with a middle-sized team. Small, medium, or large, Wooden knew his talent and tailored his approach accordingly. He was willing to adjust, to change his strategies, but his coaching philosophy remained constant. He insisted that his players be in great condition, that they play as a team, and that they have speed. Conditioning, teamwork, fullcourt pressing, and speed were the transferable parts of his coaching philosophy that were reproducible.

When attempting to help church leaders renew their churches, it is vital that we do not ask them to execute plays they are ill-equipped to run. One cannot transfer or reproduce context, personality, or spiritual qualities.

RENAMING OR REARRANGING?

The church growth movement runs a further risk of merely rearranging the furniture and calling that "renewal." In other words, it focuses on secondary "renewal" issues.

Before it is anything else, genuine church growth and renewal concern the spiritual health of the church, not just its structural practicalities. A church may be growing and successful but be utterly destitute of spiritual life and sound teaching. Renewal involves much more than humanly devised schemes. It involves prayer and confession, sorrow for sin, determined repentance, resolution of conflicts in relationships. We ought not to settle for superficial changes, which only relieve symptoms and bring temporary relief, while we ignore the deeper issues.

Church historian Richard Lovelace presents a model for contemporary church renewal that I find helpful. Never in church history has God sent revival without these two elements: "Awareness of

God's holiness and awareness of the depth of our sin."[3] The question then is, How do the internal spiritual issues come into play as they interface with church growth?

Before a church can be renewed and take advantage of church growth principles, it must come to a point of understanding God's holiness, acknowledging its brokenness in the light of that holiness, and having faith in God's provision for right standing with Him. Then that church must work out together what it means to be a forgiven and repentant congregation. Without repentance, church growth principles are humanly devised substitutes. Repentance is a Spirit-empowered process that is essential for long-term change. Twice Luke mentions "fruit in keeping [appropriate] to repentance" (Luke 3:8; see Acts 26:20). The phrase means "actions that demonstrate a change in purpose and resolve." The limitation of any seminar or event-oriented change is the lack of accountability and follow-through. Charisma will never suffice for confession; success will never paper over recognition of our sinfulness; our own cleverness will never meet the human need for justification, acceptance, and forgiveness at the hands of a holy God. The Holy Spirit's influence will linger much longer than the seminar's emotional high.

THE MOVEMENT HAS CREATED
MORE FRUSTRATION THAN GROWTH

Whereas the church growth movement has, as I stated at the beginning, contributed some valuable insights, the scales measuring results tip more toward frustration than growth.

If the research is accurate (90 percent of America's churches have 200 or fewer in attendance on an average Sunday morning worship), all of this emphasis and activity has not actually produced the intended results. Elmer Towns informs us that twenty years ago there were 100 megachurches (one thousand plus in worship); today there are 4,000.[4] Lyle Schaller believes that this number will increase in the nineties.[5] Those facts tell us two important things that touch our subject. First, since the total number of believers is not increasing, we are doing a poor job of evangelism. Second, the number of smaller churches will decrease as the number of megachurches increases. Schaller claims that 50 percent of Christians attend 7 percent of the churches. If the megachurches increase in number they will pull from the already existing 90 percent of churches (200 or fewer).[6]

Unless and until the highly talented church planters start penetrating the truly unreached, they will keep reaching the reached. Therefore, the larger churches will continue to expand, while the smaller churches will shrink. That is why George Barna predicts that 100,000 churches will close during the decade of the nineties.

If the church growth movement continues to tell pastors that they all can have growing churches while the number of smaller churches grows, then frustration will mount. I am not defending declining churches, nor am I against the growing churches! In fact, John Naisbitt, of *Megatrends* fame, states that the emergence of the megachurch is one of the three key developments of the nineties.[7] However, there is simply no way to continue to help the church unless these issues are faced.

POSITIVE CONTRIBUTIONS OF THE MOVEMENT

In addition to calling our attention to practical concerns, the church growth movement has also made some substantial contributions that ought not to be ignored in any critique.

Its focus on working models provides a visual aid. In a college class I was required to execute several moves on gymnastic rings; the teacher told us to grab the rings and then pull ourselves up to and then into several unusual positions. I hadn't the faintest idea what he meant; neither did the rest of the class. Finally, the teacher was forced to demonstrate the moves. That didn't make them any easier to execute, but it did give us a mental image of what was required.

Working models provide illustrations of principles. If the principle can be identified and then illustrated by way of a particular method, the average learner can more quickly "get a fix" on the principle. If a working model is not principle-based, then there will be problems. That means that the model itself will falter, because methods must change with culture.

The prime example of that is the Sunday evening evangelistic service. During the nineteenth century it was the cutting edge for the church to draw non-Christians to church on Sunday evenings to watch gas lights burn. Most people did not own a gas light, so the service was an opportunity to marvel at the latest technology. Innovative church leaders made use of that situation for evangelism. To this day there are churches holding Sunday evening evangelistic services, and a seeker hasn't attended in decades! The principle at work is to gain access to the people we are to evangelize. Unfortunately, too many churches have not understood the difference between the principle and the method.

If it is principle based, then change is welcome and improves the principled application (method).

Many church leaders benefit from working models because they are eager to do the right thing. The highly motivated can adapt models, glean the principles, and then make them work. I adapt better than create and have forged much of what I believe in dialogue with those who were making it work. I extracted examples of principles and then employed them. Over the years I refined both principle and method. Most people learn interactively. Once they see it done in one context, they can immediately see how it can be applied in their own.

It provides hope. Many pastors and congregations need support and a sense of hope. Although it is possible to build a large collection of people without building a church, it *is* the case that some churches that have put first things first have grown thereby. However, some churches that have also recognized the primary importance of their theology and philosophy of ministry have not grown, simply because of basic pragmatic concerns. A combination of factors—insufficient parking, lack of child care, apathetic outreach, lifeless worship, preaching that is sound but fails to be translated from seminary notes to public address—can be the dead weight that keeps an otherwise promising congregation from getting off the ground.

There really are some important lessons of practical advice we can learn, as well as some useful tools and concepts we can employ in our own context, and if we get our priorities right (theology before sociology), most of the dangers pointed out earlier in this chapter can be avoided.

It can be a terrific experience for a pastor of a smaller congregation to spend some time visiting a megachurch and interacting with the leaders there. He may realize that his church cannot be a megachurch, but such contact may give him hope that his church can be significantly better. There are some great ideas floating around out there, just as long as they *serve* the ordained mission of the church rather than *mastering* it.

It is catalytic to renewal. Earlier I argued that the church growth movement runs the risk of undermining true revival, but now let me show you the other side of the coin.

Many churches avoid renewal because they simply get stuck in a routine. Sometimes the insights a tired, frustrated pastor gains through church growth principles awakens him from his pastoral slumber, and he is able for the first time to open his eyes to the spiritual problems facing his congregation. Even in cases where church growth principles are not the answer, they can point out some of the problems.

The working model I developed gave me an opportunity to see that in action. After gaining national and international attention, the success of our model placed a tremendous burden on our church staff to handle the visitors! Pastors and lay leaders would ask if they could spend a few days with us and observe our work. Additionally, we spent many hours in phone consultation. After some time, we realized that we simply did not have the time to carry on in this way, but that led to a seminar that now is international in scope.

We ought not to be cynical about the idea of pastors and lay leaders "checking out" growing churches and observing the operations. Although theology comes first, many details of leadership and organization are simply matters of common sense and practical wisdom. There are people who have something to teach us about these matters, and we ought not to reject everything in the church growth movement simply because of the all-too-common excesses. The tools have limitations, but they also have their place in the service of proclamation.

CHURCH GROWTH:
SUBSERVIENT TO A THEOLOGY OF MISSION

I have referred rather generally to the primacy of a theology and a philosophy of ministry that is deeply rooted in Scripture, but we must also have a theology of mission. Every church growth principle must be refined by the scriptural flame. Not only does a congregation need a clear doctrinal position, it is incomplete without a functional theology of mission. The official doctrinal confession or statement of faith tells us why we are here; the theology of mission addresses the question, "We're here, *now* what?" The theology of mission is built on a classic orthodox theology, but if theology is the study of God, then who God is should lead us to ask what He expects of us as a church.

The importance of a theology of mission, therefore, cannot be overstated. Secondary renewal instruments simply do not address that core issue. Apart from internal struggles of the disciple with the world, the flesh, and the devil, a lack of theology of mission is a primary reason for church sloth and decline.

So many are asking the wrong questions about the church in North America. There is too much focus on models that work, numbers, and addressing ourselves to the unchurched. The inability to understand the culture and minister to the baby boomer is not the most basic obstacle to growth. The real killer is the compromised, weak-willed, and theologically flabby team the evangelical church is putting on the field. The question that matters, and is rarely being asked, is, "What kind of team does the evangelical church *put* on the field?" Are the people in the congregations penetrating their networks? How many non-Christian friends do we have? Why on earth should we be surprised that even though we have access to statistics and data on the unchurched, we still don't understand them enough to attract them to the church? We are substituting marketing research and statistical data for relationships. Are Christians where the non-Christians are, getting to know them in their own environments, as Jesus and His disciples did? You will remember that Jesus was *too* involved with non-Christians for the comfort of the distant and self-righteous Pharisees: "The Son of Man came eating and drinking, and they say, 'Here is a glutton and a drunkard, a friend of tax collectors and "sinners"'" (Matthew 11:19). We should not be surprised if we should be painted with this brush: we're in good company. But I doubt very seriously that the evangelical church today could be confused with being too involved.

Pastors and church leaders know they are supposed to take their church somewhere, to provide vision and direction. They know they are to engage in "winning the world" and "equipping the saints," but because they may have never worked out a theology of mission and a philosophy of ministry from an over-arching theological system, they do not have the deeper motivations and direction they need. They are stuck; they travel from seminar to seminar and read book after book in search of something that will rescue them from a philosophical "no man's land."

It's something like visiting Uncle Joe in New Mexico. First, I need to *know* Uncle Joe and know *why* it's worth visiting him in New Mexico. Next, I need to figure out a strategy for getting there. I take out my road atlas and determine the best route. Knowing I should go to Uncle Joe's house is like knowing I need to lead the church. Many of the leaders with whom I work need to develop a strategy and understand that even strategy is found in the Scriptures. There are biblically based models of how we lead the church to its prescribed destination.

BUT WHAT *IS* A THEOLOGY OF MISSION?

First, learn more about God: that's theology. There can be no theology of mission without this essential understanding. And yet, theology is often overlooked because it is viewed as impractical and irrelevant. Some pastors reason, "I got theology in seminary; what I really need is something practical right now." Thus, strategies are devised in board rooms that fail to take God's character and will into account. The church thus becomes a business and not a divinely ordained institution.

An example of this essential relationship is the fact that the deity of Christ is directly linked to the command "All authority in heaven and on earth has been given to me. Therefore go and make disciples of all nations" (Matthew 28:18b-19a). Without linking an understanding of Christ's Person and work to this famous declaration, the latter loses its steam. Why should we be motivated to serve the mission of a God about whom we know very little? As pastors, we must stop assuming that the average believer already understands the basics of the Christian faith. Any church growth strategy must begin with a fresh commitment to teaching the full range of biblical doctrine. We cannot evangelize the world if our congregations are barely evangelized themselves.

Second, develop from that a theology of mission. A good theology of mission answers the "why" and the "how" questions. "God so loved the world that He gave his only begotten Son," for instance, is the theological foundation for mission. Before we start talking about methods and techniques, we have to get a handle on the message. Based on that incredible "why" of God's love and sacrifice of His Son, we are to "go and make disciples of every nation"—that is the "how." God's method of disciple-making is telling the world about Christ.

Could you imagine the impact of the leadership of more than 150,000 evangelical churches in the United States alone having worked through and developed a theology of mission? If the churches were clearer on what they believe and why they believe it, if they consequently developed together a theology of mission, the members themselves (and not just the tired, overworked pastor at the top) would share the vision. They would understand the goals and articulate them. Where the leaders launched an aggressive program based on a well-understood, biblically based philosophy of ministry, there would be amazing results.

The bottom line in this is simple: The figures clearly demonstrate that the church growth movement is going nowhere, in spite of all its dazzling apparatus. We must get beyond growth through technology and realize that the gospel doesn't need to be marketed; it needs to be preached from the pulpit and brought personally to non-Christians in their own environment.

CONCLUSION

The church growth movement has its place—as a support to both scriptural principles and a theology of mission. But the tools do not bring revival, reformation, or renewal. They can only serve a larger, well-conceived framework.

By choosing pragmatism over theology, we run the risk of bringing further secularization to our culture instead of evangelization. Methods cannot convert; only the Holy Spirit can do that—and He does so by using the Word: "How, then, can they call on the one they have not believed in? And how can they believe in the one of whom they have not heard? And how can they hear without someone preaching to them? And how can they preach unless they are sent? As it is written 'How beautiful are the feet of those who bring good news!'" (Romans 10:14-15).

NOTES

1. Ken Sidey, "Church Growth Fine Tunes Its Formulas," *Christianity Today,* June 24, 1991.
2. James Hunter, *Evangelicalism: The Coming Generation* (Chicago: U. of Chicago, 1987).
3. Richard Lovelace, *Dynamics of Spiritual Life* (Downers Grove, Ill.: InterVarsity, 1979), p. 136.
4. Elmer Towns, 1990; interview by the author.
5. Lyle Schaller, "Megachurch!" *Christianity Today,* March 5, 1990, pp. 20-24.
6. Schaller, Address to the Leadership National Conference, August 1991; notes taken by the author.
7. John Naisbitt, *Megatrends: Ten New Directions Transforming Our Lives* (New York: Warner, 1984).

7

A Better Way: Church Growth Through Revival and Reformation

Tom Nettles

INTRODUCTION: THINGS THAT GO TOGETHER

Although it is possible to have marriage without love, and love without marriage, a popular song of the 1950s reminded us that love and marriage truly go together.

So it is with revival and reformation; when individuals pursue one without proper appreciation for and attention to the other, the results can be very ugly.

Though the two must go together, we must define them separately and be able to discern their distinctive characteristics. A clear grasp of the tendencies of each when separated from the other can be a great aid in seeing clearly just what kind of illness has invaded the Body. With care we can help to assure a prescription that does not underdose the thing most needed. The relation of reformation and revival to the growth of the church must also concern us.

This chapter contends that fragmentation between revival and reformation has increased since the middle of the nineteenth century. The expanding focus of attention on successful methods, with growing confidence in their spiritual efficacy, has minimized the apparent importance of objective truth both in preaching and in

Tom Nettles is professor of church history at Trinity Evangelical Divinity School in Deerfield, Illinois.

establishing methods. The modern church growth movement involves a pursuit of method (ostensibly revival) and finds it can create success only with a facade of theological truth.

REFORMATION

Definition. Reformation is the recovery of biblical truth that leads to the purifying of one's theology. It involves a rediscovery of the Bible as the judge and guide of all thought and action; corrects errors in interpretation; gives precision, coherence, and courage to doctrinal confession; and gives form and energy to the corporate worship of the triune God. Though it should be an ongoing enterprise in all churches and in the Body of Christ throughout the world, the most poignant displays of reformation come at times of great theological, moral, spiritual, and ecclesiological declension in the church.

A biblical paradigm from the Old Testament. Under the reign of Josiah, the book of the law was discovered in the house of the Lord. Upon hearing it read, Josiah "tore his robes" and inquired of the Lord because it was clear to him that the people had not "obeyed the words of this book" (2 Kings 22:11, 13). Josiah learned from the prophetess Huldah that God's wrath was against the people of Judah but that because his "heart was responsive" and he had humbled himself before the Lord when he had heard what was spoken against them, he would be gathered to his fathers before the day of God's wrath came (vv. 16-20). From that time Josiah engaged in extensive reforms in accordance with the book of the law.

He eliminated the vessels, figures, priests, places, and practices of idolatry in Judah and destroyed the high places in the cities of Samaria. He removed all mediums and spiritists and reinstituted the Passover "as it is written in this Book of the Covenant" (23:21). All that he did that he might "fulfill the requirements of the law written in the book that Hilkiah the priest had discovered in the temple of the Lord" (v. 24). Josiah experienced personal reformation and revival and brought reformation to Israel. Before his time "there was no king like him who turned to the Lord with all his heart and with all his soul and with all his might, according to all the law of Moses; nor did any like him arise after him" (v. 25, NASB).

The historical framework: Attempts at Reformation in the Middle Ages. How are the problems of reformation to be tackled? Attempts to bring reformation through treating the moral, spiritual, and ecclesiological dimensions while ignoring the theological always fall short. The Middle Ages saw a number of attempts to reform the church. *Moral* reform became the concern of a variety of churchmen and involved a series of monastic reforms and powerful preaching. The Franciscans sought reformation and conversion of heretics through an example of austere morality and fervent preaching. Ximines de Cisneros (d. 1517) banished more than two thousand immoral monks from Spain and used the Spanish Inquisition to enforce an ascetic morality on the clergy. In the sixteenth century, members of the Oratory of Divine Love sought moral reform in their own lives and in the lives of those around them. Their research into the morals of the clergy led to the extensive moral reforms of the Council of Trent. Erasmus, the great humanist, invested his great powers in ridicule of the morals of the clergy and even supported Luther's attack upon the bellies of the monks. However, none of those efforts served to give the needed reformation to the church but only hardened conditions.

There were also efforts at *spiritual* reform. The *Apocalypticism* of Joachim of Fiore promised freedom from the "bondage" of the external form of the church. That would be characterized by an "eternal gospel" that went beyond the one introduced by the life and work of Christ. The new age of the Spirit would be ushered in by contemplative monks. Although he advocated no revolutionary tactics, Joachim's view of history was condemned because it did not view the Roman Catholic church as the final, perfect form of the city of God.

The *principle of poverty* espoused by the Observant Franciscans highlighted spiritual ministry and eschewed the covetous spirit enhanced by ownership of private property. The principle was declared heretical in a series of bulls by Pope John XXII (1316-1334), officially ending the grasp for God through instituted poverty.

Mysticism continued this quest for God. Mystics desired a suprarational union with God that transcended the mechanical operations of the sacramental system. Though spiritually exhilarating to some, mysticism had very little chance, in fact very little desire, to challenge the prevailing theological structure of the church. The theology of mystic experience differed generically from orthodox Roman Catholicism and neither denied nor challenged its basic doctrine of salvation. In fact, mysticism's formative doctrinal assumptions were antithetical to the reformation that was needed. It was consistent with the sacramental system in that it was semi-Pelagian, emphasizing the possibility of man's contributing to his salvation by achieving justification through increasing godlikeness.[1]

Ecclesiological reform showed its greatest ardor during the periods of the Babylonian Captivity of the Church (1309-1378), when the popes resided in Avignon, France, and the papal schism (1478-1415), when two and three popes ruled at the same time. The churchmen who sought to bring about reform were known as the conciliarists because they advocated through Scripture and history the power of general councils over the pope. Their actions relieved the embarrassment caused by the Captivity and the schism but also gained a deserved notoriety by burning John Hus, a forerunner of the Reformation. No theological change appeared on their agenda; they were quite sure that none was needed.

The Reformation: The axe to the root. When reformation came, however, it came through the substantial alteration of strategic doctrines. Calvin gave credit to Luther, "who held forth a torch to light us into the way of salvation." In particular, "those heads of doctrine in which the truth of our religion" and the legitimate worship of God and "those in which the salvation of men is comprehended, were in a great measure obsolete" when Luther appeared.[2] Luther's concerns did not terminate with moral and ecclesiological issues, although he was involved with both; he went right to the theological problems that kept sinners curved in on themselves and away from the free mercy and justifying righteousness of Christ.

The doctrine of justification was central. This doctrine was defined by Luther's biblical insistence that faith not be viewed as meritorious in any sense. Fallen humans could only sin. One contributes nothing to a right standing before God, nor can one prepare himself or herself for it. Those truths constitute, as Calvin would say, "the first stage in the way to salvation, when the sinner, overwhelmed and prostrated, despairs of all carnal aid."[3] Only when the sinner sees himself in hell is he led to find hope in the completed work of Christ alone. Calvin would call that the "second stage" and speak of it passionately.

> This he does when, animated by the knowledge of Christ, he again begins to breathe. For to one humbled in the manner in which we have described no other course remains but to turn to Christ, that through his interposition he may be delivered from misery. But the only man who thus seeks salvation in Christ is the man who is aware of the extent of His power; that is, acknowledges Him as the only Priest who reconciles us to the Father, and His death as the only sacrifice by which sin is expiated, the divine justice satisfied, and a true and perfect righteousness acquired; who, in fine, does not divide the work between himself and Christ, but acknowledges it to be by mere gratuitous favour that he is justified in the sight of God.[4]

Luther's doctrine of the bondage (depravity) of the will not only was biblical but gave theological coherence to the necessity of imputed (ascribed, credited) righteousness being the sole source of our just standing before God. In his 1525 debate with Erasmus, Luther named that the "essential issue . . . the hinge on which all turns."

Calvin spoke in unison with Luther on that issue. If all hinges on something outside of man, immediately a controversy arises with reference to "the freedom and powers of the will." If one has any ability to serve God acceptably, then he is not saved only by the merit of Christ but will attribute part to himself. Their "opponents" maintained, in spite of holding the doctrine of original sin, that "the powers of man are only weakened, not wholly depraved." Therefore, the grace of Christ aiding him, the sinner has something "from himself which he is able to contribute." The Reformers maintained that the sinner "possesses no ability whatever to act aright."[5]

The Reformers called for a fundamental alteration of the Roman Catholic system; Luther was at odds with the entire reigning theological school. Had he submitted to the authority of tradition and popes he could have forgotten all about those doctrines, but he had no choice. He found no reason to trust anything but Scripture as the final and infallible authority in theological issues. Luther considered it safer to be destroyed by the powers of this world than to live by having failed to confess God's truth.

All the major Reformers agreed in those essentials. "The Clarity and Certainty of the Word of God," as Zwingli would call it, stood as the *formal* principle of reformation. The completed work of Christ issuing in absolutely gratuitous salvation through the imputation of His doing and dying was the *material* principle of reformation. Man's sinful condition made necessary a unilateral, omnipotent work of God rendering salvation a reality that is selective, certain, and effectual. Those truths, under God, brought reformation and resulted in a variety of church forms, each seeking to be consistent with this new understanding.

REVIVAL

Definition. Revival is the application of Reformation truth to human experience. It occurs one person at a time and may appear in individuals who thereby become somewhat isolated from the more general apathy around them; or it may appear on a relatively massive scale radically altering the spiritual face of an entire church, community, or even nation. Normally, therefore, revival involves three things: the presence of Reformation doctrine either preached, read, or otherwise known; the experiential application of that doctrine accompanied by loving but careful investigation of that experience; and the extension of such an experience to a large number of people.

Biblical paradigms from the New Testament. Most of the awakenings in Scripture appear to be a combination of reformation and revival, because as mentioned at the beginning, it is always difficult to separate them. The reality of their being separated at times, however, is seen in some of the addresses to the churches in Revelation.

Thyatira appears to be a church with good experience (Revelation 2:19) but with a shallow and imperceptive doctrinal base (v. 20). They were in need of reformation; the Lord, however, condescending to their weakness, required only that they hold in purity the truth that they did know (vv. 24-25). The church at Ephesus, on the other hand (vv. 1-7), appears to be doctrinally sound but in need of increased affection for the truths known. They were able even to examine and expose those who falsely claimed to be apostles (v. 2) and to persevere under persecution while affirming the truth about Christ (v. 3). The admonition they receive, however, is one for increased love: "You have forsaken your first love" (v. 4). Here we see a case of the essential truths being in place and even prompting discretion and courage; yet beyond abiding by the truth of God, they need a resurgence of love for the God of truth.

First Corinthians 9:23–10:6 contemplates the possibility of understanding and preaching the gospel, and even manifesting the external gifts of an apostle, or being the beneficiary of the powerful and godly leadership of one like Moses, and still falling short of genuine conversion. Paul indicates that his zeal for the gospel is not only that he might win those to whom he witnesses, but that he might partake of its blessings himself. Paul consistently pursued personal conformity to the gospel so that he would not prove disapproved, failing the test in the end (9:24-27).

Christian experience, though entirely dependent on the internal, efficacious working of the Spirit of God, also is entirely dependent on full involvement of heart, soul, and strength of the sinner. When asked if only a few would be saved, Jesus answered, "Strive [or agonize] to enter by the narrow door; for many, I tell you, will seek to enter and will not be able" (Luke 13:24, NASB). In a sense the answer is, "Yes, only a few will be saved; but only because the many desire the glory of the end of salvation and not the cross of the way of salvation."

Entering and staying in the way of salvation is revival. It is a sovereign work of God utterly dependent on His power and grace that engages, enlivens, and expands all the capacities of sinners to embrace Christ's redemptive work and enjoy the glory of the Lord.

The historical framework: The First Great Awakening in America. The historical standard to which all revivals of religion must be compared is the First Great Awakening in America. That is not because it was necessarily the purest of all revivals, nor the most powerful, but because of the unusual balance of its leaders: Jonathan

Edwards and George Whitefield. Jonathan Edwards was a preacher, theologian, philosopher, spiritual psychologist, and religious critic. Not only was he one of the revival's major participants, but he was also one of its most careful analysts. From his firsthand observations of the phenomena and his understanding of human spirituality and careful theological application, he developed a body of divinity pertaining specifically to human experience in revival.

Edwards was positive toward revival but careful to state clearly the distinctives that marked a movement as the work of God. He also discussed a number of other factors often accompanying deep spiritual movements but which detractors sometimes used to seek to discredit the entire work. To each of those Edwards responded that "'tis no argument that the work in general is not the work of the Spirit of God. That there are some counterfeits, is no argument that nothing is true."

Several tensions always are present in the interaction between humans and a holy God, and those become most exaggerated in a time of revival. Edwards sought to maintain the truth in both sides of the tension. First, he preached careful and detailed doctrinal messages on the major themes of the Reformation while carefully crafting pungent application to personal responsibility and experience. Second, Edwards showed great leniency toward a large number of unusual manifestations but allowed nothing to deter him from insisting on the true distinguishing traits of a work of God's Spirit. Third, he pressed the urgency of a sinner's obligation to immediate repentance and faith but would never assist the sinner in gaining comfort too quickly by omitting any truth of the gospel of redemption. Fourth, Edwards and his contemporaries took no measure designed strictly to increase the number of respondents but were nevertheless interested in growth as an evidence of a genuine and unusually powerful working of God's Spirit.

1. *Doctrinal, experiential preaching.* The series of messages under which the first movements of revival began to occur in Northampton, Massachusetts, were elaborate theological expositions of the doctrine of justification by faith. Determined to defend the biblical teaching from "Arminian" perversions of the truth, Edwards went into great detail on the relationship between repentance and

faith, how faith is best suited to be the means through which Christ's righteousness is imputed to us. He defended detailed, doctrinal preaching as entirely appropriate in light of the nature of the subject and the dangers of the times. Edwards concluded with six important applications of the discussion, which show that distinctions between his position and that of Arminius do not consist "only in punctilios of small consequence," but that the Arminians' scheme leads men to "trust in their own righteousness for justification, which is a thing fatal to the soul."[6]

George Whitefield; William, Gilbert, and John Tennent; and John and Samuel Blair, though not as turgidly philosophical in their presentations, were just as determined theologically. Whitefield, in "The Lord Our Righteousness," defended the deity of Christ against Arians (those who believe that Christ was not of the same nature as God but was created) and Socinians (those who believe Christ was only a man and deny the doctrine of the Trinity) and gave a thorough exposition of the necessity of Christ's righteousness in His human nature, both His passive and active obedience, and of His righteousness being imputed to us. Whitefield then defended the doctrine of imputation against many objections and closed with urgent appeals to all classes and ages to receive the Lord as their righteousness. In one particularly striking passage Whitefield illustrated the exclusive efficacy of Christ's work.

> Suppose I went a little more round about, and told you, that the death of Christ was not sufficient, without our death being added to it; that you must die as well as Christ, join your death with his, and then it would be sufficient. Might you not then, with a holy indignation, throw dust in the air, and justly call me a setter forth of strange doctrines? And now then, if it be not only absurd, but blasphemous, to join the intercession of saints with the intercession of Christ, as though his intercession was not sufficient; or our death with the death of Christ, as though his death was not sufficient; judge ye, if it be not equally absurd, equally blasphemous, to join our obedience, either wholly or in part with the obedience of Christ, as if that was not sufficient. And if so, what absurdities will follow the denying that the Lord, both as to his active and passive obedience, is our righteousness?[7]

Clear doctrine forcefully preached undergirded the fervent appeal and application so characteristic of the first Great Awakening.

2. *Necessary traits, indifferent phenomena.* In *The Distinguishing Marks of a Work of the Spirit of God*, Edwards discusses nine factors "that are no evidences that a work that is wrought amongst a people, is not the work of the Spirit of God." Among those matters that should not in themselves discredit a movement in general is the uncommon nature of an experience. That it produces unusual and extraordinary effects is no mark against a revival as long as it does not contradict those distinguishing marks that are necessary.

God in times past has "wrought in such a manner as to surprise both men and angels" and in the future will do the same. Nor do extraordinary effects such as groans, outcries, and agonies of body give cause for a work to be judged one way or another. In fact, Edwards reasons, men under extraordinary stress from conviction should be expected to express themselves in desperation and hope. Two months earlier Edwards had preached "Sinners in the Hands of an Angry God," and he had seen physical effects of great stress. Evidently harsh criticism had come his way for that message, but Edwards was determined to argue both for the legitimacy of the sermon and the appropriateness of such responses.

> If we should suppose that a person saw himself hanging over a great pit, full of fierce and glowing flames, by a thread that he knew to be very weak, and not sufficient long to bear his weight, and knew that multitudes had been in such circumstances before, and that most of them had fallen and perished; and saw nothing within reach, that he could take hold of to save him; what distress would he be in? How ready to think that now the thread was breaking; now, this minute, he should be swallowed up in these dreadful flames? . . . or held over it in the hand of God, who at the same time they see to be exceedingly provoked? . . . no wonder that they cry out in their misery.[8]

Edwards treats numerous other problems, including doctrinal error, scandalous lives of some who profess to be converted, errors in judgment and delusions of Satan, the conversion of others being used as examples, that it causes a "great ado," that it makes great impressions of people's imaginations, and that preaching focuses on the terrors of God's law. None of those *discredit* the work, and none are *necessary* as distinguishing marks.

Using the fourth chapter of 1 John as his text, Edwards established five things as essential in a work of God's Spirit. First, a true work of the Spirit raises the "esteem of Jesus that was born of the Virgin, and was crucified without [outside] the gates of Jerusalem; and seems more to confirm and establish their minds in the truth of what the Gospel declares to us of his being the Son of God, and the Saviour of men."[9] Second, it operates against the interests of Satan's kingdom, against sin and men's worldly lusts. Third, men are established in a greater regard for the Holy Scriptures "in their truth and divinity." Satan has ever "shewn a mortal spite and hatred towards that holy book" and therefore "hates every word in it" and would never raise one's affection to it. Fourth, the Spirit operates as a Spirit of truth. A Spirit who shows people the uniqueness and holiness of God and that they must die and that very soon, and "that they must give account of themselves to God; one who convinces them that they are helpless in themselves and confirms them in other things that are agreeable to sound doctrine," that is a Spirit of truth. Fifth, the Spirit who generates love to God and man is the Spirit of God. Edwards developed this further in a section in which he treated specific objections.

In *Some Thoughts Concerning the Present Revival of Religion in New-England* (1742) Edwards affirmed that the revival was a glorious work of God, argued that all should promote the work, defended its promoters against false charges, spoke of things that should be corrected or avoided, and gave specific suggestions as to what positive things would contribute to the work. Wherever true religion is, Edwards asserted, there are "vigorous exercises of the inclination and will towards divine objects." Those exercises are "no other than the affections of the soul." He did not think that all affections, however, were "saving affections and experiences" but warned against "those manifold fair shows, and glistering appearances, by which they are counterfeited." Revivals will never last long, he contended, until we learn to distinguish between the true and the false and become settled "wherein true religion does consist," so that we will know clearly and distinctly "what we ought to contend for."[10]

3. *A careful urgency.* Edwards sought to make matters of the soul's salvation of paramount urgency to all men. In "Pressing into the Kingdom," preached in the first wave of awakening in Northampton, he urged sinners to use all the energy they have to seek to take the kingdom of God by storm. Persons pressing into the kingdom "are so set for salvation, that those things by which others are discouraged, and stopped, and turned back do not stop them, but they press through them." The gain is so great and the loss so immeasurable that they "ought to be so resolved for heaven, that if by any means they can obtain, they will obtain."[11] In "Ruth's Resolution" Edwards enjoined his listeners to "count the cost of a thorough, violent, and perpetual pursuit of salvation, and forsake all, as Ruth forsook her own country, and all her pleasant enjoyments in it. Do not do as Orpah did; who set out, and then was discouraged, and went back: but hold out with Ruth through all discouragement and opposition."[12]

Even with all this arousing of sinners to press into the kingdom Edwards still insisted that God has obligated Himself to no one either by justice or promise no matter how hard one may strive as long as he has no "true repentance begun in him." If the extreme of despair appeared, Edwards just as surely reminded the seeker of the "infinite and all-sufficient mercy of God in Christ." In that way both fear and hope were duly experienced and "proportioned to preserve their minds in a just medium between the two extremes of self-flattery and despondence."[13]

4. *Joy in success but humility as to its source.* The great attention given to the theological issue did not make the promoters of the Awakening oblivious to the numbers that were being converted. In *Faithful Narrative* Edwards, though not "pretending to be able to determine how many have lately been the subjects of such mercy," nevertheless, hoped that "more than 300 souls were savingly brought home to Christ." He even enumerated the breakdown in ages because "it has been heretofore rarely heard of, that any were converted past middle age." Those converting influences came to

young and old alike with more than fifty of those converted being above forty years old. Of those, twenty were above fifty, ten were above sixty, and two above seventy. The very young also were "savingly wrought upon." Thirty between ten and fourteen years of age, two between nine and ten, and remarkably, one four years of age. So unusual was this last one, Phoebe Bartlett, that Edwards records a detailed description of her spiritual pilgrimage.

In November 1803, referring to the Second Great Awakening (ca. 1799-1805), the *Connecticut Evangelical Magazine* carried a twenty-two column article on a spiritual awakening in Lebanon, New York. After describing the extraordinary results of that Awakening, the reporter observed:

> One hundred and ten have been added to the church, about thirty more, we hope, have passed from death to life, and seventy-three have been baptized, in the course of the revival. Ninety-nine were received into the church in the compass on one year, sixty-four of which were received in the compass of two months.[14]

"It is visible," said the reporter, "that God hath acted as a sovereign, having mercy on whom he would have mercy."

> Numbers who were not only inveterate, but open opposers of the doctrine of election, now not only acknowledge its truth, but say if it were not true, they should not have the least hope of heaven. And I know of none who have obtained hopes in this awakening, who have not embraced the Calvinistic system of doctrines.[15]

Nothing is more obvious in these reports than that combination of many things which through the remainder of the nineteenth century increased in rarity. (1) Theology and experience flourished together. Careful and uncompromising attention to precise doctrinal matters undergirded the inception and continuance of deep religious experience. (2) There was a healthy and joyful interest in the numbers affected by the revival, including their sociological description, but without the least hint that the movements came from anything more or less than the gracious disposal of a sovereign God. (3) Personal religious perceptions and testimonies were sought and encouraged but also were examined closely in light of Scripture. (4) Awakenings marked by "regularity and order" as well as those in which people were impressed in an "extraordinary manner" were seen as coming from the same God and the same truths but into different social situations and different levels of maturity in personality. A movement was not deemed genuine or spurious solely on the basis of external affectations.

The pressures of apparent conflict between these respective sets of factors could not be held together much longer. Jonathan Edwards devoted his life to maintaining doctrinal and experiential equilibrium both in how one carried on revival and in how one subsequently evaluated revival. Humpty Dumpty was soon to break, however, and none was able, and very few even willing, to put him together again.

THE NECESSITY OF UNITY

Unity of the truth and love in salvation. Reformation is truth, revival is love. Truth without love oppresses, mocks, scorns, and eventually decapitates everything else. In the process, it loses itself because it is fearsome and not beautiful. It eliminates the context in which it can be communicated. "Speak the truth in love" we are admonished, and the psalmist teaches us that "lovingkindness and truth go before Thee" (Psalm 89:14, NASB). Of the descendants of David, God says, "I will visit their transgression with the rod, and their iniquity with stripes. But I will not break off My lovingkindness from him, nor deal falsely in My faithfulness" (vv. 32-33, NASB). In His lovingkindness God establishes a way to redeem the covenant people without enervating the full impact of His truth. If we understand all mysteries and have all knowledge but do not have love we are nothing (see 1 Corinthians 13:2). Truth itself is lovely—is worth being loved because of its moral and aesthetic excellence. It can make its home, therefore, in a congenial way only in those who approve of and enjoy it for its excellence and loveliness. And if they enjoy truth because it is excellent and lovely, they themselves will live in love. Truth without love ceases to be truth because it excludes from itself the sum of all moral perfection.

Love without truth melts into formlessness; it is goal-less motivation and duty-less sentiment. A love that remains insensitive to the necessity of truth eliminates its own essence. Love does not take into account a wrong suffered; but that spirit of forgiveness assumes a standard of right or it could never realize that a wrong had been done. Truth-less love would have no joy, for love rejoices in the truth. No matter how much supposed love one may exert, without truth it is only a damning affection. Those who perish do not receive the love of the truth (see 2 Thessalonians 2:10) but are given up to believe a lie. Those who are chosen to salvation, however, find deliverance through belief in the truth. If not exactly synonymous, belief in the truth and love of the truth are nonetheless indivisible.

In the same way, when a church seeks expansion at the expense of careful attention to both reformation (truth) and revival (love), it can become an empty shell or a whitewashed sepulcher. The book of Acts documents the increase in the size of churches and the geographical expansion of the gospel. Paul's zeal was to "preach the gospel, not where Christ was already named" (Romans 15:20, NASB), but in places destitute of the word of truth. Enormous thanksgiving welled up in his spirit when he heard of the faith spreading "in all the world . . . constantly bearing fruit and increasing" (Colossians 1:6).

Yet the increase of numbers did not in itself signal a healthy situation. Others who imitated gospel preachers were able to draw large numbers after themselves so that Paul and John and Peter had to warn against them (e.g., 1 Timothy 6:3-5). They "went astray from the truth" and led others after them (2 Timothy 2:18, NASB). They introduced "destructive heresies" (2 Peter 2:1, NASB) and did not "abide in the teaching of Christ" (2 John 1:9, NASB). Among their heresies were false teaching about the character of God (2 Peter 2:1), creation (1 Timothy 4:3-5), the Person of Christ (1 John 4:2-3), the work of Christ (Galatians 2:21), justification by faith (Galatians 2:16, Philippians 3), resurrection (1 Corinthians 15; 2 Timothy 2:18), and the second coming (2 Peter 3).

Not only teachers but listeners sought to escape the truth-claims of the gospel. In some places they stoned or imprisoned ministers of the gospel and other believers. In other situations, strangely enough, they did not work overtly to destroy the church but sought the church community as a haven for their egocentrism. Paul had encountered some who loved flattering words and would pay dearly to hear them. And there were preachers enough ready to be prostituted to such a task. Paul's confidence as one "approved by God to be entrusted with the gospel" who spoke not "as pleasing men but God" alienated those who liked to buy their sermons (1 Thessalonians 2:4-6, NASB). Paul's description of a preacher who held "fast the faithful word which is in accordance with the teaching, that he may be able both to exhort in sound doctrine and to refute those who contradict" (Titus 1:9, NASB) embodied little attraction for these who wanted approval, fun, and comfort from their religion instead of repentance, cross, and truth. Those who resisted sound teaching were zealous to employ acceptable teachers in order to confirm them in their own moral propensities (2 Timothy 4:3). Any church growth not built on the truth is spurious, and all systems that can cause growth apart from the truth should be feared.

The New Testament church also addressed the issue of experiential problems. The doctrine of grace was turned into lasciviousness on more than one occasion (Romans 6:1; 2 Peter 2:19; 1 John 3:1-6). Doctrinal correctness was mistaken for saving faith (James 2:19-20).

The spiritual issue involved in those errors is the subject matter of Jesus' interview with Nicodemus. Jesus said that spiritual life cannot be reduced to a mental comprehension in which proper conclusions are drawn from miraculous signs. More is involved than speculative knowledge. The new birth gives not only rational clarity to the things of the kingdom of God, but a genuine sense of their beauty and loveliness. Subjects of the new birth, along with John the Baptist, rejoice when they hear the bridegroom's voice and say, "This joy of mine has been made full. He must increase but I must decrease."

All the evidences and proofs that may convince a person that Christianity is right will not change the heart to embrace Christ as lovely and desirable. Only the light that comes from God Himself does that. Even believing the Bible to be true falls short of true saving faith. Evidences can be compelling, and the Bible certainly is true; and true faith requires both elements. But mere assent is often present, as in demons, without salvation.

Nor will salvation be secure in the presence of an excitable revivalistic biblicism resulting in many an external decision but without any accompanying change of heart or alteration of affection. What is needed is a change of heart to see one's sin, the infinite excellence of God, and the justice of God in all His judgments. Sin, innate and voluntary, blinds us to the beauties and wisdom of God's redemptive activity. Only one thing can make us see it.

Paul describes it in 2 Corinthians 4:6, "For God who said, 'Light shall shine out of darkness,' is the One who has shone in our hearts to give the light of the knowledge of the glory of God in the face of Christ" (NASB). At that point all the evidence collapses into an intuitive and compelling sense of the beauty of knowing God. That goes beyond, though it is connected with, the mental apprehension of how the death and resurrection of Christ give perfect harmony to the attributes of holiness, justice, righteousness, and truth and the works of mercy, grace, reconciliation, and redemption.

It all resolves into the response of faith—a resignation of all hope in one's self, an affirmation of the justice of God in His verdict of "guilty" on sinners, a confidence in Christ's ability and willingness to save, and an embracing of Christ's work and way for sinners.

Historical ambivalence. The controversies of the first Great Awakening resulted in ambivalence toward revivalist practice.

1. *Wariness toward "enthusiasim."* Genuinely concerned that true doctrine find full exposition in revival preaching and that "discriminating discourses" clearly distinguishing true religion from every counterfeit be at the heart of public exposition and private counsel, the next generation of revival promoters and observers had virtually no toleration for "enthusiasm." Bennet Tyler, a leader of the New England portion of the Second Great Awakening, was pleased that the "fanaticism and delusion which succeeded the [revival] in the days of Whitefield and Edwards" did not mar the one of which he was a part. Tyler spoke of "temporary excitements, which, like a tornado, sweep through the community, and leave desolation behind them," and believed that "all religious excitement is injuri-

ous, which is not the result of clear apprehensions of Divine truth." The preachers preached the doctrines of grace and had no fears that "the preaching of these doctrines would hinder the progress of a revival." They insisted on the utter sovereignty of God, justification by faith, the necessity of regeneration by the Holy Spirit, and that the heart of man was enmity against God; but just as clearly "demolished all their vain excuses, and pressed upon them with great plainness, the duty of immediate repentance." When converted, the people saw from their own experience "the truth of all the great fundamental doctrines of the gospel." Tyler called on all who loved Zion to pray unceasingly "that pure revivals may increase in number and power, till the whole world shall be converted to Christ."[16]

2. *Reformation—yes; revival—?* Tyler's prayers to the contrary, revivals became increasingly human-centered and emotion-oriented. The result was that those chiefly concerned about truth frowned on revival, while revival became increasingly independent of any doctrinal system. Many who initially supported revivals became so cautious about the possibility of abuses that they seemed to yearn for a situation that never called for the necessity of an extraordinary work of God. Archibald Alexander contemplated a situation in which there would be a "continuous lively state of piety; and an unceasing progress in the conversion of the impenitent." Then such increasing prosperity would be the case "that revivals shall no longer be needed"; or perhaps it could be referred to as a state of perpetual revival. Alexander Proudfit preferred catechizing (systematic teaching) as a means of maintaining spiritual vitality and regularity of conversion. It is best adapted to support the regular order of the church without resort to "extra or protracted" meetings.[17]

That sort of hesitance merged with outright resistance in the person of John W. Nevin. The colleague of the great Philip Schaff at Mercersburg, Nevin fired one of the most formidable shots in the battle against the "new measures" introduced by Charles Finney. Nevin's intent was stated clearly: "The very design of the inquiry now proposed, is to show that the Anxious Bench, and the system to which it belongs, have no claim to be considered either salutary or safe, in the service of religion." All the arguments in favor of the system based on its supposed effects Nevin considered as worthy of no confidence whatever.[18] He considered it pure quackery and a mildew on the face of congregations and churches whose blighting presence threatens the perfection of any fruit."[19]

The anxious bench creates a false issue for the conscience, unsettles true seriousness, usurps the place of the cross, and substitutes actions, decisions, and committals for true repentance toward God and faith in our Lord Jesus Christ. In short, it is in contrast with Nevin's understanding of a true biblical ministry that he calls "the system of the [Heidelberg] *Catechism.*"* The two systems involve two different theories of religion; they are antagonistic to each other.[20] The Catechism stands for the regular teaching ministry of the church, consistent doctrinal preaching, and the biblical use of the sacraments. By this means, true Christian experience with fruit unto holiness may be expected. The other system "has much to answer for, in the occasion it has given, and is giving still, for the name of God to be blasphemed, and for the sacred cause of revivals to be vilified and opposed."[21]

3. *Doctrinal dalliance for revival results.* Charles Finney constructed the "new measures" system that gained such energetic opposition. Much of the opposition came because he reduced revival to the "purely philosophical result of the right use of means."[22] Finney maintained that "the most useful and important things are most easily and certainly obtained by the use of appropriate means." Included in those means for Finney early in his ministry was "excitement sufficient to break up the dormant moral powers."[23] Other excitements in the world attract the attention of the people and "these excitements can only be counteracted by religious excitements."[24]

Finney believed that the moral means for revival were not beyond the present capabilities of man in his fallen condition. They simply needed to be awakened; the use of unusual means could do it. He also seemed to deprecate the normal channels of church ministry in favor of his concept of revival. "Better were it for them," he

---

* The chief sixteenth-century Reformed catechism, still used to this day in a number of denominations.

179

says of children, "if there were no means of grace, no sanctuary, no Bible, no preaching, than to live and die where there is no revival."[25]

In his later years Finney realized that he had placed too little emphasis on the "necessity of divine influence upon the hearts of Christians and of sinners." With admirable candor Finney added, "I am confident that I have sometimes erred in this respect myself," and instead emphasized "the natural ability of sinners to the neglect of showing them the nature and extent of their dependence upon the grace of God and influence of his Spirit."[26]

Finney also came to amend his views on "excitements." In an 1845 letter on revival he addressed this issue in detail.

> I have sometimes witnessed efforts that were manifestly intended to create as much excitement as possible, and not unfrequently have measures been used which seemed to have no tendency to instruct or to subdue the will, or to bring sinners to the point of intelligently closing in with the terms of salvation; but on the contrary, it has seemed to me to beget a sort of infatuation through the power of overwhelming excitement. I cannot believe that this is healthful or at all safe in revivals.[27]

That does not represent a complete alteration, however, for he still advocated the use of "extra and exciting efforts" to promote revivals but in the context of wisdom against "indiscretion, and means of an *unnecessarily* agitating and exciting character." His concern was to use means that would secure attention to the truth, not divert attention from the truth.[28]

Reticence about Finney in a major part of the evangelical church did not really arise from his introduction of "new measures." Those were but a symptom of a changed theology. Finney did not accept Reformation theology. He rejected the teaching that Christ received in his death a punishment that justly was due for those who died ("It is naturally impossible, as it would require that satisfaction should be made to retributive justice [which] . . . can never be satisfied."[29]), justification by faith ("The doctrine of an imputed righteousness, or that Christ's obedience to the law was accounted as our obedience, is founded on a most false and nonsensical assumption"[30]), bondage of the will ("Depravity of the will, as a faculty, is or would be physical, and not moral depravity. . . . [Moral depravity] cannot consist in anything back of choice, and that sustains to choice the relation of a cause."[31]), and, thus, the necessity of regenerating grace.

Regeneration was for Finney one's alteration of mind due to the influence of truth upon it. That was not mere intellectual belief, for the devils have that, but a purposeful, volitional change of the ultimate preference or choice of the soul.[32] The sinner changes his heart by changing his mind when given a sufficient amount of convincing truth. Finney saw the preaching of those like Edwards as the source of much discouragement and ruinous error in the management of revivals:

> Sinners . . . have been perplexed and confounded by abstract doctrines, metaphysical subleties [sic], absurd exhibitions of the sovereignty of God, inability, physical regeneration and constitutional depravity, until the agonized mind, discouraged and mad from contradiction from the pulpit, and absurdity in conversation, dismissed the subject as altogether incomprehensible, and postponed the performance of duty as impossible.[33]

In the end, however, Finney was not too experiential and emotional, but too cerebral. He relied too little on altered affections as a foundation for true faith, and asserted too plainly the purity and power of the mind of man in religious matters. Nothing lay behind the mind of man as a cause of action; not only were sinners commanded to make themselves a new heart, they were entirely capable of doing so.

When, in accordance with his own observation, churches affected by his revivals became shallow spiritually, he advocated the doctrine of entire sanctification as a remedy. Ministers formerly open to his approach refused to admit him to preach that doctrine; he, therefore concluded that they "refused to be searched . . . and the result is that the Spirit of God has left and is fast leaving them."[34]

Archibald Alexander was just as passionate about Finney's assertions as was Finney, but in the opposite direction. Entire sanctification (perfectionism) would never answer the problems of the churches. The problem was not in sanctification but in the initial gospel message.

> And here I cannot but remark, that among all the prepos-terous notions which a new and crude theology has poured forth so profusely in our day, there is none more absurd, than that a dead sinner can beget new life in himself. The very idea of a man's becoming his own father in the spiritual regeneration is as unrea-sonable as such a supposition in relation to our first birth. Away with all such soul destroying, God-dishonouring sentiments![35]

4. *From alteration of theology to evacuation of theology.* If theology can be manipulated to submit to the purposes of a reviva-list, then perhaps it can be dismissed altogether. A group of revival-ists followed in the wake of Finney who placed little importance on distinctive theology as a necessary foundation for revival. Samuel Porter Jones (1847-1906) is a paradigm of those who minimized the-ology in quest of what was hoped would be revival. "Oh, that preach-ers would preach less of doctrine and more of Jesus Christ," he pleaded. Jones could characterize the "little Presbyterian preacher" as standing in his pulpit "preaching about the final perseverance of the saints and the elect, and not half his gang have anything to per-severe on." The Baptists he painted as "hollering, 'Water, water,' and half his crowd going where there is no water." The Episcopalians ring the changes about apostolic succession when they "better be looking to where they are going than to where they came from." Jones felt sorry for the preacher "who has a creed that needs de-fense."[36]

In reality, Jones's theology was not nonexistent, just ill-formed and naive. The elect are the "whosoever wills," repentance is "doing your whole duty," evangelism is getting "men to see how merciful God is to the man that wants to do the clean thing." Some-how, for Jones, the origin of the atonement in the love of God eli-minates any aspect of wrath from it. When speaking of the wrath of God being poured on the Son, Jones cried, "It's a lie! It's a lie! God never was mad, nor did He ever shoot the javelin from His great hand at the heart and body of His Son."

If a traditional Christian protests that if the Son had not received the Father's wrath, He would have to pour it on us, Jones replies, "It is false! It is false! It is false!" He then can quote 1 John 4:10 and completely ignore the concept of "propitiation." Is it uncharitable to contemplate whether some in this camp may be among those of whom Paul said, "One comes and preaches another Jesus whom we have not preached"(2 Corinthians 11:4, NASB)?

5. *New "new measures."* In light of the development of reformation and revival in the last two hundred years, it is worth asking if the contemporary church growth movement is simply an advanced species of "new measures." Among the commitments the movement shares in common with historic Reformation theology are the desire to be obedient to the Great Commission, a passion for the salvation of individuals, and the numerical growth of the church. Church growth leaders have been at the forefront in insisting on the furtherance of cross-cultural missions. Also, they have sought to maintain the priority of evangelistic and church planting missions, whereas others have been pressured into what is called "holistic missions," which more often than not substitutes social action for evangelism. Their work in analyzing cultural anthropology has given a necessary reminder that we must not transport Western culture into mission areas, but we must be sure that we do all things for the sake of the gospel, and to the uncircumcised become as uncircumcised. The structuring of *strategy* in evangelizing both the world and the church field has been seen as a legitimately spiritual task.

Given those strengths, there are also some cautions necessary to be stated. First, in the same mentality with Finney, there is a tendency to compete with the world by imitating its values and developing greater excitements than the world. An analysis of what people like and are accustomed to as a model for what the church should give them tends to minimize the head-on conflict that the gospel always has with the world.

Second, that tendency has an admittedly pragmatic feature, which can be harmless, but can also be compromising. Biblical evangelicalism combines three things: a purpose of glorifying God, a goal of salvation for sinners, and an unchangeable message that focuses on convincing them of their sin and misery and enlightening their minds in the glories of Christ. Sometimes church growth principles focus only on the goal, redefined in terms of movement toward Christ, and bypass the purpose and the message.

Third, this pragmatic tendency many times leads to a minimizing theology. In reformation and historic revival, clear and precise theology held a place of preeminence. That was seen as a matter of eternal life and eternal death. No careless dealing with souls was permissible. Church growth advocates do not forsake the vocabulary of repentance and faith, but close analysis of these concepts appears to have very little place in church growth concerns. C. Peter Wagner, for example, has said, "Church growth principles have intentionally been kept as atheological as possible, on the assumption that they can be adapted to fit into virtually any systematic theological tradition."[37] This principle may be harmless in some areas, but in others, when creating a theory that has to do with confronting sinners with the claims of God and the gospel, an atheological approach is inadequate simply because it *is* atheological.

Fourth, church growth emphases tend to assume that initial conversions will be of such a nature that deep spirituality will only be attained by a subsequent system of follow-up. That is similar to Finney's development of his brand of *sanctification* to accomplish that which his *gospel* could not do. Obviously, continued teaching is in order for growth in grace, but the gospel of the Reformers, Edwards, Whitefield, and others, had at its heart a principle that drove people toward the pursuit of holiness. Establishing principles that create a large body of nominal Christians in need of a second work or a "secret" of happiness and holiness is hardly friendly to the biblical gospel.

Fifth, in some cases church growth principles become more than a framework into which the gospel can be more widely disseminated. At times, the principles themselves become the drawing power. The means have become the end. So attractive a situation is established by the use of sociological tools that many people are drawn simply on the basis that they find a social group with which they feel comfortable. The preaching becomes void of the offense of the cross in order not to undo the success of a sociological principle, and an increasing number are received into the church through the broad way and not through the narrow gate.

In many American churches, as we have seen, that produces a shifting in the arrangement of church members and has created megachurches and killed neighborhood churches. Too often the megachurches grow, not because they are superior in their evangelism or better in their preaching or more apt to produce genuine discipleship, but because they have the resources to create special activities appealing to the desires of many different types of groups. That situation is not intended by any of the church growth advocates but follows very naturally from some of the methods. What is "atheological" has at times become tremendously *devastating* theologically.

CONCLUSION

As the reformers and the revivalists move further apart—the former often afraid of experience; the latter often afraid of theology, especially Reformation theology—we must pray for zeal and wisdom, love and truth. We should encourage and practice teaching and preaching that unites reformation *and* revival. Likewise, all that tends to erode true reformation or pollute true revival must be resisted and corrected. Perhaps all that is needed in some cases is gentle persuasion of those who are sincere but nisguided.

In any case, we live in the confidence that God will undertake the protection of His truth and the progress of His work and will raise up a company to accomplish it (2 Timothy 1:11-14). Without being insincere or melodramatic, we should not fear to emulate the examples of Luther and Calvin in one of the most strategic and dangerous of all times for the church and claim as our own intention that of Calvin before Emperor Charles V:

> In regard to ourselves, whatever be the event, we will always be supported, in the sight of God, by the consciousness that we have desired both to promote his glory and do good to his Church; that we have laboured faithfully for that end; that, in short, we have done what we could. Our conscience tells us, that in all our wishes, and all our endeavours, we have had no other aim. And we have assayed, by clear proof, to testify the fact. And certainly, while we feel assured, that we both care for and do the

work of the Lord, we are also confident, that he will by no means be lacking either to himself or to it.[49]

NOTES

1. Pelagians (after the fourth-century monk Pelagius) generally maintained the belief that humans are not born inherently fallen and are therefore capable, by nature, of obeying God perfectly. Semi-Pelagians deny natural perfectibility but believe that grace and free will cooperate toward bringing a person into God's favor.

2. John Calvin, "The Necessity of Reforming the Church," in *Selected Works of John Calvin*, ed. and trans. Henry Beveridge, 7 vols. (Grand Rapids: Baker, 1983; repr. of Edinburgh: Calvin Translation Society, 1844), 1:125.

3. Ibid., 1:133-34.

4. Ibid., 1:134.

5. Ibid., 1:159.

6. Jonathan Edwards, *The Works of Jonathan Edwards*, 2 vols. (Edinburgh: Banner of Truth; 1976 repr. of 1834 edition), 1:652-53.

7. George Whitefield, *Whitefield's Life and Sermons* (n.p.: n.p., 1834), p. 321.

8. Jonathan *Edwards, The Distinguishing Marks of a Work of the Spirit of God in The Great Awakening*, ed. C. C. Goen (New Haven, Conn.: Yale U., 1972), pp. 231-32.

9. Ibid., p. 249.

10. Edwards, *Works*, 1:235.

11. Ibid., 1:656.

12. Ibid., 1:668.

13. Edwards, *Faithful Narrative* in *The Great Awakening*, p. 168.

14. *The Connecticut Evangelical Magazine*, November 1803, p. 185. The report is by Silas Churchill and extends from pp. 179 to 189. It is typical of several that occur in the magazine from July 1800, when it began, through at least 1804.

15. Ibid., p. 188.

16. Bennet Tyler, *New England Revivals as They Existed at the Close of the Eighteenth, and the Beginning of the Nineteenth Centuries* (Boston: Massachusetts Sabbath School Society, 1846; repr. Wheaton, Ill.: Richard Owen Roberts, 1980), pp. vii-xi.

17. W. B. Sprague, *Lectures on Revival* (Edinburgh: Banner of Truth, 1978; repr. of 1832 ed.), Appendix, Letter XVIII, pp. 82-85.

18. John W. Nevin, *The Anxious Bench* (New York: Garland, 1987) pp. 7, 18. The anxious bench was a bench at the front of the church to which Finney invited all who had anxiety about their spiritual confidence. They would be exhorted directly during the sermon and often prayed for by name.

19. Ibid., pp. 19-28.

20. Ibid., pp. 55-56.

21. Ibid., p. 10. Herman Hanko, a contemporary theologian also in the tradition of the *Heidelberg Catechism,* has taken Nevin's view one step further and rejected the concept of revival totally (Herman Hanko, "Ought the Church to Pray for Revival?" in *Trinity Review,* no. 79 (May-June 1991), published by The Trinity Foundation, Jefferson, Md.). He views the superfluous manifestations that have accompanied various revivals through history as the essence of revival. He sees the theology of Wesley, Finney, and,

in my opinion, a wrongly described Puritan theology as foundational to revival. He considers the Puritans as "wrong, desperately wrong, in their conception of Christian experience." Revival also leads unalterably to Roman Catholic mysticism and the charismatic movement. In his opinion revival has a wrong view of conversion and of the covenant. He affirms that "the children of the church are covenant children, themselves already regenerated. In their lives conversion is a daily turning from sin and turning to God in humble repentance." Revival theology mocks that concept, he contends, and substitutes an unbiblical emphasis on crisis prompted by the preaching of the law, conviction of sin, preparatory grace, and an eventual "closing with Christ." Therefore, "revival is wrong. Revival is contrary to the Scriptures. Revival is at odds with the Reformed faith. To pray for revival is to go against the will of God and is to grieve the Holy Spirit." Hanko's statements illustrate how difficult it has become, both for pro- and anti-revivalists, to separate the incidental from the essential. That difficulty leads many simply to quit trying.

22. Charles Finney, *Revivals of Religion* (Westwood, N.J.: Revell, n.d.), p. 5.
23. Ibid., p. 4.
24. Ibid., p. 3.
25. Ibid., p. 22.
26. Charles Finney, *Reflections of Revival,* comp. Donald W. Dayton (Minneapolis: Bethany Fellowship, 1979), pp. 17-18.
27. Ibid., p. 41.
28. Ibid., pp. 82-84, 119-23.
29. Charles Finney, *Systematic Theololgy* (Minneapolis: Bethany, 1976), p. 207.
30. Ibid., p. 321.
31. Ibid., pp. 165, 167.
32. Finney, *Revivals,* p. 414.
33. Charles G. Finney, "Sinners Bound to Change Their Own Hearts," in Robert L. Ferm, *Issues in American Protestantism* (Gloucester, Mass.: Peter Smith, 1976), p. 169.
34. Finney, *Reflections,* pp. 104-10.
35. Alexander, *Religious Experience,* p. 22.
36. Samuel Porter Jones, *Sam Jones' Revival Sermons,* p. 232.
37. C. Peter Wagner, *Church Growth and the Whole Gospel* (San Francisco: Harper & Row, 1981), p. 83.
38. Calvin, *Selected Works,* 1:233.

PART 4
POWER WITHIN

"They dress the wound of my people
as though it were not serious.
'Peace, peace,' they say,
when there is no peace.
Are they ashamed of their loathsome conduct?
No, they have no shame at all;
they do not even know how to blush. . . .

"This is what the Lord says:
'Cursed is the one who trusts in man,
who depends on flesh for his strength
and whose heart turns away from the Lord. . . .

"But blessed is the man who trusts in the Lord,
whose confidence is in him. . . .

"The heart is deceitful above all things
and beyond cure."

Jeremiah 8:11; 17:5, 7, 9

I know that nothing good lives in me, that is, in my
sinful nature.

Romans 7:18

POWER WITHIN

8

Integration or Inundation?

David Powlison

Christians in every time and place must answer particular crucial questions of intellect, conscience, and practice. Given the real problems of poverty and social inequity, Latin American Christians must ask if and how biblical Christianity comports with Marxist eschatology and revolutionary politics. German Christians in the 1930s had to ask how biblical Christianity related to the ideology and practices of National Socialism. European Christians in the nineteenth century had to face the higher criticism of the Scriptures. Mediterranean Christians in the late first century had to wrestle out whether objective biblical faith opposed gnostic philosophy. Judean Christians in the mid-first century had to ask how old covenant Israel related to the nations, given the stunning new covenant of the Person and work of Jesus the Messiah. Ephraimites in the tenth century B.C. had to decide if they would worship Jeroboam's calf YHWH in Bethel or cross the border and worship the invisible YHWH in Jerusalem.

What crucial questions of faith and practice face North American Christians in the late twentieth century? Each section of this book tackles a signal issue. This section on the popularization of psychology within evangelicalism is no exception. How does biblical Christianity comport with the popular psychologies that increasingly

DAVID POWLISON is lecturer in practical theology at Westminster Theological Seminary in Philadelphia and a counselor at Christian Counseling and Educational Foundation, Laverock, Pennsylvania.

claim to be biblical, doctrinally sound, Christ-centered, or spiritually oriented? How does biblical Christianity relate to the psychologies which increasingly shape the language and practices of those churches that claim to be Bible-believing?

PSYCHOLOGICAL THEORY AND PRACTICE
HAS EMERGED INTO THE EVANGELICAL MAINSTREAM

The Christianity and psychology question is both old and new. Any good seminary library fills yards of shelf space already with books on Christianity and psychology written over the last one hundred years. People who did not believe in historic, biblical Christianity wrote most of those books. They were religious people, however. They found modern psychology to be a fascinating and persuasive friend. It was useful for informing an intelligent modern spirituality. It was useful for forming effective pastoral practice. Before the 1950s only theological and ecclesiastical liberals embraced the psychologies and psychotherapies.

In the twentieth century pastoral counseling became virtually synonymous with liberalism, and such pastoral counseling was intellectually and methodologically subordinate to secular psychology.[1] Authority in the "personal problems" sphere was handed over to the expanding mental health professions. Speaking of the 1920s, Andrew Abbott has written,

> There emerged in this period a clinical pastoral training movement aiming to give young clergymen direct experience with the newly defined personal problems. Seminarians would learn the rudiments of human nature from psychiatrists, psychologists, and social workers who "knew" those rudiments, that is, from the professionals who currently controlled the definitions of them.[2]

Conservatives, meanwhile, virtually ignored counseling. The very subject was tainted by strong associations with men like Harry Emerson Fosdick.[3] Conservatives neglected to develop thoughtful pastoral care. They evangelized. Higher Life conferences dealt with the residual problems in living. The dropouts, failures, and burnouts either suffered in silence or covertly found their way into the secular mental health system. Evangelicals lacked both intellectual and institutional resources to address people's problems in living.

Since the 1950s, all this has changed. Evangelicals face two new forms of the psychology and faith question. First, people who say they do believe in historic, biblical Christianity have been writing an increasing number of those books on the library shelf in recent years. Many evangelicals have found modern psychology to be a fascinating and persuasive friend. They claim that psychology, properly appropriated, can inform intelligent spirituality and form effective pastoral practice. In the past quarter century we have witnessed the creation of a "Christian mental health establishment"[4] under the banner statement "the integration of psychology and Christianity." It claims to remain Bible-believing. It claims to appropriate contemporary psychology as an adjunct to and servant of the faith. How should we evaluate this integration movement?

Second, psychology has increasingly become popularized in evangelical churches. Psychological conversation happens in new locations, breaking out of the psychologist's office and professor's classroom. Psychology has hit the street in evangelical neighborhoods, becoming the language of life in many pews, small groups, conversations, and pulpits. The shelves of Christian bookstores—a location more significant than the libraries!?—overflow with popular self-help books. This mass movement is not a theoretical attempt to integrate psychology and Christianity. It is an overt psychologization of the faith and life of professedly Christian people. How do we evaluate the recent mass fascination with psychology's concerns, terms, and practices at the popular level?

I identify three stages in the emergence of psychological theory and practice into the mainstream of evangelicalism. First, the 1950s and '60s was a period of budding interest and rudimentary institutional development, climaxing with controversy. A few voices called the evangelical church to wake up: Christians had personal and interpersonal problems that needed to be addressed by counseling. A few evangelicals warmed to psychology as the source of wisdom for such problems in living.

Clyde Narramore was the first evangelical Christian well-known as a psychologist. Narramore utilized a trichotomist view of human nature to legitimize a new division of labor in the helping professions.[5] He allocated different parts of human nature to different expert professions. The medical doctor continued to treat bodily problems. The rest of human needs were parceled out in two directions. The pastor handled "spiritual" problems (how to be saved or to gain assurance, doctrinal teaching, prayer). The psychotherapist was granted "emotional and psychological" problems. By this definition a new profession first claimed legitimacy in evangelical circles.[6]

Several institutions were founded. A small group of Midwestern evangelicals in the mental health professions founded the Christian Association for Psychological Studies (CAPS) in 1952 to provide professional fellowship. Fuller Seminary founded its Graduate School of Psychology in 1965 with a theoretical mandate to integrate the Christian faith and modern psychology, and with a practical mandate to train clinical psychologists, who could become accredited professionals.[7] Meanwhile, pastoral counseling training in seminaries during the 1950s and '60s was wholly under the sway of Carl Rogers's psychology. Liberal pastoral theologians mediated Rogers to conservative as well as liberal seminarians.[8]

This initial period of interest in counseling and psychology ended in sharp controversy. The first counterattack to the dominant pastoral psychology came in 1970. Like Karl Barth's "bombshell in the playground of the theologians," Jay Adams's *Competent to Counsel* shattered the existing consensus. Adams argued chiefly for the minds and practice of pastors and of seminary professors teaching pastoral counseling. However, the budding Christian psychotherapy professions could not ignore his attack on their very existence.

Adams perceived psychology and psychiatry as threats to conservative Christianity in three main ways. First, psychology's influence neutered the "in the office" theology of pastors. Once a pastor left his pulpit he became a de facto Rogerian. He no longer proclaimed the claims of Christ and called to repentance. Second, the mental health system offered a persuasive rationale for referring troubled parishioners to secular experts. The province of pastoral care supposedly did not include psychologically, emotionally, or mentally "sick" people. Third, evangelicals in the mental health professions were functionally secular in their ideas and practices. They were intruders into and usurpers of the pastor's role. In Adams's eyes the phrase "Christian psychotherapy" was an oxymoron.

When Adams first wrote, the problems he perceived were issues of professional truth and turf. Psychology was not yet "pop psychology" for Christian folk. Psychology did not claim the popular Christian mind. It had not begun to define the working theology of laypeople and preachers in Bible-believing churches. It was not the language of the pew and Sunday school class. Psychology had not yet laid claim to *be* what the Bible was teaching. That has all changed since 1970. The groundwork was laid by the response of Christian psychotherapists to Adams.

The 1970s and into the mid-'80s was a period of marked professional development among Christian psychologists. This was the second stage of psychology's emergence into the evangelical mainstream. A new generation of "Christian psychologists" came of age and into influence. As professing Bible-believers, they felt the force of Adams's charges of secularism.[9] They recognized the weaknesses of current integration theory, which in effect simply rationalized a wholesale appropriation of secular ideas. They recognized the precariousness of the trichotomist rationalization for their professional existence.

However, they disagreed with Adams in at least five major ways. First, as epistemologists, they disagreed with Adams's presuppositionalism and biblicism. For Adams, even psychology's observational data was theory-laden and theory-selected. Hence it should be viewed critically and used tentatively and in a distinctly secondary way. He believed that all the significant underpinnings for counseling could be exegetically derived from the Bible. Under the banners "All truth is God's truth" and "common grace," integrationists viewed psychology as a source of legitimate and even necessary knowledge. Psychology was part of God's "second book" about human beings, supplemental and complementary to Scripture. To criticize particular unbiblical aspects of psychology did not mean viewing the whole endeavor with suspicion. The Bible was not a book on counseling per se but provided certain resources for counseling.

Second, as lay theologians and exegetes, integrationists disagreed with Adams's "atomistic" and selective use of Scripture. They saw the Bible as providing general theological themes to describe human life. Important counseling problems could not be found in a concordance. The solution to problems could not be connected to proof texts. They saw Scripture as exemplifying a multiplicity of styles of ministry, without mandating one style. Frequently criticisms turned on Adams's choice of the word *noutheteo* rather than the word *parakaleo* to summarize the Bible's approach to counseling.

Third, as licensed professionals, integrationists disagreed with Adams's ecclesiasticism. He viewed counseling as a frankly pastoral activity aiming at sanctification. Extra-ecclesiastical counseling was in direct competition with the church. Its goals of personal exploration, psychological healing, wholeness, and self-actualization were deceptive. Integrationists envisioned and sought to rationalize professional counseling as a legitimate activity by Christians, separate from the direct oversight of the pastoral ministry. They saw sanctification and psychological renewal as complementary but different ends, attained by different means.

Fourth, as theoretically committed psychologists, they perceived an ironic affinity between Adams and behavioral psychology. This contradicted Adams's claims to be distinctively biblical. Adams seemed to be a crypto-integrationist who simply would not see or admit the fact. Adams's evident kinship with behaviorism was kinship with an unpopular species of psychology. Critical of behavioral psychology, Christian psychologists were typically more interested in the implications of psychodynamic, cognitive, and humanistic psychologies for understanding and helping people.[10]

Fifth, as therapists, they disagreed with Adams's confrontational and didactic style of relating to counselees. They were committed to a generally supportive and affirmative mode of counseling —unconditional positive regard. They sought to elicit insights and healing forces from within the counselee. Adams's style of counselor was too directive, controlling the counseling session agenda too tightly. Authoritative counseling could too easily become authoritarian counseling. Christian psychologists saw counseling as a place where moral judgments and explicit guidance had little or no place.

These men (and, as the movement developed, a growing number of women) aimed to wed two identities never before joined. During the 1970s "Bible-believing evangelical" became one flesh with "professional psychologist." "Christian psychotherapy" could now be a legitimate calling. Christian psychotherapists sought to develop that calling, both cognitively and professionally. Both CAPS and its journal, *The Journal of Psychology and Christianity,* expanded under the leadership of Harold Ellens.[11] Rosemead Graduate School of Psychology and the *Journal of Psychology and Theology* were founded under the leadership of Bruce Narramore and John Carter. The Psychological Studies Institute was founded to train Christian psychologists under the umbrella of Georgia State University. The Fuller Graduate School of Psychology continued to grow, with Newton Maloney and Hendrika Vande Kempe. Wheaton College's psychology department recruited and developed a respected faculty: David Benner, Stan Jones, Steven Evans. Calvin College's Mary Stewart Van Leeuwen and Mary VanderGoot, and Hope College's David Myers became respected academic and experimental psychologists. Clinical psychologists became prominent at a number of theologically conservative seminaries: Larry Crabb at Grace, Gary Collins at Trinity, Frank Minirth and psychiatrist Paul Meier at Dallas, Roger Bufford at Western Conservative Baptist.

Psychologists also became influential beyond the circle of academic discourse and professional training. A number of psychologists—for example, Gary Collins, Bruce Narramore, James Dobson, Larry Crabb—joined Clyde Narramore in gaining respected mass pulpits. Through books, articles, seminars, videotapes, and radio broadcasts they became the evangelical authorities for solving problems in living. The evangelical psychotherapy community built its scholarly, institutional, and popular base during the '70s and '80s.

The logo for this growing professional community was the word *integration.* Through articles and books the integrationist agenda was hammered out.[12] Psychology and theology would mutually stimulate one another. Liberals had simply bowed to psychology as a superior authority. In contrast, integrationist evangelicals sought to interact with psychology in a sophisticated manner, hoping to weed out the tares of error from the wheat of truth. They sought to plunder psychological data and explanatory categories, utilizing a grid of general scriptural themes. They sought to profit from psychology's practices and institutional arrangements, under the guidance of general scriptural principles.

A growing pool of evangelical psychotherapists set up practices and established referral networks with local churches. By the 1980s conservative churches in most major population centers no longer needed to refer troubled members to secular therapists. Christians trained in psychology could treat their own. The integration movement accomplished two things. First, it formulated and fine-tuned an intellectual rationale for wedding psychology and evangelical theology. Second, it created a professional and institutional network to carry into practice a professedly evangelical psychotherapeutic.

The third stage of psychology's entry into the evangelical mainstream occurred during the mid to late 1980s. In a way no one anticipated, psychology went popular and epidemic. Speaking of an earlier fad, historian Edwin Boring once said, "In the 1920s all America had gone behaviorist."[13] We might almost say today, "In the late 1980s all evangelicalism had gone psychodynamic." Ideas that were once the province of professionals now inundated popular Christian literature. Most significantly, psychological categories increasingly became the language of daily life in evangelical circles. Words such as *self-esteem, dysfunctional family, codependency, support, unconditional love, needs, damaged emotions,* and *victimization* suddenly seemed to capture the most significant things about life and God and the Bible. Pop psychology increasingly became the vernacular in which significant parts of daily life were transacted. Psychology increasingly has become the language for discussing personal problems and struggles, the causes and the cures of difficulties in living, and the sources of help. Popular psychologies, inevitably "integrated" with biblical language and proof texts, increasingly claimed the loyalty not only of Christian therapists, but now of evangelical parishioners and pastors.

The breakout has occurred. The psychological river has been slowly rising up the levee since the mid 1950s. It went to flood stage in the late 1980s. Psychology entered evangelical religion in almost every setting. The authoritative, compelling, and interesting ideas are derived from psychology. The best-selling self-help books in Christian bookstores are psychologically flavored (e.g., David Seamands, Larry Crabb, Minirth and Meier, et al.). A colleague recently told me of his conversation with the manager of a large Christian bookstore. When asked, "What's hot these days?" the man replied, "Anything with 'pain' in the title. I can't keep the shelves stocked because they sell so fast." Almost every major evangelical book publisher has recently featured titles dealing with recovery, dysfunctional families, adult children, and the healing of psychological pain.

The seminar and conference circuit, both in person and on video, finds psychologists filling roles once filled by Bible expositors, prophecy teachers, and victorious life preachers. Pastors still fill local pulpits, but many of the new mass pulpits are filled by psychologists. Psychologists, not pastors or theologians, maintain cultural authority in the evangelical church with respect to people and their problems. They are the experts, with the authority to define what is right and wrong, true and false, good and bad, constructive and destructive.

Not only are the leading ideas coming from a new quarter, but numerous evangelical practices have also been transformed into the psychological mode. The theology and exegesis proclaimed from many pulpits unfolds psychological themes: self-esteem, the meeting of psychological "needs," the gospel as unconditional and undemanding love, healing as the mode of understanding personal transformation, and the like.[14] Discipleship, prayer, or Bible study groups have frequently evolved into support groups or 12-step groups. Even InterVarsity's traditional "Urbana" missions conference downplayed Bible exposition and made dysfunctional families a major focus of its 1990 conference. Speaker after speaker testified in the psychological mode ("Here are the painful things I went through") in startling contrast with the standard missionary witness mode ("Here is what Jesus is doing behind the Iron Curtain").[15]

In many churches the concerns of committed laypersons have noticeably shifted. Formerly there was a characteristic extrospection and activism: building faith, discovering gifts, pursuing ministries, studying the Bible, praying, seeking ways of self-sacrifice, denying desires, and the like. Those concerns have been noticeably replaced by an introspection concerned to explore old wounds, to get psychological needs met, to avoid enabling and doormat behaviors, to nourish desires, and the like.

The interfaces between the professional and the popular continue to be developed. A network of new Christian in-patient clinics has sprung up nationwide in the past several years (e.g., Minirth-Meier Clinic and Rapha). Their existence registers a new level of both popular and professional support for "Christian" in-patient hospitalization. The critical mass of popular interest to sustain such clinics has not only been reached but quickly surpassed. Small groups in churches and communities are being created to provide extramural care for troubled people. They act as feeders into the clinics and as after-care groups for discharged patients. Books, workbooks, and study guides advertise and reinforce the clinics' message and practice.[16]

The institutional network to furnish psychologically trained professionals and para-professionals is also in place. Psychology and counseling programs in Bible-believing colleges and seminaries continue to expand and to attract increasing numbers of students. "Christian psychologist" is an increasingly viable role for those who want to "go into ministry," but who do not want to become pastors, teachers, or missionaries.

WHY HAS PSYCHOLOGY BECOME SO POPULAR IN EVANGELICALISM?

The popularization of psychology within the evangelical subculture is so recent that it is only just being noticed.[17] The implications have not been wrestled with. What should we make of the "integration" of psychology and biblical truth? What should we make of the mass movement of evangelical lay people to embrace psychotherapeutic categories and methods? Why has that happened? I see two major factors contributing to the current situation.

First, the church has been weak in the domain of personal and interpersonal problems. Evangelical churches and theologians have typically not grappled with the problems in living that Christian people have. The church has either misconstrued, oversimplified, or avoided facing the existential and situational realities of human experience in the trenches of life.

Since the nineteenth century what passed for pastoral counseling in the conservative church blended three things. Troubled people were offered pietism: "Let go and let God" and "die to self" to enter the higher or victorious life. They were offered rationalism: biblical truth would be compared with errors in thinking or philosophy.[18] They were offered voluntarism: the ethical teaching of the Bible led to calls to obedience and ministry service.

The nineteenth-century evangelical view of the Christian life, of "truth, faith, obedience, and service," became a caricature of the real item. The hands-on and case-wise feel for the outworkings of many doctrines was lost: justification, progressive sanctification, repentance, discipleship, total depravity, the reality of remaining sin, temptation, spiritual warfare, suffering, eschatology. Eschatology provides a striking example that can be briefly summarized. In the Bible, eschatology is specifically treated in contexts where people are suffering situationally and are struggling with their own sins.[19] The Bible's eschatology is pastoral, providing a framework of truth, hope, warning, and meaning for strugglers. Eschatology is tailor-made for counseling. Yet most evangelical circles since the nineteenth century have not used or discussed eschatology for pastoral purposes. Eschatology has been fuel for intellectual controversy and even an excuse for disengagement from the hard problems of real people in a real world.

Such pastoral weakness did not always exist. For example, the Puritans developed a massive and profound literature on a wide range of personal and pastoral problems. They wrote numerous, detailed case studies. They had a sophisticated diagnostic system that penetrated motives. They had a well-developed view of the long-term processes, the tensions, the difficulties, and the struggles of the Christian life. They carefully addressed what the twentieth century would term addictions to sex, food, and alcohol; the gamut of problems in marriage and family relationships; depression, anxiety, and anger; perfectionism and the drive to please other people; interpersonal conflict; priorities and the management of time and money; unbelief and deviant value systems.

The Puritans not only discussed diagnostic and conceptual aspects of these problems, they tackled many methodological issues, seeking to apply pastoral care to struggling people. Possessing a keen sense that the wise counselor had wrestled through in his or her own life the very same issues, the Puritans were empiricists in the best sense of the word, attuned to cases. It is not accidental that Jonathan Edwards, "The Last Puritan," provided the model and inspiration for William James's pioneering empirical work in secular psychology. Edwards's *Treatise on Religious Affections* is a masterpiece of observational acuity wedded to biblical truth.

In a provocative article, Timothy Keller has written about Puritan pastoral counseling:

> The Puritans probably would not find themselves fitting in comfortably to most of the existing "schools" in the evangelical counseling field. They probably would find some counselors overly concerned to "raise self-esteem" when man's main problem is self-worship. Yet, on the other hand they would not be in agreement with those who completely ignore or even reject the importance of reprogramming the self-understanding through the penetration of gospel truth. They would find many biblical counselors are being far too superficial in their treatment of problems by merely calling for surface repentance and behavioral change. But they also would be quite uncomfortable with the "inner healing" approaches which virtually ignore behavior and the need for mortification. In fact, the Puritans would be quite unhappy talking about people's "unmet needs" because at bottom they believed a man does not have abstract needs, only a necessity for worship. . . .
>
> Above all, the Puritans' "spirit" would differ quite a bit from other counselors today. Most modern evangelical counselors simply lack the firmness, directness and urgency of the Puritans. Most of us talk less about sin than did our forefathers. But, on the other hand, the Puritans were amazingly tender, encouraging, always calling the counselees to accept the grace of God and extremely careful not to call a problem "sin" unless it was analyzed carefully. One of their favorite texts was: "A bruised reed he will not break, and a smoking flax he will not quench."[20]

Such sophisticated and careful wisdom was lost. In the century after Jonathan Edwards, American Protestantism divided roughly in three: Reformed orthodoxy, revivalism, proto-liberalism. None of those engaged the issues of the human heart in a detailed way.[21]

Secular psychology exploded into a spiritual vacuum at the end of the nineteenth century. The old saying that heresies are the unpaid debts of the church has rarely had a better exemplar. The mental health professions became the new "secular priesthood," in Perry London's provocative words.[22] Even more graphically, they became the new secular theologians studying the soul: psychologists. They became the new secular pastorate practicing a cure of souls:

psychotherapy. Counterfeits of pastoral care filled the vacuum for the scientifically enlightened and liberal. Progressive sanctification became a psychotherapeutic process of healing neuroses and other psychopathologies. The liberal church frankly embraced the new psychology, justly earning the well-known criticisms of secular psychologists O. Hobart Mowrer and Karl Menninger. Mower asked, "Has evangelical religion sold its birthright for a mess of psychological pottage?" Menninger wrote a book whose title is the provocative query, *Whatever Became of Sin?*[23]

Evangelicals did little better. They sounded the same old notes well into the twentieth century. Greater yieldedness, Bible study, ethical obedience, and dedicated service would cure all. They still believed in sin and in that birthright of the grace of Christ to "be of sin the double cure, cleanse me of its guilt and power."[24] They did not become secular psychologists. But though they did not sell their birthright, they did not develop it to tackle new challenges. They did not become wise, penetrating, and persuasively biblical counselors. The vacuum in pastoral theology and pastoral counseling set the stage for the psychological invasion we are now experiencing.

Psychology is persuasive existentially because it is case-wise, empirically detailed, and practiced in talking about and facilitating change processes. That is the second major factor contributing to our current situation. Psychology rings bells experientially. It comes in the ideological guise of "science." Psychology is persuasive in exactly the areas where the evangelical church is weak and has been weak for more than two centuries. As a result, segments of evangelicalism that would spot and reject deviations in justification by faith, the doctrine of Christ, millennialism, or biblical authority have embraced psychological categories and practices unwittingly.

On the one hand, the church has been relegated to the superficial and external. It calls people to moral uprightness, assent to a few doctrinal essentials, acts of will-power, and commitment. On the other hand, the church has been relegated to the mystical and intangible. It invites people to spiritual experiences of yieldedness, second blessing, charismatic overpowering, miracles, and visions. So how does the church deal with the compulsions of severe addiction or the massive anguish and chaos within marital or familial breakdown? How does the church deal with the slough of depression or the volatility of panic attack? More simply, how does the church advise parents to raise their kids? In effect, evangelical resources have been orthodox and moral—but superficial and irrelevant to the magnitude and practicality of the problems. Or they have been deep and mystical—but irrational and irrelevant to the magnitude and practicality of the problems.

Psychology has staked out everything in the middle. It has claimed the "interesting stuff," the things that are deep, significant, and yet rationally explorable: the intricacies of motivation, defensiveness, interpersonal conflict, communication, problem solving, anger, anxiety, depression, guilt, the grieving process, parenting, sexuality, addictions. Psychologists are the twentieth century's designated experts in these domains. They know the intricacies. They work with the problems. This is their expertise, where they are relevant, and an externalistic or pietistic church is irrelevant.

Notice the heartbreaking irony of our current situation. That "interesting stuff" is precisely the cognitive and practical domain of the Bible itself. This is the domain that the Holy Spirit has chosen to write about and where He works fruit. The Bible is not concerned with promoting external morality, lip-service professions of faith, and deeds of service done from fundamental blindness to one's hypocrisy and self-righteousness. The Bible does not seek to promote sensuous mystical experience, irrational and contentless ecstasies, and pieties. In fact, the Bible opposes those things. In effect, when it comes to making real sense of people and promoting significant change in people, Bible-believing evangelicals have aligned themselves with domains the Bible is designed to destroy. That Bible is centrally about domains in which secular psychologists have laid claim to truth and competency.

I can summarize this way. North American psychology has acquired a threefold authority in contemporary American society. First, psychologists have gained cultural authority. Human beings can be and have been "explained" in any number of ways. In our time and place, psychologists "are right" in their descriptions and theories, their explanations of causality, their therapeutic agenda. As Andrew Abbott put it, mental health professionals became identified as the experts who "knew" the rudiments of human nature, which is to say they "currently controlled the definitions of them."[25]

Second, psychologists have gained social authority. Human beings can be "helped" by any number of different kinds of people. In our time and place, psychologists are seen as the ones who "have the right" to help people. They care. They are the experts. They are called to help. Their institutions are the places to go for understanding, love, wisdom, help, and cure.

Third, psychologists have gained pragmatic authority. Any number of things can "make a difference" in how people act, think, and feel. In our time and place, psychologists are seen as the ones who "can make it right." They claim and demonstrate pragmatic efficacy. They seem to back up their claims to knowledge and responsibility by producing results. The net effect is that psychology, in its threefold authority, offers this world truth, love, and power.

Does the church offer truth—or shallowness, ignorance, superstition and errors that harm people? Does the church offer love—or fear, avoidance of difficult questions, avoidance of problem people, censorious accusation, or simplistic moralizing? Does the church offer power—or outworn formulas urging external reformation or producing mystical experience? Psychology offers the modern gospel. The church's historic message is mere words.

Evangelical psychologists sense this dilemma. In conversations with CAPS members I have been struck by a repeated theme. They grew up in culturally conservative, anti-intellectual, "fundamentalistic" homes and churches. Their pastors and parents offered simplistic formulas and truisms to describe what was wrong with people and how to change. When they came of age intellectually, psychology provided the "revelation" that people's motives were complex, that people had suffered and been affected by that suffering, that change was a process, that you had to get your hands dirty and be patient in order to help people. I once heard Harold Ellens describe how he and the generic CAPS member were "running from the fundamentalist shadow of our past." Christian psychotherapists have wanted to "reform fundamentalism" by engaging the psychological world and bringing home its best fruits.[26]

The church was weak where psychology was strong. The current breakout of psychology into the evangelical mainstream began in the minds and practices of Christian psychotherapists impressed with that relative weakness and strength. Evangelicals sought to redress the church's weakness by engaging the psychotherapies. But the conversion process has gone the wrong way. Instead of portraying the biblical vision of people first to the church and then to psychologists,[27] integrationists imported secular visions into Christianity. Personality theory, psychopathology, health, and therapeutic change have replaced biblical anthropology, sin, grace, holiness, and sanctification. Psychology's cultural, social, and pragmatic authority proved too strong. Biblical truth seemed insufficiently applicable.

Christian psychotherapists generally believe that the Bible is insufficient when it comes to exploring and explaining the significant goings on in the human psyche. For example, integrationists repeatedly cite the Bible's failure to offer a "personality theory."[28] Because Scripture does not detail how individual differences arise— in motivation, behavior, cognition, affective expression—it is presumed deficient when it comes to counseling.[29]

That view rests on the massive assumption that explaining the differences between people provides the key to counseling. The Bible proclaims the opposite. The deep-seated commonalities between people are far more crucial to counseling than the extensive variations between people. For example, Christians across all times and places have found that "there is no temptation that has overtaken you that is not common to all" (1 Corinthians 10:13). The social, cultural, historical, and individual differences between Hebrew herdsmen and Corinthian cosmopolitans—and between both of them and contemporary American readers—can hardly be exaggerated. What do people in Irian Jaya and in New York City suburbs have in common? Yet Paul freely recited Exodus stories to urban Greeks and then said, "These things happened to them as an example, and they were written for our instruction" (10:11). Though the visible content of life's struggles is widely variable, the core themes in people are identical.

Observations and descriptions of individual differences are, of course, extremely valuable in making counselors mature and case-wise. An appreciation of differences nourishes a godly disenculturation from the assumptions of ego- and ethno-centricity. But we should be agnostic about personality theories. On the surface such theories are speculative, prone to intellectual fashion, and prejudiced by their hostility to what is true and significant about people.

Even more important, personality theory turns out to be absolutely unnecessary for effective counseling. Personality theory is even a distraction because it directs attention to the wrong questions. It mistakes the fascinating but superficial for the significant. It buries significant clarities that the Bible provides beneath superficial ambiguities that psychology attempts to explain. The questions that personality theory tackles are interesting subjects for general scholarship. They are perennially vexed because they are inherently ambiguous. But the Bible addresses in practical detail the significant things good counseling must address. The diverse fruit on the human tree arises from generic patterns of idolatry or faith and exhibits generic patterns of sin or righteousness.[30]

The integration movement has thought that the gold mine of significant truth for counseling was in the secular psychologies and psychotherapies. So integrationists diligently exegete psychology for relevant and needed truth. In effect, the Bible contains only "control beliefs" at a high level of generality: creation in the image of God, fall into sin, redemption in Christ. Psychology contains exegetical riches of great specificity and practicality for understanding and transforming human functioning.

Of course, even at a level of generality, biblical control beliefs are helpful. The best integrationist thinkers are troubled by the current mass psychologization of the Christian faith. For example, Stan Jones and Richard Butman write, "Too much of what passes for integration today is anemic theologically or biblically, and tends to be little more than a spiritualized rehashing of mainstream mental health thought."[31] But integrationists do not provide vigorous and perceptive biblical categories both for explaining people and for stemming the psychologizing tide. The center of gravity and interest for even the most careful and theologically astute integrationists is psychology.[32] The center of gravity for effective counseling and depsychologizing the evangelical church must be Scripture. Integrationists underestimate the Bible. Their conviction of the deficiency of Scripture logically mirrors an inadequate perception of how the sufficiency of Scripture works in practice.

HOW DOES SCRIPTURE RELATE TO PSYCHOLOGY?

The core issue theologically is the "sufficiency of Scripture." That is not simply a flag that narrow-minded faith waves contrary to all facts. Biblical categories *explain* the facts. Rich biblical truth explains human nature concretely and helps people specifically. Psychology's speculative myths reconstruct human nature in ways that are fundamentally false and misleading. Christians who counsel need categories that are concretely biblical. Let me illustrate how such biblical categories work by a case study.

"Low self-esteem" is one of those pieces of pop psychology jargon that has become street talk among Christians. The "self-esteem" concept is the core of the explanatory system for many Christian psychologists. There is no doubt that "low self-esteem" accurately describes a common syndrome. There are people who are depressed, lack self-confidence, deprecate themselves, feel hopeless, and the like. However, the term "low self-esteem" explains nothing at all. It only restates one of the symptoms. It masquerades as significant knowledge, as a cause that can be addressed to bring about change. It is deceptive and unhelpful to the very people it targets: people who are desperately and hopelessly attempting to be or become something either in their own eyes or in the eyes of others. It fails to wrestle with what really is going on with people who express self-loathing and a sense of failure. The words "low self-esteem" are a tag, loaded with supposed explanatory power.

For explanations and causes, biblical categories alone shed light. Dig deeply into the life of any person—child or adult—with "low self-esteem" and you will find at least three of the common themes of idolatry of the heart. The first common idol theme is "I haven't met the standards, expectations, and desires of others." That is a form of the fear of man. People drink in faulty and idolatrous value systems from "significant others" (the dynamics of "the world"). They fail to live up to those standards, images, and demands. Perhaps they reap abuse and criticism. They believe the authority of their accusers. Hence they suffer symptomatic low self-esteem before the eyes of significant others. They feel like sinners and failures in the eyes of parents, peers, or wider society. Such low self-esteem is symptomatic of a far more profound and objective sin. The sinful fear of man makes other people the source of affirmation or stigma. The Bible cuts deep in its diagnosis.

What happens in the therapy of such undiagnosed idolaters? Psychologists offer unconditional positive regard and the support of a group of fellow sufferers. These new significant others are pleasable others, full of affirmations. They offer a standard—the real you whom they accept—against which you can never fail. Psychologists accurately observe that people with low self-esteem place inordinate hopes and fears in the opinions of others. But they do not identify that as deeply ingrained idolatry. They offer another idol—therapeutic acceptance—as the cure for low self-esteem. Even God-talk is brought to bear in affirmations such as "God doesn't make junk" and "Jesus accepts you just as you are." If you believe in the acceptance of this therapist, this group, and this benign God, you will be delivered from the tyrannical demands of unpleasable others. You gain a "healthy self-esteem," living in the eyes of pleasable others.

Such therapy rehabilitates the fear-of-man idol. It does not overthrow it. The idol affirms you now instead of accusing you. The true sin of idolatry, which produced the distorted "sense" of sinful failure, is never addressed. The living God is misrepresented. God did make us part of His good creation. But if we are honest, that fact ruins our self-esteem rather than building it. We have trashed human nature. Jesus does accept us just as we are in one sense: "Just as I am . . . ." But that acceptance also ruins our self-esteem. It is *despite* who *we* are and *because* of who *He* is: "without one plea but that Thy blood was shed for me." The holiness and love that met on a cross are transmuted by Christianized psychologies into cosmic, unconditional, positive regard. The Bible cuts deep in its rebuke of psychotherapy in order to heal the sin-sick soul.

The second typical idol theme is "I haven't met my own standards, expectations, and desires." That is a form of pride and the compulsive drive towards self-righteousness that operates in everyone. People generate their own faulty expectations and idealized images of what or who they ought to be. Sometimes they fail to meet them. Their own lie-distorted conscience accuses them. Hence they suffer symptomatic "low self-esteem." The Bible cuts deep diagnostically.

Psychotherapists speak to them of "false guilt" and attempt to help them set realistic standards for personal accomplishment and self-image. As that succeeds, people gain a "healthy self-esteem and self-confidence." The idols of personal performance are rehabilitated. Pride now sets reasonable and attainable goals. The true guilt of idolatry, which produced the deceptive guilt feelings, is never addressed. Repentance from self-righteousness unto a crucified Savior is never enjoined. The law (Become wise! Love your neighbor! Praise God! Pay your taxes! Rejoice in your wife!) is not reinstated as the true standard the Holy Spirit empowers us to obey.

The third common idol motif is "Other people and God Himself have failed to meet my standards, expectations, and desires." Low self-esteem is almost invariably accompanied by a low esteem for God and others. That is pride and demandingness succeeding all too well, and yielding a harvest of anger, bitterness, self-pity, grumbling, self-centeredness, and fears. Three hundred years ago such a person might well have been diagnosed as an ingrate. The victim identity that sufferers of low self-esteem find so seductive—wounded heart, adult child, damaged emotions—is belied by the all too evident and active sins that accompany it. Psychotherapy recognizes hostilities and lovelessness only as secondary developments. But rebuilding self-esteem and self-love is seen as primary to loving God and others. The Bible, again, pierces to the twisted underpinnings both of the human soul and of the answers the psychotherapies construct.

Those three idol patterns are among the common sins of the human heart. They bear diverse fruit, among other things in the depression and self-hatred that goes by the label "low self-esteem." Jesus' love in dying on the cross for sinners meets our true need for mercy, for power, for hope, and for a change in what we worship. Great esteem for Christ results! Jesus never meets a supposed self-esteem need. Both creation and redemption (the doctrines usually cited as "nourishing" to self-esteem) are in fact shattering to human self-esteem.

Notice how biblical faith and psychology "integrate" in this case study of the phenomenon "low self-esteem." Biblical thinking engages psychology in a multifaceted way. First, psychologists make acute observations and have valid concerns. For example, psychologists have accurately described people who are depressed and observed patterns in social and personal history that are frequent correlates. They have described the various manifestations of "low self-esteem": cognitive, behavioral, affective. Psychologists also have valid concerns. Depressed people need help. Someone must give them help. Biblical thinking agrees that the phenomena cry out for attention and help.

Second, those observations and concerns may be provocative to Christians. If Christians have not looked closely into the lives of depressed people, psychologists challenge us. If Christians have avoided depressed people or have done a superficial or poor job of counseling them, psychologists challenge us. Biblical thinking recognizes the incompleteness of current wisdom. Psychology may be a catalyst for greater wisdom.

Third, the interpretive categories that psychologists use are highly distorted. The very things that are perceptive and provocative are also highly selected. Psychological systems wear blinkers, excluding many significant facts. Psychological systems wear distorting lenses as well. For example, they typically give *causal* status to some *symptom* or aspect of the environment. Are problems caused by low self-esteem, distorted cognitions, altered blood chemistry, a depressive personality type? Are problems caused by traumatic or non-nurturing primary relationships, nonrewarding or punitive contingencies of behavior? Because psychologists are blind to the rich and penetrating biblical view of motivation and personality, they juggle externals. They inevitably end up feeding covert or overt idolatries.

Explanations are signposts to solutions. The solutions— boost self-esteem, change self-talk, create a nurturing re-parenting environment, and the like—logically derive from the explanations offered. Many different sorts of solutions may create pragmatic, symptomatic relief, as noted in the example of self-esteem. People whose idols are rehabilitated will feel better and function better (according to criteria of desirable social adjustment). Biblical thinking is deft with the most fundamental question of all: Why do people do, think, and feel as they do? Biblical thinking is deft in exposing the noetic effects of sin that pervert all psychological explanatory systems.

Fourth, psychology's descriptive riches, valid concerns, provocative exposure of the church's failings (real or apparent), and pragmatic effectiveness combine to make psychological systems persuasive. Those are the typical characteristics of any system of falsehood that opposes itself to biblical truth about God and man: from the serpent in the garden to Rabshakeh outside Jerusalem's walls to gnosticism to Marxism to liberalism to the current psychologism. That persuasiveness makes the church vulnerable. Integrationist thinking typically surrenders to such persuasion. It is easy to relegate biblical truth to the periphery of one's conceptual and methodological interests. It is easy to make psychology the driving force of thought and practice. Such syncretism has an inertia in the direction of a practical atheism and idolatry, whatever the residual professed and personal faith. Biblical thinking, on the other hand, destroys speculations "and every lofty thing raised up against the knowledge of God" (2 Corinthians 10:5, NASB).

Fifth, biblical truth places a specific paradigm shift on all that psychologists see. For example, the biblical view of motivation sees specific God-substitutes that rule the human heart. Such biblical categories *causally* explain the *phenomenon* "low self-esteem." Biblical categories also explain the pragmatic success of secular (or secularized "Christian") counsel. Biblical thinking is not dependent on the self-selection of counselees who perceive themselves as needy, struggling, or suffering. Biblical categories are as insightful into the idolatries of happy people as they are regarding unhappy people. Biblical thinking exposes both dysfunctional idols (producing low self-esteem) and eufunctional idols (producing healthy self-esteem and pragmatically effective therapies). Biblical thinking exposes the deceitfulness that masks both the real issues in counselees and the noetic distortion contained in secular psychological answers. Biblical thinking shows specific ways in which a checked and repentant psychology could be extremely useful. Valid psychology is neither a psychotherapy nor a speculative pseudoscience competing with biblical truth. Valid psychology is an exploratory and illustrative science that must be submitted to biblical categories. Biblical thinking turns psychological interpretations and psychotherapeutic interventions inside out and upside down.

The provocative role of psychology in exposing the church's weakness must not lead to buying secular categories. The Bible's explanation of low self-esteem phenomena is frankly and specifically coherent with the cognitive orthodoxy and the pastoral practice that lies on the face of Scripture. The crucified Savior and repentance from sin and lies are instrumental to the sanctification of the person with low self-esteem. Biblical thinking even restores the much abused metaphor of "healing" to usefulness. In the current psychological flood, the figure of speech has taken on a life of its own, burying the antecedent it was meant to illumine. The metaphor is meant to capture the liberty and blessing of the gospel in contrast to the bondage and misery of living accursed as sinners in a sinful world. The Bible never contemplates a medical model of psychic "dis-ease" or trauma. *Biblical thinking is the paradigm shift that affects all seeing, not simply a filter trying to screen out the bad from the good.* Thoughtful integrationists filter out a lot more than careless integrationists. But no integrationist sees the complete paradigm shift that the sufficient Scripture offers.

Sixth, evangelicals call psychologists to cognitive and practical repentance. The biblical encounter with psychology must not issue in the psychologization of church and Bible. Psychologists will be converted when and if they open their eyes to the lies that guided and structured even their best observations. That conversion is not simply a matter of individual faith and moral reformation. Their whole explanation of people and their problems must be turned inside out. Sin is the problem, in a way that cuts deeply and specifically to the motives and kinks of the human heart. Their whole model of counseling must change. They cannot operate in a medical/therapeutic model that pursues healing by experts for the problems in living. They must operate with a moral model and pursue sanctification via the counseling ministry of the gospel. We understand their observations better than they do, and we address their valid concerns more deeply than they do. Biblical thinking is the crucible to make conversions.

Through this entire process of encountering psychology, the church is humbled and made wiser. To their credit, integrationists see that this must happen. The entire process affirms that secular psychologists are not stupid. It recognizes that the church is imperfect, ignorant, and loveless in certain pivotal ways. But Christians must not praise or sit at the feet of psychologists as if they had discovered "truth." We call them to specific and thorough repentance for having consistently distorted everything they saw so acutely, cared about so intensely, and accomplished so effectively. This encounter with psychology also challenges Christian psychotherapists, who embrace and promulgate psychology in the guise of Bible words and theological generalities. The specific truth of the Bible will be exalted and vindicated. The Christian critics of psychology have rightly seen that that must happen. Specific texts come to life. Counseling gains exegetical power. Theology and pastoral practice acquire the mind, tongue, hands, and feet to tackle the issues of counseling. The integrationist agenda of the Christian psychotherapy establishment is too enamored of psychology. It is too weak in specific biblical thinking ever to challenge secular psychology to a noetic and methodological repentance. It is too weak to stem the pop psychology flood, because it is fundamentally symptomatic of the problem rather than corrective.

CONCLUSION: WHICH INUNDATION?

A pastor made a comment to me recently that set me to some hard thinking. "The next great heresy will come from within evangelicalism. Classic liberalism is dead intellectually. Liberals haven't had a great thinker since Tillich. Liberal churches are withering institutionally, and lack any authority of truth or morals. The vitality is in the evangelical church. Persuasive error will come out of vitality." We agreed that a Christianized psychology is one likely candidate for that "next great heresy."

As I reflected on our conversation, my thoughts moved in a more ominous direction. What if the great heresy is not "next" but is "present"? What if in barring the front door against liberals, New Agers, Mormons, secularists, and the rest, evangelicals have thrown open the back door to psychology? What if our theology, morals, counseling practice, small groups, pastoral training, popular literature, and daily conversation have been already significantly turned?

J. Gresham Machen, the Presbyterian theologian who broke away from Princeton on the grounds of its liberalism and one of the founders of Westminster Theological Society, wrote his classic *Christianity and Liberalism* almost seventy years ago. He demonstrated that the ecclesiastical and theological conflicts in the early twentieth century were not really intramural. They were not between "fundamentalist" and "liberal" brands of Christianity. The conflict was between real Christianity and a wholly different religion, a modernist religion that denied all that Christianity was about. Certainly liberals sounded Christian and biblical. They talked of God, love, Jesus Christ, the kingdom of God, faith, the Spirit, even of sin. The personal faith of many of them in the early years appeared genuine. But all the words had been altered to mean other things. The faith of their successors has proved spurious.

The Christian psychologists often sound Christian and biblical. Many of the theological words are there.[34] But the meanings are different. The current mass psychologization of Christian life and thought is the popular fruit of the integration movement. The logic and drift of the integrationist movement has not been a biblical logic and drift. The church is reaping the consequences. Integration or inundation? The deluge is upon us. If Machen wrote his book today, he would entitle it *Christianity and Psychologism*. The modern psychological evangelicalism, the intellectual flood in which we float or against which we swim, is not Christianity.

"The earth will be filled with the knowledge of the glory of the Lord, as the waters cover the sea" (Habakkuk 2:14). There is another deluge that the God of truth promises. Intellectual fashions come and go, and psychology is such a fashion, but the Word of the Lord endures forever. The evangelical church must wage the current cultural war for the minds, hearts, and practice of Christian people. The human phenomena that necessitate counseling are comprehensible within frankly biblical categories. The constructs and practices of psychology differ from those of Scripture. Unquestionably, psychology may play a provocative and descriptive role. But it may never play a constitutive role, except to the peril of genuine evangelicalism. The current mass infatuation with psychology and the intellectual and institutional heritage of the integration movement place us precisely in that peril.

NOTES

1. See E. Brook Holifield's *A History of Pastoral Care in America: From Salvation to Self-Realization* (Nashville: Abingdon, 1983). The historical drift of pastoral counseling from the seventeenth century to the twentieth is captured by his subtitle. Conversation

replaced conversion; psychotherapy replaced the cure of souls. Holifield concludes that psychological modes of thinking "have tended to refashion the entire religious life of Protestants in the image of the therapeutic," as Protestants forget that the Bible is a "text that resists reduction to the psychological" (p. 356).

2. Andrew Abbott, *System of Professions: An Essay on the Division of Expert Labor* (Chicago: U. of Chicago, 1988), p. 308. Abbott concludes the chapter "The Construction of the Personal Problems Jurisdiction" (pp. 280-314) with a telling analysis of the capitulation of mainline Protestantism to psychology.

3. Fosdick's unbelief in "the fundamentals" made him the cause célèbre in the church splits of the 1920s. He was closely allied with the Mental Hygiene Movement. This was the first epidemic pop psychology. Many of its themes—defining personal problems in health metaphors rather than in moral terms, encouraging people to think well of themselves—have been repeated in subsequent pop psychologies. Fosdick determined to reform preaching into a mass-scale psychotherapy to produce healthy, positive thinking.

4. Stanton Jones and Richard Butman, *Modern Psychotherapies: A Comprehensive Christian Appraisal* (Downers Grove, Ill.: InterVarsity, 1991), p. 414.

5. Trichotomy views human beings as composed of spirit, soul, and body. Commonly the soul is subdivided into mind, will, and emotions. The alternative view, dichotomy, views human beings as a fundamental unity, composed of a body and an inner being that may be understood from many angles: heart, soul, mind, inner man, spirit, conscience, reins, and so on.

6. Clyde Narramore, *Encyclopedia of Psychological Problems* (Grand Rapids: Zondervan, 1966), pp. 14ff. In recognition of his groundbreaking work, Narramore was presented an award as a pioneer in Christian counseling at "Atlanta '88" (The International Congress on Christian Counseling, Atlanta, November 9-13, 1988).

7. George Marsden, *Reforming Fundamentalism* (Grand Rapids: Eerdmans, 1987), pp. 233-37.

8. Seward Hiltner, *Pastoral Counseling* (New York: Abingdon-Cokesbury, 1949); Paul E. Johnson, *The Psychology of Pastoral Care* (New York: Abingdon-Cokesbury, 1953); Carroll Wise, *Pastoral Counseling: Its Theory and Practice* (New York: Harper, 1951).

9. In the early 1980s I had a fascinating discussion about Adams with one of the leaders of CAPS. He said, "I totally disagreed with Adams's system, but on one point he was absolutely right and brought me up short. When I entered my counseling office the fact that I was a Christian made no difference at all in how I treated patients. Ever since, I've tried to change that." Adams became the foil for the self-definition of the Christian psychotherapy community. That explains the otherwise curious fact that he was given a special award (along with Clyde Narramore, Norman Wright, et al.) as a pioneer in Christian counseling at "Atlanta '88." See n. 6.

10. For example, Gary Collins has often expressed admiration for Paul Tournier's gentle mentoring of clients: listening, comforting, guiding. Tournier's methods have a humanistic flavor in comparison to Adams's directive counseling. Collins commented: "Adams brings secular principles through the back door. The best description of behavior therapy that I've ever read—Skinnerian type therapy—is in Jay Adams' *Competent to Counsel"* (*The Wittenburg Door* 47 (February-March 1979), p. 13. In a recent example, Jones and Butman discuss the many resemblances between Adams's methods and the methods of cognitive-behavioral therapy (*Modern Psychotherapies*, pp. 164, 219).

11. Ellens's tenure began in 1974. CAPS membership grew from 350 to almost 2,000 in fifteen years (*Journal of Psychology and Christianity* 7, no. 4 [Winter 1988], p. 3). *The Journal of Psychology and Christianity* began as *The CAPS Bulletin* in 1974 and was renamed in 1982 to reflect its mission and its maturity as a journal.

12. Seminal publications include Bruce Narramore and John Carter, *The Integration of Psychology and Theology: An Introduction* (Grand Rapids: Zondervan, 1979) and Gary Collins, *The Rebuilding of Psychology* (Wheaton, Ill.: Tyndale, 1977). The latest and most sophisticated statement of the integrationist position is Jones and Butman, *Modern Psychotherapies.*

13. Edwin Boring, *A History of Experimental Psychology,* rev. 2d ed. (New York: Prentice-Hall, 1950), p. 645.

14. The best known representative of this trend is Robert Schuller. In *Self-Esteem: The New Reformation* (Waco, Tex.: Word, 1982) he radically reconstructs theology around his view that "the core of sin is a lack of self-esteem" (p. 98).

15. Ken Sidey "'Twentysomething' Missionaries: Urbana 90," *Christianity Today,* February 11, 1991, pp. 52-55.

16. See Robert McGee, *The Search for Significance* (Houston: Rapha, 1985, 1990) and Robert Hemfelt, Frank Minirth, and Paul Meier, *Love Is a Choice* (Nashville: Thomas Nelson, 1989). McGee's book concludes with a twelve-page advertisement for Rapha, complete with an 800 number.

17. James Hunter has written provocative descriptions of this trend, gathering data from publishing statistics (*American Evangelicalism: Conservative Religion and the Quandary of Modernity* [New Brunswick, N.J.: Rutgers U., 1983], pp. 91-99) and extensive surveys and interviews (*Evangelicalism: The Coming Generation* [Chicago: U. of Chicago, 1987), pp. 64-71. He notes that the differences in substance between pop psychologists such as Schuller and the more high-brow integrationists are only "superficial" (p. 95).

18. The follow-up counseling of evangelist R. A. Torrey is a particularly striking example of this. His *Personal Work: A Book of Effective Methods* (USA: Fleming Revell, n.d.) addresses dozens of common human problems. He supplies proof texts that argue rationalistically with each problem. Cf. Holifield's discussion of the rationalism and voluntarism of nineteenth-century pastoral theology.

19. This wedding of hardship and temptation with the internal struggle to believe and obey is one of the ground themes of all of Scripture. Think in particular of Psalms, Job, Jeremiah, Hebrews, Romans, Revelation, 1 Peter—and of the entire life of our Lord.

20. Timothy Keller, "Puritan Resources for Biblical Counseling," *The Journal of Pastoral Practice* 9, no. 3 (1988), pp. 11-44.

21. Puritans are not the only repository of what Jones and Butman have called the church's "rich corporate history in the field of pastoral care" (*Modern Psychotherapies,* p. 415). Thomas Oden has provided some fascinating resources in *Pastoral Theology: Essentials of Ministry* (San Francisco: Harper & Row, 1983) and *Cure of Souls in the Classic Tradition* (Philadelphia: Fortress, 1984). Novelist Fyodor Dostoevsky gives a provocative glimpse into Eastern Orthodox pastoral care through the person of the wise elder, Father Zossima (*The Brothers Karamazov,* trans. Constance Garnett [New York: New American Library, 1957]).

22. Perry London, *The Modes and Morals of Psychotherapy,* 2d ed. (New York: Hemisphere, 1986), p. 148.

23. O. Hobart Mowrer, *The Crisis in Psychiatry and Religion* (Princeton, N.J.: Van Nostrand, 1961), p. 61. Karl Menninger, *Whatever Became of Sin?* (New York: Hawthorn, 1973).

24. Augustus Toplady, "Rock of Ages Cleft for Me."

25. Abbott, p. 308.

26. George Marsden's telling phrase: *Reforming Fundamentalism: Fuller Seminary and the New Evangelicalism.* Marsden comments that Fuller Seminary is a case study of a

much larger phenomenon in evangelicalism. His analysis of what drove Fuller Seminary is largely true of the Christian psychotherapy community. They saw the practical and intellectual poverty of evangelicalism and the contrasting riches of the world. They sought to remain faithfully evangelical, yet enrich their counseling through interaction with psychologists.

27. The test of a truly biblical engagement with psychology is wisdom for apologetics and evangelism.

28. Personality theories seek to explain now the individual differences between people arise.

29. Jones and Butman offer the latest restatement of this point (*Modern Psychotherapies*, pp. 32-35, 39-42, 58-60. In some ways their book's thesis hinges on the assertion that the Bible is insufficient to explain what is concretely going on with people.

30. See my "Idols of the Heart and 'Vanity Fair,'" *Areopagus* 2, no. 1 (Summer 1991), pp. 2-21) for a panorama of the Bible's theory of human motivation. I believe that article strikes the appropriate balance between clarities and ambiguities.

31. Jones and Butman, *Modern Psychotherapies*, p. 415. Cf. the first paragraph of Jones's editorial "Demonizing the Head Doctors," *Christianity Today*, September 16, 1991, p. 21. Jones sees many of the same phenomena I have mentioned, but considers their net effect less ominous.

32. Jones and Butman decided that the first stage toward a Christian view of counseling is to make a "critical evaluation" of psychology. This is the prelude to a second stage of "theory-building," which will "bear the imprint of Christian presuppositions" (*Modern Psychotherapies*, p. 22). Their book performs stage one and waves a hand in the direction of stage two. That is a fundamental misstep. The stages should be reversed. How can one critically evaluate without a theory? Biblical theory-building about people, problems, and solutions must be first. The ongoing critical evaluation of psychology will then create a feedback loop that will continue to prod theory construction.

   In fact, Jones and Butman do have an a priori theory guiding their evaluation of psychology. It is a theory significantly saturated with unevaluated psychological assumptions. For example, their core definition of counseling assumes a "distressed" client in a collaborative relationship with a perceivedly expert helper (*Modern Psychotherapies*, p. 12). This definition is theory-blinkered, reductionistic, and highly dubious biblically. The Bible has a far more comprehensive view of counseling in which Jones and Butman's definition is embedded as one subcase. Consider the old definition of the preacher's goal: to comfort the disturbed and disturb the comfortable.

   Because they absorb certain assumptions unexamined, Jones and Butman's evaluation of psychology ends up analogous to the intramural critiques psychologists make of each other. They pick and choose rather than radically turning theories inside out and upside down. Consistent biblical thinking will reformulate even the keenest observations and most constructive practices of psychologists.

33. But many of the words are not there, as well. Noteworthy by their absence are significant mention and treatment of the nature of the human heart, God's wrath, the law, discipleship, the lordship of Christ, repentance, the cross as the specific form of God's love, the sovereignty of God, holiness, the power of the Holy Spirit, the return of Christ, the biblical view of suffering and evil. All of these are integral to the growth and encouragement of struggling Christians.

9

Codependency and the Cult of the Self

Edward Welch

O f the pop-psychology movements that influence the Christian community, none is currently more influential than *codependency*. Only five years ago the codependency movement consisted of a small group of counselors in the substance abuse field. Today the self-help literature on codependency fills the shelves of both secular and Christian bookstores. *John Bradshaw On: The Family*, a text for codependency, sells about forty thousand books a month, and *Codependent No More* has broken all records for longevity on the *New York Times'* best-seller list. In our churches the language of codependency fills the pulpit, and codependency support groups can be found in a growing number of church basements.

Any literature that captures attention so quickly certainly deserves closer examination. Why is it so popular? Does the church need to respond? If so, how? An understanding of codependency's popularity will most likely expose weaknesses in the evangelical church and challenge us to speak more persuasively to a twentieth-century audience. Also it will provide a case study in how the church has, in many instances, once again uncritically adopted a popular secular trend. At root, codependency is a self-conscious, theological, and anthropological revolution intent on offering a new view of God

EDWARD WELCH is director of counseling for the Christian Counseling and Educational Foundation, Laverock, Pennsylvania, and is a licensed psychologist.

and ourselves. It wants to remake the soul, offering a religion that is explicitly a cult of the self. And since this thinking fills the air we breathe, it has affected us all in ways that might surprise us.

HISTORY AND DEFINITIONS

Everyone knows something about codependency, but very few can define it. It is even difficult to find consensus in the movement's literature. That ambiguity is not surprising, considering its populous roots. Codependency does not come to us out of the laboratory, with its associated technical definitions. Rather, it comes to us out of the marketplace—off the street, where words are flexible and rest on shared experience more than on professional research and testing.

Although popularization of the concept is rather new in terms of marketing, the attitudes underlying it have been around for some time. I would suggest that there are three critical historical precursors to the codependency movement: the Romantic period of the late eighteenth and nineteenth centuries, the psychodynamic revolution associated with Freud, and the grass roots movement of this century known as Alcoholics Anonymous. The Romantic period was an ideological revolution, given its initial shape by Jean-Jacques Rousseau (1712-1778). Although it included a wide variety of beliefs, most historians would agree that that period emphasized the following features:

- The innate goodness of humanity
- The centrality of feeling over against reason or faith
- The dethroning of the supernatural while looking for the divine in creation and in the self
- The importance of the spiritual over the material realm

The interest in the spiritual was secular, indeed, a pagan interest. It had nothing to do with belief in the historical Jesus and His death and resurrection, but referred to a feeling of the infinite, an ineffable experience or sense of oneness with nature. It was not even dependent on a conviction of God's existence.

Codependency represents not so much a revival of the Romantic worldview as it does a continuation and popularization of it. Modern culture remains a Romantic culture, and no ideology has broken its grip.

Freud's influence is somewhat veiled because codependency has not retained his language, but the Freudian stamp is everywhere to be found in codependency writings. Freud's fixations of psychic energy are now "frozen emotions." (Freud had a machine, or hydraulic, model for the mind. Using that metaphor, problems were seen in part a result of dammed up, restrained, or fixated psychic energy that needed to be released.) Freud's view of the importance of emotional catharsis is now paraphrased popularly, "I have to experience the pain of my child within." Freud's view of the hazardous effects of repressive parenting, which grew out of the Romantic notion that evil only comes from without, not from within, flowers into full bloom in codependency writings. His view of instincts translates into the person-as-needy. Just as Freud's instincts clamor for expression, so the codependency movement suggests that our inner emotional needs constantly demand gratification. If they are not satisfied in various relationships, one is driven to various addictions to meet felt needs. Thus every addiction is attributable to the fault of someone or something else. Finally, and perhaps most important, Freud psychologized guilt. He rendered guilt an experience that had no Godward reference. Guilt, for Freud, was an intrapsychic process during the Oedipal period. Here again, codependency follows Freud's lead. In codependency, guilt is essentially false guilt that is due to low self-esteem. Guilt is purely intrapsychic. It is not objective and real, but subjective and illusory. It has nothing to do with the person-before-God, but only with the person-within-himself.

Within the historical traditions of the Romantic movement and Freudian thought, the basic outline of codependency was already in place: problems come from without rather than from within; the person-as-divine-child; the person-as-needy; the centrality of emotional experience; and spirituality as an intrapsychic phenomenon. It is likely, however, that those two strands would never have merged into the modern codependency movement were it not for the impetus of Alcoholics Anonymous (A.A.).

The A.A. stamp is the most obvious of the three historical influences. In a sense, A.A. gave the codependency movement its God, its Bible, and its language. For its God, A.A. offered the "higher power," a God of man's own imagination who makes no demands—something akin to a benevolent but somewhat senile grandparent who remembers all the good and forgets all the bad. The Bible of recovery groups is The Twelve Steps, a set of laws that have moral overtones but are divorced from atonement, forgiveness, justification, and the power of the Holy Spirit. The language of codependence is the language of physical disease and health. At times one wonders if a rapist is any more responsible for his own actions than a cancer patient is responsible for his or her disease. Codependents have a disease or an addiction; never will you hear of personal sin and repentance. In recovery groups people are now "healing," "recovering," or "addicted." They have experienced "pain," or "woundings." Notice, in this sort of language, they have not themselves done anything for which they are responsible. Even the addiction has an excuse. Innate, biological "needs" leave us "sick" if they are neglected, and "toxic parents" are part of the problem.

In 1951 A.A. spawned Al Anon, the support group network for spouses of heavy drinkers. Almost immediately the two groups noticed that there were experiences and feelings they shared. One shared experience was the sense that spouses and children demonstrated addictive patterns themselves. For example, as the substance abuser was obsessed with the drug, so the family was dependent on, obsessed with, or addicted to the substance-abuser. As substance abusers could devote their lives to the next drink, so families could devote their entire lives to their hope for sobriety, or at least, damage-control, in the home. As the substance-abuser's identity was shaped largely by the bottle or pill, so spouses' identities were forged by the substance-abuser. As a result, words like "co-alcoholic" emerged for spouses, and the well-known label "adult children of alcoholics" was employed. Today, both phrases are subsumed under the burgeoning heading of codependency.

Out of this A.A. tradition came the original definition of codependency. Codependency referred to the complex web of relationships that exist around substance-abusers. The field of meaning for the term had to expand, however, in order for it to have the grass roots impact it currently enjoys. By the late 1970s the concept of addictions was expanding to include activities such as gambling, sex, and eating. During the 1980s it expanded even further, until the literature now assures us that we all have an addiction.[1] (Having replaced sin with addiction, it appears that there are as many addictions as there used to be sins.) Again, I am not critical of this movement because I am an enemy of psychology. I am a licensed psychologist and a professional researcher and professor in that field. But the codependency movement is the product of marketing more than sound research. Just as the mixture of Christianity and literature often creates books that are neither theologically sound nor particularly good writing in the name of "integration," so many who would integrate pop-therapeutic trends with Christianity will find that the result is neither sound theology nor sound psychology.

In her best-selling book *Codependent No More* Melodie Beattie cautiously attempts a broader definition of codependency that has become the standard. She suggests that "a codependent person is one who has let another person's behavior affect him or her, and who is obsessed with controlling that person's behavior."[2] Her basic idea is that we are all either controlled or controlling. *Love Is a Choice,* the best-selling Christian book on codependency, has a similar definition. The authors state that codependency is "an addiction to people, behaviors, or things. Codependency is the fallacy of trying to control interior feelings by controlling people, things, and events on the outside."[3]

Finally, to broaden the definition one more time, on the most popular level codependency can refer to anyone who either is not in a satisfying relationship or has come from a "dysfunctional family."[4] That definition is so ambiguous that, on first glance, it seems useless. Has any of us not come from a family with some problems? How many problems must a family have before it is declared "dysfunctional"? All of the codependency writers see codependency as the result of "low self-esteem" provoked by inadequate "nurturing." Their view of the person is that all persons are good and needy. There is never any mention of sin and redemption. God is viewed as a being with only one attribute: benevolence. To "change" is to go from placing one's dependency on others to placing one's trust in oneself. It is this system that remains largely unexamined by

Christians, and it is here one finds that codependency is ultimately committed to finding power through the cult of the self.

In the following section of this essay we will take a closer look at the codependency movement. We will begin with the descriptive riches of codependency and examine the assumptions that are consistently wedded to those descriptions. Then we will offer a biblical response.

THE DESCRIPTIVE POWER OF CODEPENDENCY

Listing 234 symptoms, *Codependent No More* is an example of vivid descriptions that reach out and grab the reader. The author begins by reminding the reader that he or she was hurt in the past. Someone has let him or her down. At this point, most people are putty in the hands of codependency literature. Who cannot recall painful memories, given the proper opportunity and encouragement. The list can go from the trivial ("My parents made me go to bed by ten when I was a teenager") to the most severe, such as incest.

The literature then connects those hurts with present emotions, thoughts, and behaviors. Many codependency books suggest that the following feelings and behaviors are common when there has been relational disappointment in the past. Codependents tend to:

- feel a sense of low self-esteem as a result of being criticized
- feel intimidated by angry people and personal criticism
- be either very responsible or very irresponsible
- procrastinate
- judge themselves and others
- suppress their feelings
- feel not quite good enough
- feel guilty
- wish others would like or love them
- blame others for the way they feel
- get frustrated and angry
- think their lives aren't worth living

Codependency hooks its readers, including many Christians, with descriptions that inevitably leave people exclaiming, "That's me!"

That presents a challenge for students of Scripture. They can only agree that everyone has those experiences and that a person's history has a profound influence on his present feelings, thoughts, and behavior. Students of Scripture can also see that the secular community has taken the lead in providing descriptions that seem to be more captivating than their own.

THE CODEPENDENCY SYSTEM

A second glance at the descriptions provided by the codependency movement reveals another challenge to evangelicals. Codependency exists with mandatory assumptions about the cause of the problems, the nature of persons, and the character of God. It is impossible to adopt the concept of "codependency" without adopting the larger Romantic-Freudian-A.A. system. Codependency is as much about one's worldview and fundamental beliefs as it is about "recovery." Believing that the Christian view of persons is hopelessly outdated, the codependency literature has replaced the view that we are sinners-in-need-of-redemption with a concept of the "true self," popularly known as the "child within." Those who wish to be relevant will argue that the replacement of sinners-in-need-of-redemption with codependents-in-need-of-self is merely a modern way of saying the same thing, but the two systems are worlds apart.

Beyond explicitly offering a pantheistic religion (God, or the "higher power," as a part of creation or a divine element in the person), much of the literature concentrates on this "true self" or "inner child" as possessing two essential qualities: it is *good,* it is *needy*.

The codependent has been declared morally blameless. Unkindness can be attributed to one of the many "needs" left unmet in one's life. Blame is placed on the "dysfunctional" home. But the members of that dysfunctional home were themselves not responsible because they, too, came from a dysfunctional home where needs were not sufficiently met, and so on in infinite regress. Perhaps the blame could reach as far back as Adam, who blamed his sin on "the woman you [God] put here with me" (Genesis 3:12), and to Eve, who pointed to the serpent's deceit (v. 13). What a dysfunctional race!

The closest the codependency literature comes to talking about being born in sin is its reference to people being "imperfect,"[5] as though humans were flawed by creation rather than corrupted by the Fall. Imperfection simply means that the child needs education and experience in order to mature.

The anthropological companion to the *good* inner child is the *needy* inner child. That idea, the cornerstone of the system, is the one most likely to reshape popular thinking about the soul. Recognized by various labels such as "yearnings" and "thirst," the concept is vividly captured by Hemfelt, Minirth, and Meier in their book *Love Is a Choice.* They write that we are "love cups" and experience "love hunger" if our need is not met.

Although Christians tend to feel a little uncomfortable if the person-as-morally-good doctrine is too pronounced, they appear quite comfortable with an anthropology (view of humans) that says we are needy. After all, we *are* certainly needy before God. But, as we will make clear later, the needs of codependency are absolutely unrelated to being morally bankrupt and in need of grace. The codependency concept is actually much closer to "I want" or "I must have." It is not intended to lead us in submission to Christ and service to others, but to exalt our own desires. It is all an aspect of what Christopher Lasch calls *The Culture of Narcissism,* the cult of the self.

Listen carefully and you will hear the language of need: "Church isn't meeting my needs." "My spouse isn't meeting my needs." Sometimes the language might be an inner voice that says, "I deserve more respect from her," or, "I have a right to be treated better." Sometimes it is frustration or anger that one's desires are not met by other people. All of those statements are evidence of a "need theology" in which the focus is on oneself rather than on Christ.

Unquestionably, we all experience a need or strong desire to be loved (respected, healthy, financially secure, and so on) and we are disappointed if the person whose love we desire does not return the favor. The question, however, is this: do we build a doctrine of the person on our needs and desires, or do we allow biblical categories to interpret and critique those desires? Codependency has reified our sense of need; that is, it has explained need by simply saying that it is a real "thing"—a natural and good thing—that exists within. That is a weak base logically for a new anthropology, but strategically it is quite powerful. It locates one's felt needs in the "true self"; so placed, those needs now share the self's alleged moral excellence. Suddenly, meeting one's needs becomes the highest calling.

Notice how the "need theology" introduces the new morality of codependency. When emotional cravings are labeled as needs they become sacred objects. The highest good in life, according to that morality, is to meet those needs. What gratifies emotional cravings is "right," and what ignores or demeans them is "wrong."

Nothing is new or original about that approach. Hedonism— the satisfying of the self's cravings and pleasures—has been the ruling principle in a number of ethical systems throughout history and is probably the most popular. As a result, the language of need inevitably moves toward the much stronger language: "I deserve love," or, "I have a personal 'bill of rights.'" Charles Whitfield, in his book *Healing the Child Within,* lists thirty-seven of those rights. Included are the following:

- I have a right to say no to anything when I feel I am not ready, it is unsafe, or it violates my values.
- I have a right to dignity and respect.
- I have a right to make decisions based on my feelings, my judgment, or any reason that I choose.
- I have the right to be happy.[6]

If any of those rights are violated, addictions, controlling behaviors, or any of the hundreds of other codependency symptoms are said to result.

In the codependency system it is essential that people "get in touch" with their needs. To do that they are to listen to and obey their feelings. Feelings pave the royal road to one's true needs. Codependency's Romantic roots are most apparent in this exaltation of feelings. The German Romantic Goethe made a distinctly modern statement when he said, through his character Faust, "Feeling is all." Faith having been declared irrelevant and reason questioned, the Romantic period looked to feelings as the route to self-fulfillment. That was the natural consequence of a theology that insisted that the soul was godlike. Why go outside of the self for revelation when what is most important resides within? In the Romantic tradition, feelings were the inarticulate mutterings of what was considered to be the divine soul.

Religion in the Romantic period was also reduced to feeling, as the German theologian Schleiermacher suggested that "religion is a feeling of absolute dependence."[7] The language of religion was retained, but its content was gone.

Codependency has diligently preserved that tradition. "Keep dealing with your feelings, go to a recovery group, and everything will be OK." That is the common codependency prescription. John Bradshaw talks about emotions as the tools that allow one to be fully aware of his needs and sees that awareness as critical for self-actualization. He also sees suppression of emotion as one of the cardinal sins of the culture; only an increased acceptance of one's feelings, by oneself and others, will rescue one from certain codependency.

Curiously, the most precious feeling in the codependency system is pain. It appears even to be worshiped in some quarters. All orthodox codependency writers make pain and grief central to recovery. Of Bradshaw's own recovery he states, "I had to experience that [his own] child's pain."[8] In the system, freedom from codependency is impossible without grieving over the perceived injuries to the child within. People are called to "embrace legitimate suffering" and "enter into grief." As a result, most persons who choose the codependency route are guaranteed that they will experience strong emotions, and those emotions will make them even more prone to believe in the validity of the system.

Feelings are also the grid through which spirituality is evaluated. The system follows the Romantic and A.A. traditions by including a great deal of God-talk and spiritual language, but that language is unrelated to the knowledge of a personal God. Spirituality is "the actual immediate experience of God" that "comes through deepening insight into my being."[9] It is "relying on your own understanding of what a loving God is and does for you. . . . This is the discovery of your sacred identity and it is holy work."[10] The feeling—

the self-focus—is central. Any experience that is ineffable, any sense of the infinite, will constitute a redemptive spirituality. There is no objective relationship with God in the codependency system, even though it sets out to teach spiritual truth.

Given this mystical background, "God as you understand Him" is much further from the biblical portrait than it first appears. The emphasis is not on God; rather, it is on "how you understand Him," "how you imagine or want Him to be," or "how you feel Him to be." The only limitations the system places on our view of God is that this God must be only nurturing and never a judge, and He must meet every need or at least be delighted when we meet our own.

Those are the basic assumptions of the system. Now we will take a look at the codependency system in action.

CODEPENDENCY IN ACTION

Compulsions, worry, a life punctuated by extremes, and a miserable view of self have their cause, according to the codependency literature, in the subtle rejections of the dysfunctional family.

> The child in us believes we are unlovable and will never find the comfort we are seeking; sometimes this vulnerable child becomes too desperate. People have abandoned us, emotionally and physically. People have rejected us. People have abused us, let us down. People have never been there for us; they have not seen, heard, or responded to our needs.[11]

Our present relational difficulties are said, therefore, to be a result of people's failing to meet our needs.

The journey into codependency, according to the system, goes like this. When our "love cup" is not being consistently filled by nurturing parents, the person gradually feels unworthy of love and feels shame. Self-protective walls soon follow. The task of recovery is to move from that sense of shame, which is a result of relying on the judgments of other persons, to self-love and nurturing the child within. "The whole adult child movement is about reclaiming the lost child and nurturing it with self-worth and helping it grow up."[12] Or, in other words, the goal is to move from being codependent (dependent on another) to being self-dependent. As the A.A. literature indicates, "We are recovering through loving and focusing on ourselves."[13] Melody Beattie is even more explicit in proclaiming a cult of the self:

> We can cherish ourselves and our lives. We can nurture ourselves and love ourselves. We can accept our wonderful selves, with all our faults, foibles, strong points, weak points, feelings, thoughts, and everything else. It's the best thing we've got going for us. It's who we are, and who we were meant to be. And it's not a mistake. We are the greatest thing that will ever happen to us. Believe it. It makes life much easier.[14]

How does that happen? It is here where the literature becomes a bit ambiguous. One step might be to interview the dysfunctional family with the hope that the codependent can see them as victims as well. Sometimes therapists will even talk about forgiveness, but it usually consists of "giving back" to the person who victimized you the traits that you don't want. Sometimes a therapist might assign the following:

> Looking at pictures of yourself as a youngster can help you to connect with that child within. . . . Find a snapshot of yourself taken in childhood. . . . Just let your feelings be your guide. Choose the photo that you feel most sympathetic toward. . . . Think about what you, as an adult, would have done to love and protect that helpless child from the buffets of the world; that's precisely what you need to do for yourself today. . . .
>
> You may find writing a letter to yourself, addressing that child within, very nurturing and validating. It can be a kind of nice gift to yourself. After all, letters do take time and effort; and directing that effort to that child inside you . . . can enhance your self-esteem.[15]

Ultimately the task of recovery is a mechanical attempt to flood oneself with praise and love.

A BIBLICAL RESPONSE
TO THE CODEPENDENT DESCRIPTIONS

When one attempts to examine the deep beliefs of popular movements it is usually necessary to read between the lines. Most popular movements either are unaware of their philosophical or doctrinal commitments or leave them unexpressed. That is not the case with the codependency movement. In it the view of persons and God are clearly presented. Because key concepts in the movement move beyond attempts to scientifically or clinically identify problems and solutions and because the movement makes overtly religious statements that are to be accepted on blind faith, it is a movement especially open to biblical criticism. The codependency literature is so "spiritual" and "religious" in nature, making direct assertions about the nature of persons and God, that it is amazing to realize that many Christians have failed to think critically and biblically in the face of its distortions.

A biblical response must do more than criticize the codependency dogma, however. True, the dogma must be exposed, but an even larger goal is to demonstrate the *sufficiency* of Scripture for faith and practice. Moreover, one needs to demonstrate that Scripture must be heard not only because it is our only rule for faith and practice, but because it explains the data better and offers deeper, more meaningful, and more profound solutions than are available in any other literature.

The effects of the past. The first challenge from the codependency literature is its discussion of the effects of the past. Codependency writings make persuasive and even brilliant connections between past experiences and present emotions and behaviors. Many persons who have been captured by the codependency system feel understood when reading the descriptions. They feel as though the descriptions are about them. On the other hand, when they go directly to the Scriptures or to a pastor they sometimes feel as though they are not uniquely understood.

Codependency has provided an important challenge to the church. It reminds us that past influences can be very powerful. Undoubtedly the church can do better at studying individuals and describing patterns and making relevant applications of biblical categories. We must realize that our ministry task is twofold: we must study people, together with the insights we glean from culture, science, and so on; and we must study the Bible more deeply. We have to know both well enough to recognize what it takes to make timeless answers relevant without trivializing and distorting the biblical message. To do that, counselors *must* be able to describe the unique experiences of others in a way that leads people to recognize, "That's me!" Otherwise, biblical truth (regardless of how accurately it is presented) will seem irrelevant. However, as David Powlison pointed out, we share more experiences than pop psychology seems to want us to believe, underscoring the unique nature of *my* problem.

Scripture actually has a great deal to say about the effects of our personal histories. In fact, it surpasses the codependency literature in its breadth. Under the categories of "trials," "testing," "temptations," and being sinned against, the Bible presents a much broader field of historical influences. Certainly it includes the influence of parents and spouses, but it also includes the influence of peers, church and political leaders, teachers, persecution, and physical and material well-being. Moreover, it includes the most powerful influences in our lives, influences codependency knows nothing about.

Scripture indicates those influences are important in shaping our lives. They can create difficulties and occasions for sinful responses, situations that make us more susceptible to sin's tyranny. Therefore, it is important that we know of those influences if we are to understand people.

But God's Word discusses these influences in a context that communicates hope. The Bible tells us that past influences, no matter how severe, can never make us sin. Even in the middle of personal tragedy we have been given God's grace to avoid sinful responses when the opportunity presents itself. Our sufferings can be a catalyst for a change of focus. Instead of looking to the past, feeling condemned and defined by our childhood, persons of faith can look back to the cross where sin's guilt and tyranny were remedied. As justification is the answer to guilt and condemnation, with all of the anxieties and neuroses related to Divine-human alienation, so also a doctrine like the sovereignty of God is calculated to guide us through the pressures of modern living with the confidence that there is a purpose in everything, including suffering and pain. Such biblical doctrines, and many others, can be of so much more value than the superficial answers provided by codependency.

If we are not to use categories of "self-esteem," "unmet needs," "codependency," and the notion of the basically good "child within," what descriptions rise out of biblical categories? According to Scripture, we are sinners by birth (original sin) and sinners by choice. Sin is a condition arising from a fallen nature that is hostile to God, and this condition produces personal choices and actions that are sinful. But because we are all sinners, there is a third element: although we are sinners by birth and sinners by choice, we are also *sinned against.* There is a legitimate place in Scripture given to the idea that we both victimize others and are ourselves victims of the sinful actions of other people or institutions. Contrary to the accusations of the codependency movement, the Scriptures encourage a full range of feelings, not denial. If we have difficulty calling out to God, even in outrage at what is going on all around us, the Psalms are perhaps the most descriptively rich book we could study in this vein. Without question, there are psalms that will lead us to respond, "That's me!"

Ezekiel 37 describes the experience of being sinned against by those in authority. People become weak and injured. They have no one to guide and protect them. They are frightened and prone to be influenced by false shepherds. The passage, however, does not leave people in their suffering. God comes to the aid of the victimized as the God of justice (vv. 20-28). God is against the victimizer and stands for the oppressed. He will avenge injustice: "It is mine to avenge; I will repay" (Deuteronomy 32:35). He will shepherd His people and He will guide them to good pasture.

That is absolutely foreign to the codependency system, which knows nothing about the mercy of God satisfying His own justice in Christ. There is no one outside of the victim who can save, so the codependent must save himself or herself by turning inward. And, by declaring sin to be a subjective psychological impression rather than an objective reality of guilt, the system cannot allow a sense of relief at justice being fully met in the sacrifice of another, namely, Christ. No one is morally responsible; one's victims are merely victims themselves. Therefore, the sense of condemnation we all stand under (both objectively and subjectively) being lost, there is no sense of genuine forgiveness and acceptance.

The dynamics of controlling and being controlled. A second category from Scripture is particularly powerful in describing and interpreting the dynamics of controlling and being controlled. The biblical category is *idolatry,* the immoderate or inordinate devotion to an object or person. By no means an exclusively Old Testament problem, idolatry has been a part of the human fabric since the Fall and is probably one of the chief marks of modern life. Its nature is simply manifested differently in various cultures. In the United States it rarely takes the form of bowing down to a man-made image, because the "spirit of independence" would not tolerate such appearances. Instead, our idolatry has taken on a more dignified garb. We erect idols of money, health, beauty, thinness, respect, power, pleasure, comfort, and the idol enshrined in the codependency movement: being loved.

The characteristic strategy of idolatry is to take something that is fine in itself and exalt it so that it rules the person. Money, for example, is a blessing. It can be used to provide food and shelter and various opportunities for work and leisure. It can also further the work of God's kingdom. However, as Scripture constantly warns, it can also easily become a god. One's entire life can be shaped by the love of money. Likewise, being loved is a blessing. However, when it moves from godly desire to ruling passion or need, it is evidence of the sinful tendency to serve other gods, all ultimately in an effort to worship oneself.

The root of idolatry can be summarized as "I want." It is more than bowing down to a created object. Rather, it is the expression of a heart that says, "I want what I want—*now!* Since God won't give me what I want (or what I feel I need) I will get it from my idols."

Idolatry seems like a strange path to self-gratification. After all, as we live in humble obedience to and faith in God we have an exalted status as His image-bearers and, better yet, as His adopted children. Given a choice between worshiping the living God or a dime store idol of the latest fad, I for one see more honor in pursuing a relationship with the King. That is not to say that there is no perceived payoff in idolatry. The purpose with all idolatry is to manipulate the idol so that it gives one what one wants. It is a form of magic. For example, when Elijah confronted the Baal worshipers on Mount Carmel (1 Kings 18), the prophet-magicians of Baal tried to manipulate the idol to do their bidding. They wanted nothing above themselves, including their idols. Their fabricated gods were intended to be puppet kings.

Therefore, when people worship money, their goal is not to be subservient to it but to manipulate it so that it will meet their felt needs. When one worships the feeling of being loved, one's goal is to exalt oneself and one's own desires above God. For Christians, that does not mean outright disavowal of the gospel; rather, it often takes the mode of a quiet, unspoken conviction that because God does not meet all one's needs, one can divide one's allegiances and trust in idols in *addition* to God. That is what happened when the Israelites erected the golden calf (Exodus 32). The mighty God was not enough for the Hebrews, even though they had just seen the display of His awesome sovereignty. Their rampant desires and fears outdistanced their faith.

Sometimes, too, we even create in our imagination an idol we *call* "God." That idol serves the purpose of the puppet-king, who does our bidding and succumbs to our manipulation. He exists to help us meet our felt needs, such as the feeling of being loved. In that subtle and seductive way, we end up worshiping an idol at the same time we are convinced it is the right God we are honoring.

The reason idolatry is forbidden and the reason it is occasionally used as a summary for all sin is that it is an expression of the self-exalted heart. As persons who are instinctive worshipers, we can only express our prideful independence in a distinctively *religious* form, and idolatry is that form. But there is a cruel paradox in idolatry, much like the so-called Hedonistic Paradox: although idols promise so much more than the real God in terms of immediate self-gratification, what they actually deliver is slavery instead of freedom; self-hatred instead of self-love; guilt instead of pleasure. When we offer ourselves to idols we become their slaves: "Don't you know that when you offer yourselves to someone to obey him as slaves, you are slaves to the one whom you obey—whether you are slaves to sin, which leads to death, or to obedience, which leads to righteousness?" (Romans 6:16).

That is idolatry: seeking to control, but being controlled.

Maureen was a faithful Christian in a difficult marriage. Years of strife finally brought her to a counselor. As she reviewed her story Maureen noticed a pattern of rage followed by depression, and the trigger was always the same. The cycle of anger and despair was always preceded by her husband's ignoring her. As Maureen thought biblically about those experiences she began to realize that she had begun to worship something other than God. Her idol was the god of being loved. Like most forms of idolatry, it had a religious and pious appearance, making it more difficult to detect. Maureen had the reputation for being the self-sacrificing, exemplary wife, but her emotional cycles began to expose the fact that her love for her husband was more manipulation than godliness. She wanted to manipulate her husband-idol to give her the love, admiration, and attention she thought she must have in order to live. When her idol let her down, her life started falling apart.

Certainly nothing is wrong with being loved or wanting to be loved. It is a godly desire we all share. But with Maureen the desire had become a compulsion, a ruling lust. The result was the paradox of idolatry. On the one hand, while she was spiritually unaware, Maureen quietly set up an idol that she sought to manipulate for her own ends. In her pride, she was actually worshiping herself and demanding that others do the same. But that god would not be manipulated, and it was controlling her. Her idol, erected to provide pleasure, only led to bondage. When she could not control it she was enraged; when it mastered her she was depressed. Aware of the activity of her heart, she realized that her only path to freedom was through turning away from the goal of self-exaltation and turning to Christ in dependent faith.

It is important to point out here that Maureen did not simply turn *from* dependence on her husband to meet the need of self-exaltation *to* Christ for the meeting of the same idolatrous "need." Sometimes Christian versions of codependency offer Christ as the only one who can truly meet felt needs. In that application the answer is simply to transfer dependence on a husband to dependence on Christ. In that scenario Maureen would have remained in slavery to self-worship and self-exaltation. The only change would have been in *who* was expected to give it to her! The Scriptures take another course. We must not simply exchange the manipulation of this or that person for the intended manipulation of Christ in the pursuit of getting our "needs" met. Christ will not be manipulated; He will always resist our attempts to control Him in an effort to wrest from Him what others have failed to provide. Christ tells us what our real needs are and meets those, but He does not exist to help us exalt ourselves.

Maureen's frustration in relation to her husband has been duplicated countless times in thousands of relationships, and it is exactly that experience that the codependency literature attempts to describe. No wonder the codependency movement has such a universal appeal—it is simply observing a feature of the human heart. But whereas we should not be surprised that her experience strikes a chord in nearly every human heart, we *should* be alarmed at codependency's apparent secularization of idolatry. Codependency has rendered idolatry an intrapsychic dynamic associated with unmet needs, instead of a problem rooted in a person's relationship with God.

When behavior is described as idolatry instead of codependency our perspective immediately changes. Family background and the personal histories of our relationships are no longer the primary focus. Instead, we see only our own hearts and the face of a holy and jealous God. Our self-exalted images are shattered. But the Spirit speaks gently to us in our helplessness and leads us to call out for forgiveness and then the power to dethrone reigning idols. He shows us Christ. Then we can know something of the apostle Paul's comments: "It is for freedom that Christ has set us free" (Galatians 5:1), and we can learn to practice "faith expressing itself through love," instead of practicing self-esteem expressing itself through idolatry. Liberated persons know the bent of their hearts. They know that although justification by grace through faith is a once-and-for-all event, sanctification is a daily battle with idols that slowly and deceptively master us. Therefore, there is never a time when we can return our confidence to ourselves. We are always in need of forgiveness and abandonment to the righteousness of Christ that alone can make us acceptable before a holy God.

The "treatment" for codependency is much different. People are implored to cast off one idol and replace it with one that will hopefully work better. They are encouraged to free themselves from a person and to worship themselves instead. That may make people feel better for a while, but the self is a fragile entity. It is not sturdy enough to stand apart from God, especially while the conscience constantly reminds it that it stands *coram Deo,* "in the presence of God."

This essay gives only a sampling of biblical categories that respond to the descriptions of codependency. Yet even in those few categories, the Bible is richer and more meaningful. It paints a broad landscape of the influences of our past, and it goes on to say that those influences can be exceedingly difficult stumbling blocks. Those sufferings are not insurmountable, however. They can strengthen us and become fruitful, serving to remind us of our glorious, eternal hope. They can also serve to disclose the idolatrous tendencies of our hearts. When that happens, only the Bible can truly explain the paradox of controlling and being controlled.

That thought brings us to a recasting of the definition of codependency. Using a biblical lens, one can say that codependency observes thoughts, feelings, and behavior that join together the influences of our past and the idolatrous tendencies of our hearts. The symptoms that emerge at that junction tend to manifest themselves in two ways. One manifestation consists of a set of symptoms derived from our self-exaltation or self-centeredness and includes emotions such as anger, rage, or frustration; words such as "rights" and "needs"; and an attitude of "I deserve." The other symptoms are a result of the bondage of idolatry and are characterized by words, thoughts, and feelings of powerlessness, despondency, hopelessness, and loneliness.

On a more popular level, the field we are examining could be defined as "loving others for selfish (sinful) reasons, and its associated consequences (curses)."

A RESPONSE TO THE CODEPENDENT SYSTEM

Many of the deeply held beliefs of the codependency system are implicit in the descriptions we have already discussed. However, if we are to appreciate the robust nature of biblical truth, those deeply held beliefs must be examined by deeply held *biblical* beliefs.

The good child within. The movement's anthropology (view of human persons) is based on the conviction that humans are morally good. More specifically, the child within is good. Occasionally, that guiding principle will come with biblical proof texts. One common reference is Matthew 22:39, "Love your neighbor as yourself," taken by codependency to mean that if we are to love ourselves, we must be worthy of love. But does the verse command self-love? And does it command self-love on the basis that we are worthy of such love? Certainly not. It is a command for us to love others because we do not do so automatically. "No one ever hated his own body, but he feeds and cares for it" (Ephesians 5:29); therefore, our love for others must rival our own self-interest. What is being taught here is not self-love but self-sacrifice, and that is confirmed by the clear teaching of Christ and His apostles elsewhere in Scripture. Scripture never calls us to self-love but constantly calls us away from our own self-absorption to care for the interests of others. Indeed, the Scriptures characterize the *wickedness* and *ungodliness* of the last days as consisting in self-love (2 Timothy 3:1-4).

That is not to say that we do not experience something that feels like self-loathing. Indeed, most do. But that experience is often the result of our idols' failing us or our dejection over the fact that we do not have what we want—in other words, we aren't beautiful enough, rich enough, smart enough, respected enough, successful enough.

A second category of proof texts addresses children and is used to illustrate the goodness of the child within. One such passage is Mark 10:14: "Let the little children come to me, and do not hinder them, for the kingdom of God belongs to such as these." But does that statement support the idea of the good child within? It appears rather that Jesus is using children as an illustration of persons who must rely on others in order to live (Matthew 18:4). Children are not self-sufficient, and they know it. For all their threats to run away from home, they choose not to because they know they need the care of parents or other adults. Their circumstances place them in a position of being humbled before others. It is their self-conscious dependence on others that makes them excellent examples of kingdom humility. Jesus holds no illusions about the sinlessness of children. He knows that children are gifts from God, but He also understands that they are sinners from birth (Psalm 51:5), whose hearts are full of foolishness (Proverbs 22:15). His hearers knew that as well.

The codependency emphasis on the morally good child within, who is hurt, is understandable. When they were children many adults were harshly criticized and constantly demeaned, and they do need to be lifted up. However, that lifting up will not come through declaring children to be morally upright, nor will it come from an evanescent positive thinking; instead it will come from the reality of being united with Christ by faith in His obedient life, death, and resurrection. Christ is the only human being who was born innocent, lived a perfectly upright life, and achieved complete success before God. Now, by virtue of their union with Him, believers have the history of Jesus Christ rather than their own. Their failures become His cross, and through His agony they are set right with God. Such a gospel is unavailable in the codependency model. There is no real guilt and no real salvation. The closest that codependency can come to the gospel is to say that Christ died for good people, for people who were worth His death. The Scriptures, however, inform us that "God demonstrates his own love for us in this: While we were still sinners Christ died for us" (Romans 5:8). Christ did not die for good people or for worthy people. He died for the wicked. That is good news for those of us who know that we are indeed wicked.

Codependency is weak and impotent by contrast. It is no wonder that the literature rarely talks about loving others. Apart from Christ we simply cannot get beyond loving ourselves.

The person as needy. The second part of the codependent doctrine of persons does not have such a straightforward biblical response. Is the person-as-needy concept a biblical way of defining people? Articulating a biblical response is challenging because the answer can be yes or no depending on how "needs" are defined. One sense of the word *need* refers to those things that maintain physical health: food, clothes, and shelter. Without those we would die. In popular language, *need* can also refer to an emotional craving stirred by the absence of something that is good and desirable. If you are accustomed to having a vacation at the beach, and you can't go this year, you might say, "I need a vacation at the beach." That kind of need is typically present only after we experience it and it has fanned our desire. It is unlikely that a person who has never seen a beach would say the same thing. That has nothing to do with life or death. You don't need a week at the beach in order to survive but are simply using the concept of need to communicate the intensity of your desire.

Similarly, children who lived with both parents and then experienced divorce will often feel a "need" for the absent parent. The Scriptures indicate that those experiences are very difficult, and God has deep compassion for those who have had difficult losses, but this sense of need is not something we have by way of creation; it is not part of our constitution but is a desire that develops with experience. Therefore, it is not surprising that many persons who were reared by a single parent can feel very loved and nurtured and not have the sense of needing another parent.

A third use of *need* takes us back to earlier comments we have made on idolatry. "Need" can be a euphemism for lust or idolatrous demands. The idea is that we desire something intensely, and the sating of this desire is of paramount importance. That is the predominant meaning of "need" in the codependency system.

By changing the language from lust to needs, codependency is revolutionary. It glorifies what Scripture identifies as our flaw; it elevates our sinful tendencies of self-centeredness. It attempts a deathblow to the life that seeks to imitate Christ, and it flies in the face of such texts as Philippians 2:3: "Do nothing out of selfish ambition or vain conceit, but in humility consider others better than yourselves."

The fruit of that revolution is increasingly apparent. People not only experience anger or despair in relationships with others, there is an epidemic of anger with God. Many people feel justified in their demanding rights before God. When God does not supply their lusts (which they call "needs"), they are offended that God did not serve them. A need-oriented theology turns their relationship with God upside down. Instead of being servants who live in humble reliance on and thankfulness to the King of kings, they demand that He be their servant and give them the things that they passionately believe they need.

Considering this opposition to the clear truths of Scripture, how is it that a need-theology is so rampant among evangelicals?

One reason is that there exists such a slippery slope between our needs (lusts) and godly desires. How can anyone say that the desire to be loved is sinful? Neither Scripture nor our experience suggest it. The dilemma lies in distinguishing when something is a strong desire and when it is idolatrous. One indicator might be the sense of being controlled. The clearest indicator, however, would be our responsiveness to what Christ has done for us. Can we look toward Christ, know of God's grace, and have a vision for expressing that in love to others? If not, it is time to examine the motives of our hearts.

There is at least one other meaning for the word *need,* and that meaning has no counterpart in the codependent system. We do have a genuine, objective need that must be met if we are to live. It is truly our desperate need. Unbelievers are not consciously aware of that need, but at some level everyone knows it because everyone knows God (Romans 1:21) and everyone falls short of the standards of his or her own conscience. In unbelievers that need—the need for Jesus Christ—comes out as fear, guilt, walls of protection keeping people from God and others, despair from ineffective idols, and hopelessness. For followers of Christ, that need is expressed in other ways. Perhaps it is most beautifully described by the psalmist.

> As the deer pants for streams of water,
> so my soul pants for you, O God.
> My soul thirsts for God, for the living God.
> (Psalm 42:1-2)

How then do we provide an alternative to the codependency cult of the self? Persons-as-created-in-God's-image is one alternative, but there is too much debate over the meaning of the image of God in humans. Persons-as-needing-Christ is great, but the ambiguity of "need" makes it a weak alternative. Persons-as-sinners, or persons-as-idolaters, is certainly true, but the expression misses God's original design for us, skipping creation and going straight to the Fall. A view that encompasses all those attempts is to say that we are persons-who-are-called-to-respond-to-God. We are responders.[16] God is the initiator; we respond to His loving initiative.

That perspective reminds us that our environment is God-centered rather than autocratic. It leads us to thankfulness and dependence instead of creating demanding personalities. It points to the profound solution for what has been called "codependency": "We love because He first loved us."

NOTES

1. For example, Anne Wilson Schaef, *When Society Becomes an Addict* (San Francisco: Harper & Row, 1987).

2. Melodie Beattie, *Codependent No More* (San Francisco: Harper & Row, 1987), p. 31.

3. Robert Hemfelt, Frank Minirth, and Paul Meier, *Love Is a Choice: Recovery from Codependent Relationships* (Nashville: Thomas Nelson, 1988), p. 11.

4. For example, Lynne Bundesen, *God Dependency* (New York: Crossroad, 1989), p. 33.

5. Pia Melody, *Facing Codependence* (San Francisco: Harper & Row, 1989), p. 66.

6. Charles L. Whitfield, *Healing the Child Within* (Deerfield Beach, Fla.: Health Communications, 1988), p. 171.

7. Freiderich Schleiermacher, *On Religion: Speeches to Its Cultured Despisers* (New York: Harper & Row, 1965), p. 36.

8. John Bradshaw, *Bradshaw On: The Family* (Deerfield Beach, Fla.: Health Communications, 1988), p. 171.

9. Ibid., pp. 234, 236.

10. Bundesen, *God Dependency*, p. 59.

11. Beattie, *Codependent No More*, p. 90.

12. Dennis Wholey, *Becoming Your Own Parent* (New York: Doubleday, 1988), p. 104.

13. Friends in Recovery, *The Twelve Steps—A Way Out* (San Diego: Recovery, 1987), p. 133.

14. Beattie, *Codependent No More*, p. 113.

15. Emily Marlin, *Hope: New Choices and Recovery Strategies for Adult Children of Alcoholics* (New York: Harper & Row, 1987), pp. 134-35.

16. Also see Tony Walter, *Need: The New Religion* (Downers Grove, Ill.: InterVarsity, 1985).

10

A Better Way:
Christ Is My Worth

Don Matzat

I
f you were to walk into a room and see Sigmund Freud, Carl Rogers, Carl Jung, Abraham Maslow, and Jesus Christ seated together, to which would you go and what would you consider your greatest problem needing a solution?

Your answer to the former is dependent largely on how you
answer the latter. If your greatest problem is codependency, Jesus
Christ may not be your answer. If you perceive your deepest need to
be self-esteem, it is more likely that you will hear what you are looking for from Carl Rogers rather than from Jesus Christ. If, however,
you are convinced that your deepest need is to be accepted, loved,
and forgiven by a holy God who is justly angry with sinners, Jesus
Christ is the only one of the five who came "to save that which was
lost" (Matthew 18:11, NASB).

In this "better way" chapter, I intend to point us away from
two extremes: one is to deny any validity to psychology as a legitimate, natural discipline in society; the other, to integrate secular
psychology with the theology of the church.

DON MATZAT is the host of a daily radio program, "Issues, Etc,"™ and has been in parish ministry in the Lutheran Church–Missouri Synod for twenty-seven years.

THE RISE OF THE SELF-ESTEEM MOVEMENT

For the past one hundred years, secular psychologists have proposed a number of theories to explain human behavior. Until recently, behaviorism and Freudianism were the dominant schools of thought. Both viewpoints reduced man to a creature whose behavior was determined by outside forces. The behaviorist theories of B. F. Skinner, based upon the responses of animals to external stimuli, concluded that human behavior was conditioned by rewards and punishments. Sigmund Freud, on the other hand, perceived human beings as primarily sexual beings whose behavior was largely determined by unconscious, repressed desires. Neither of these theories was popular within Christian circles, and for good reason. They left no room for God, nor did they promote human dignity.

Reacting against these two schools of thought, the "third force," also known as "humanistic psychology," arrived on the scene in the late fifties and early sixties. Led by Carl Rogers and Abraham Maslow, the humanistic psychologists sought to return to man the power of his own life. Man is a conscious, responsible being, they taught, able to control his own destiny, behavior, and emotions. Out of humanistic psychology came the notion that developing self-esteem and striving to maintain a positive self-image would determine behavior, emotions, productivity, and the like.

According to the self-esteem advocates, our behavioral and emotional problems are largely the result of a negative self-image created by those who have influenced our lives. Parents who called us "bad boys and girls," and teachers who made us feel inferior in class when we failed a test, found their way to the top of the list of self-esteem offenders. And the Christian church, a major culprit, stirred up within us deep feelings of guilt, referring to us as poor, miserable sinners.

As a result of those influences, we have gone through life without feeling good about ourselves. Our subsequent behavior, emotions, social interaction, and productivity merely followed and reinforced a negative self-perception. But no matter what the limitations others imposed on us, the humanistic psychologists argued, we should take control of our lives and adjust our self-image by developing positive feelings toward ourselves, moving toward a state of self-esteem.

Many believe that humanistic psychology has finally solved the human dilemma. The state of California, for instance, after investing three quarters of a million dollars in studying the positive effects of self-esteem, concluded that making people feel better about themselves would benefit the entire nation. "Employees will then become more productive, teenagers will be less destructive, crime will decrease and welfare recipients will move toward financial self-sufficiency."[1]

IS SELF-ESTEEM AN UNBIBLICAL CONCEPT?

Any Christian criticism of this approach must clearly distinguish between what the Reformers called life *coram Deo* (before God) and life *coram homnibus* (before humans). Another way of putting it is in terms of the so-called two-kingdoms theory. On one hand is the kingdom of nature in which all human beings share. A physician does not have to be a Christian in order to perform a successful operation; that activity takes place in the realm of natural, shared knowledge common to everybody. On the other hand is the kingdom of grace. In that kingdom, the answers to life's ultimate questions are given in the biblical revelation. Only those who are "in Christ" can understand spiritual things (see 1 Corinthians 2:14-16; Ephesians 2:1-7).

In the kingdom of nature (that is, on the horizontal level, "before humans") is it wrong to agree with the state of California that a positive view of one's abilities and value in society, the family, school, the church, and the workplace is an essential and worthwhile goal? Does the doctrine of total depravity mean that people are as bad as they could possibly be, or that they are helpless in securing God's favor by their own righteousness? Evangelicals have consistently maintained the latter position and disavowed the former. Each of us, created in God's image, though fallen, retains a marred reflection of the truth, goodness, and beauty of the Creator. The point the Scriptures are anxious to maintain is that those qualities are not capable of being used to the glory of God apart from Christ and are, therefore, utterly worthless as attempts at the righteousness God requires.

That means, for instance, that we ought to affirm a son or daughter for getting a B on an exam, even when we really were hoping for an A; as parents and teachers we ought not to attach destructive labels to our children; we should encourage the unemployed and unskilled person to discover and cultivate his or her talents instead of contributing to a defeatist posture that withholds the dignity of being human. James, presumably including non-Christians in his view of those to whom we have a responsibility, complains that with the same tongue "we praise our Lord and Father . . . and curse men, who have been made in God's likeness" (James 3:9).

Thus, every person possesses dignity and value as an image-bearer of God. From this bedrock evaluation we derive the dignity of work and the family. Not to view oneself as created in God's image is to create a defective personality in those arenas. The state of California correctly recognized the problem, but did not understand it deeply enough to provide a sufficient solution.

If I met my friends at the golf course and muttered to myself as I was about to make a three-foot putt, "Why do you keep thinking you're going to make these three-foot putts?" my game would reflect that attitude. There is nothing unchristian or unscriptural about having a positive view of one's abilities, talents, personality traits, and so on, so long as we, as believers, acknowledge God as the giver of all good things. Even a Christian salesperson would never (or should never) introduce himself or herself by saying, "I know that you won't buy this car from me because I am a poor, miserable salesperson."

Before the doctrine of self-esteem became a buzzword and point of controversy among Christians, the necessity for self-confidence and a positive self-image in the arena of normal, daily human activity was taken for granted. Many Christian parents have read to their children the story of *The Little Engine That Could*. When our children took their first steps or attempted to ride their first bicycle did we not bolster their self-confidence? "C'mon, Johnny, you can do it!" parents shout at Little League baseball games. It has never been considered inappropriate for Christians, any more than for non-Christians, to encourage their children or boost their self-esteem in this way. The Bible nowhere expects Christians to tell their children,

"Johnny, realize that you are a poor, miserable shortstop." And yet, we are all poor, miserable sinners.

That is what brings us we to this other matter—our value *coram Deo,* or "before God," in the kingdom of grace. The Scriptures declare that "all our righteousnesses are like filthy rags" (Isaiah 64:6, NKJV*), that "there is no one righteous, not even one; there is no one who understands, no one who seeks God. All have turned away, they have together become worthless; there is no one who does good, not even one" (Romans 3:10-12). Before God we are regarded as "dead in trespasses and sins, . . . by nature children of wrath" (Ephesians 2:1, 4, NKJV). That is not because God is less forgiving than our friends and family on earth, but because God is holy. Therefore, whatever the basis of our relationship with God is to be, it cannot be in the slightest measure dependent on anything we have to offer in this relationship; all of our righteousness must be found in someone else's moral perfection.

This, therefore, is where much of the current debate gets confused. On one side are those who argue that any inculcation of a positive self-image is idolatry, whereas others insist that this is the gospel. Rather, we ought to argue that positive thinking on the purely human level is an altogether different matter than positive evaluations of our moral worth before God. By creation, we are endowed with God's image and possess dignity, but the Fall marred that image, and we ourselves invent new ways of effacing it. Thus, in the matter of redemption (the kingdom of grace) God will tolerate no self-esteem, no self-assertion, but only self-despair as the believer turns to Christ for his or her righteousness and worth before God.

The concept of "righteousness before man" was also called by the Reformers "civil righteousness." Luther writes the following:

> Now it is true and undeniable, however, that for himself and by virtue of his own powers a man can accustom himself to decency, respectability, and virtue. One observes this in the case of the heathen. As you see, not all men are murderers, adulterers, fornicators, thieves, wine guzzlers and loafers; there are many pious and honorable people in this world. These people have splen-

New King James Version.

did, beautiful virtues; they do splendid, beautiful works. Everyone should be encouraged to have such virtues and do such works.[2]

John Calvin also points out that distinctively human virtues cultivated by natural man are even rewarded by God:

> Hence this distinction between honorable and base actions God has not only engraved on the minds of each, but also often confirms in the administration of his providence. For we see how he visits those who cultivate virtue with many temporal blessings. Not that that external image of virtue in the least degree merits his favor, but he is pleased thus to show how much he delights in true righteousness, since he does not leave even the outward semblance of it go unrewarded.[3]

It is therefore a legitimate exercise for psychology to observe the obvious behavioral differences that exist among natural human beings, Christians and non-Christians alike, and seek to understand and promote virtues. However, psychology is a science belonging to the kingdom of nature. Like medicine, biology, astronomy, and physics, psychology can collect observable data, but it cannot offer any insight into the ultimate questions. Those answers are found only in the kingdom of grace, only in the gospel, which itself is found only in the text of Holy Scripture.

Rejecting the determinism of Freud and the conditioning of behaviorism, humanistic psychology, as the result of extensive research, teaches that our self-image, or the manner in which we perceive ourselves, to a great extent influences our success. If that assessment is accurate, and if humanistic psychology is successful in fostering more responsible behavior within society, that would be pleasing to God inasmuch as it served civil righteousness. God might commend the state of California for wanting employees to be more productive, teenagers less destructive, citizens less prone to commit crimes, and welfare recipients more successful at moving toward financial self-sufficiency. The apostle Paul, for instance, instructed us to pray for the success of human government so that the church of Jesus Christ could live in peace and security (1 Timothy 2:2). But is self-sufficiency and self-confidence in the workplace the same as self-confidence before God? Does the gospel promise greater self-confidence?

Although the Scriptures commend civil righteousness, they also clearly affirm that the virtues produced by human nature can contribute nothing to our righteousness before God. Calvin points out that such human virtues are motivated by "ambition, or self-love, or some other sinister affection."[4] Luther states that civil righteousness "contributes no more to a Christian's righteousness than do eating, drinking, sleeping, etc."[5] He compares civil righteousness to hay and straw required by cattle: "A cow must have hay and straw. This is a law for her, a rule without which she cannot exist. But through this law she does not become a child, a daughter, or an heiress in the house; she remains a cow."[6]

Even though a sense of self-worth and a positive self-image might be helpful if we are to successfully interact in society, before God such success is nothing but hay and straw. Martin Luther commended human civil righteousness and applauded the virtue often found among the heathen, but when it came to one's standing before God, his words were rather different:

> You hear your God speaking to you how all your life and deeds are nothing before God, but that you, together with everything in you, must perish eternally. If you believe this aright— that you are guilty—you must despair of yourself. . . . But in order to come out of and away from yourself, that is, out of your doom, he puts before you his dear Son, Jesus Christ, and has him speak to you his living, comforting Word: You should surrender yourself to him in firm faith and trust him boldly.[7]

THE REAL PROBLEM

The controversy in the church today over the issue of self-esteem has not been created by secular psychologists, many of whom have no intention of having their theories underwritten by Christianity. The problem has been created out of the tension Christian psychologists discover between the secular theories of their profession and the biblical revelation. However, when psychology is the professional's first and primary interest, theology can often be used to justify rather than to critique one's professional conclusions.

One should not doubt the honesty or integrity of Christians who wrestle with the integration between the two disciplines, but distinctions such as the one we have made in this chapter between "civil righteousness" (before man, in the kingdom of nature) and "divine righteousness" (before God, in the kingdom of grace) are absent from such discussions. Hence, it is impossible to entirely affirm civil righteousness as sufficient, but we feel compelled to affirm the basic human value of individuals. So what often happens is a blending of civil and divine righteousness. We feel uneasy giving unequivocal support to the idea of self-esteem (even before man), but we cannot believe "worm theology" any longer, so we steer a middle course. What I am suggesting is that we resist that temptation, affirming the full dignity, self-worth, and grandeur of humans as created in the image of God, encouraging our children in their self-image, and at the same time pointing out the fact that before God, because of our sinfulness, we are worthy only of condemnation apart from Christ's worth.

Therefore, to take the position that we ought to remove not only destructive labels from children in the classroom but also biblical references such as "sinner," "wretch," "miserable," and "unworthy" from our hymnody and from Christian discussion is to seriously misunderstand and, in fact, to undermine the biblical gospel. The doctrine of creation (all humans bearing the divine image) may be used as the basis for self-esteem before man (civil righteousness), but the gospel may not. The gospel comes to those who feel miserable about themselves, not to those who think of themselves as "basically good" (see Mark 2:17).

Even within secular psychology there is opposition to the confusion of psychology and theology, often called "integration" by well-intentioned brothers and sisters. Witness Karl Menninger's famous diatribe asking the church, *Whatever Became of Sin?* Of course, we know, don't we? It has been psychologized away even within the church. We are codependent and others have failed to meet our needs or we have a wounded inner child. Secular answers have replaced biblical ones, and this is not integration, but outright subversion of the Christian message. Then there is Jewish psychiatrist Viktor Frankl's insistence that "any fusion of the respective goals of religion and psychotherapy must result in confusion." He correctly states that although the effects of psychotherapy and religion might seem to overlap at points, the intentions are different.[8]

One must ask those who are engaged in Christian psychology where integration ends and confusion begins. They cannot answer that question without an abundant appeal to theology. Unfortunately, in many cases those who practice psychology know their respective psychological schools and theories better than they do their systematic theology, with the result that they end up "integrating" a Sunday school training in theology with a graduate school training in psychology. No wonder such popular works tilt in favor of psychological concepts and phrases, notwithstanding the abundance of proof texts and Bible words. Such efforts are little more than props in a play in which psychology is queen of the sciences.

A CONTROVERSIAL INTRUDER

Here is where the church is afraid of making waves. Services are often created to minimize discomfort for the unbeliever so that he or she begins to accept Christianity as an affirming influence. People ought to leave church feeling good about themselves, it is said, instead of being called to self-examination, sincere repentance, and faith toward God.

Although the church must affirm human dignity *coram homnibus*, or before man in the kingdom of nature, it must equally report the biblical facts concerning human depravity *coram Deo*, or before God in the kingdom of grace. When Robert Schuller writes that "the most serious sin is the one that causes me to say 'I am unworthy,'"[9] he confuses self-worth before man and self-worth before God. Did not Jesus affirm the very opposite in His illustration of the tax-collector and the Pharisee? "And the tax collector, standing afar off, would not so much as raise his eyes to heaven, but beat his breast, saying, 'God be merciful to me a sinner!'" (Luke 18:13, NKJV). Whereas the Pharisee was affirming himself and nurturing himself with positive, uplifting "self-talk," the tax collector was committing Robert Schuller's cardinal sin: calling himself "unworthy." "I tell you," Jesus concluded, "this man went down to his house justified rather than the other; for everyone who exalts himself will be abased, and he who humbles himself will be exalted" (v. 14, NKJV).

The intrusion of the secular concept of self-esteem, therefore, faces us with the temptation to create new gospels that offer solutions to whatever the world has decided is humanity's fundamental problem—this week—while the timeless revelation of human despair and hope waits to be reappropriated and reapplied in each new generation.

Christians are urged to draw from knowledge, whatever its source. Following Augustine's famous dictum, "All truth is God's truth," we can expect to learn things from the social sciences that the Bible is not concerned to tell us. But what we see today in so much of the literature and preaching of Christian pop psychology is not *integration* of biblical-theological and natural-scientific knowledge, but a *replacement* of biblical views of humans, God, and salvation with purely secular notions, baptized with noncontextual verses from the Bible.

If "all truth is God's truth" and God has seen fit to lead humanistic psychologists to discover something about God, man, and salvation that Christians have overlooked, underemphasized, or ignored altogether, we should expect such insights to fit nicely with biblical revelation. The Holy Spirit would not provide us with conflicting truths; therefore, where the Bible clearly addresses any issue or concept it is the final authority, regardless of how impressive rival theories might appear.

THE CROSS: GRACE OR MERIT?

The central focus of Christianity is the grace of God bestowed upon sinful human beings through the death and resurrection of Jesus Christ. This is the gospel, and its proclamation justifies the existence of the church as an institution. In order to preach God's grace, one must also clearly explain the hopeless condition of sinful humanity. To believe in grace, one must be convinced there is nothing in himself or herself that merits or deserves God's favor or makes the person worthy of God's fatherly care. "If by grace, then it is no longer by works; if it were, grace would no longer be grace" (Romans 11:6).

However, the self-esteem focus has popularized a theory within some Christian circles that implies we do have moral worth and justification before God. I have heard more than one pastor declare in a sermon that Christ's death proves our self-worth. The impression is given that if we had absolutely nothing to offer and no merit, God would not have wasted his time and energy on us. Christ died for us, we are told, because we were worth it. One writer argues, "It is as if Christ had said, 'You are of such worth to me that I am going to die; even experience hell so that you might be adopted as my brothers and sisters.'"[10]

Another popular writer states, "Of course, the greatest demonstration of a person's worth to God was shown in giving us his Son."[11] Again, that confuses the issue. The cross is a demonstration of God's love, mercy, compassion, justice, and goodness—not ours.

The Bible clearly defines the death of Christ as a vicarious act. He died in our place. He took the punishment that was rightfully ours. We were worthy, to be sure—worthy of eternal death—but He took our unworthiness upon Himself and gave us His worth, His merit in our place. He did not give His life for us because we were worthy, but in order to render us worthy before the Father. The cross reveals the depth of our sin, not the height of our worth before God. The apostle Paul declared, "If One died for all, then all died" (2 Corinthians 5:14, NKJV). In other words, the cross is a demonstration of the spiritual bankruptcy of humanity before God: "They have all gone out of the way; they have together become unprofitable" (Romans 3:12, NKJV).

In addition, the death of Christ was a judicial act. It was a divine sentence leveled against sinful humanity and carried out against the Son of God. How, therefore, can one suggest that the severity of the judicial sentence against us for our sins and assumed by another reminds us of our self-worth? If it were possible for the death of Jesus Christ to have been even more cruel and horrible would we be thereby granted even greater self-worth?

A recent television newscast reported the arraignment of a serial killer who has admitted responsibility for at least fifteen murders. The judge set his bail at $5 million! Would we use the same sort of reasoning to conclude that this man should feel good about himself and regard himself as an especially valuable human being, since the judge set his bail so high? After all, he is worth $5 million to society!

The $5 million bail obviously does not reflect the value of the murderer, but the severity of his crime. Similarly, the death of our Lord Jesus Christ on the cross is not a statement of our worth but indicates the depth of our sin and guilt before God. Again, if Jesus died for us because He saw something in us worth dying for, then there was something in us that merited His death somehow. But we are saved because of something good in God, not because of something good in us.

I have often heard it said, "If I had been the only person on the earth, Jesus would still have died for me." Although our Lord could have given His life for just one person, it most certainly would not have been because that person was so valuable, but because God was so gracious. Such an occurrence should hardly, therefore, be regarded as a source of pride or self-esteem. For me to argue that Jesus would have died for me if I were the only person on the earth simply indicates that my sins alone, without the rest of you contributing your share, were sufficient to demand the severe punishment Jesus Christ vicariously assumed in my place. When faced with that reality, we ought to weep for the selfless sacrifice of our Lord instead of finding in it one more opportunity for feeling good about ourselves.

And yet, the very approach I am suggesting, which has been characteristic of evangelical preaching and teaching for centuries and lies at the heart of the biblical revelation, is anathema in many evangelical circles today. Ray Anderson, who teaches a course on the integration of self-esteem and theology at Fuller Theological Seminary in Pasadena, California, complains about the psychological battering of the cross: "If our sin is viewed as causing the death of Jesus on the cross, then we ourselves become victims of a 'psychological battering' produced by the cross. When I am led to feel that the pain and torment of Jesus' death on the cross is due to my sin, I inflict upon myself spiritual and psychological torment."[12]

There is no doubt that the cross of Jesus Christ does inflict upon us a "psychological battering." Theologically, we have considered that to be part of the process leading to repentance. The law reads like a series of algebra problems we have failed, and the failing grade is read aloud: "For all have sinned and fall short of the glory of God" (Romans 3:23). It is a measure of just how greatly secular concepts have revolutionized our daily discourse as Christians when evangelical seminary professors can look at the cross of Christ and His suffering and physical and spiritual battering and then warn Christians about the danger of being psychologically battered by the event. Consider rather Martin Luther's attitude toward the cross: "The main benefit of Christ's passion is that man sees into his own true self and that he is terrified and crushed by this. Unless we seek that knowledge, we do not derive much benefit from Christ's passion. . . . He who is so hard-hearted and callous as not to be terrified by Christ's passion and led to a knowledge of self has reason to fear."[13]

THE RIGHTEOUSNESS OF CHRIST

God does not inflict upon us the psychological battering of the cross in order to leave us in a tormented condition. It is at the cross where we are offered through the gospel the very righteousness of Jesus Christ. We are granted a new identity in Him. This biblical doctrine of justification by grace through faith is God's answer to the human identity crisis. God has made us right with Him by imputing to us the very righteousness of Christ Himself. This righteousness we receive from God is neither of our own making, nor is it based upon our good works or efforts. It is an "alien" righteousness found in the Person of Christ and imputed to us by God. Luther referred to this righteousness as a "passive" righteousness that is received, rather than an "active" righteousness that is the result of one's own doing. It is a righteousness that comes from God and is found in Christ, not a righteousness that comes from self. Therefore, the focus of justification is never upon self, but always upon Christ Jesus.

If you study the doctrine of justification by grace through faith as it is found in Scripture and was clearly taught by the Reformers, you will discover that it is not possible to merge that teaching of justification with self-esteem before God. Luther and Calvin would be outspoken opponents of this doctrine in our day, as they were of the human-centered challenges to the gospel in their own.

Remarkably, however, the historic, Reformation, evangelical position toward self is exactly the opposite of much of what is passing for evangelical preaching and teaching today. The Reformers taught that the professed goodness of "self" hinders faith from grasping the righteousness that God has provided in Christ. We begin to feel just good enough about ourselves to conclude that we do not need such a radical gospel remedy, but then we find ourselves trapped in disillusionment, anxiety, shame, and fear all over again shortly thereafter. Luther wrote that faith in Christ demands that you "come out of yourself and away from yourself."[14] In our age, C. S. Lewis echoed those thoughts. In *Mere Christianity* he writes, "There must be a real giving up of the self. You must throw it away 'blindly,' so to speak."[15]

It is important to point out that this "throwing away" of "self" is not self-destruction. We ought not to become preoccupied with self-hatred instead of self-esteem. We do not lose our identity when we become Christians. Although we have become "new creations" in Christ, we are nevertheless still the same people in terms of personality and physical, emotional, and psychological characteristics. It is not the obliteration of personal identity to which the gospel calls us but to the realization that our worth and merit before God come to us from outside, not from within, as a gift, a charitable donation. Whereas we can never say, this side of heaven, "God has made me righteous," we can say, "God has made Christ my righteousness" (see 1 Corinthians 1:30). The apostle Paul, though he had a number of marks in his favor of which to be proud, was more than happy to "count them but rubbish" before God in order to "gain Christ, and . . . be found in Him, not having a righteousness of my own derived from the Law, but that which is through faith in Christ, the righteousness which comes from God on the basis of faith" (Philippians 3:7-9, NASB).

This turning away from self-righteousness and self-esteem before God toward justification and acceptance before God because of Christ requires that we accept the sentence the law levels against us and recognize that we are indeed unworthy sinners who deserve nothing but God's eternal wrath and judgment. Apart from that, the cross of Christ is a meaningless distraction from the business of contemporary narcissism.

OBJECTIVE REALITY VERSUS SUBJECTIVE ILLUSION

The secular doctrine of self-esteem is a feeble alternative to the truth of justification. The righteous identity that God provides for us is based upon the objective facts of Christ's righteous life and sacrificial death. When faced with depression, worry, or fear, we can look to the Word of God and focus our thoughts upon Jesus Christ. We can sing, "Jesus, thy blood and righteousness, my beauty are, my glorious dress," or, "My hope is built on nothing less than Jesus' blood and righteousness." Even though we know that all our righteousness is as filthy rags, we can trust the perfect righteousness of someone else who attained it for us. The profound manner in which God has made us right with Himself makes the secular alternative look pitifully inadequate by comparison.

The feelings of guilt, shame, fear, and lostness are not merely subjective impulses to which we choose to yield, but real facts about ourselves. We are guilty, shameful, and lost; and the fear we feel is a natural and, in fact, proper anticipation of what our guilt requires in terms of a divine response. To deny this or downplay it is to deny ourselves and those we try to influence any hope of resolving the conflict once and for all and setting the conscience at peace with God. Realistic solutions require realistic appraisals.

In Christ we are already seated in heavenly places. In Him we have a solid, weighty, and positive identity that constantly raises our minds from the passing assurances and positive platitudes of this world to the heavens where we hear the promise of One who has issued us with these "new papers." Instead of concentrating on our shame, or denying it, we accept it and then exchange it for Christ's integrity. For God has made Jesus Christ our wisdom, our righteousness, our holiness, and our redemption (1 Corinthians 1:30).

That does not mean, however, that Christianity is at odds with psychology as a social science any more than it is at odds with physics. It is when psychology dons the theologian's gown or the pastor's robe that it becomes a rival. When it usurps the authority reserved for revelation, the kingdom of nature makes itself into a rival religion to the kingdom of grace. Geologists may explain the age of the earth, but they will never explain the purpose or meaning behind its existence and ours. Psychology may help people with deep emotional problems related to multiple personalities or a severe depressive condition, but it will never explain the truth about our deepest needs or help us understand our relationship to God.

Therefore, a Christian need not feel guilty about seeing a psychologist about a sleeping disorder, for instance, but he must be aware that psychologists transgress their competence when they address issues such as guilt and forgiveness.

As with pragmatism in church growth, ideology in politics, and signs and wonders in missions, biblical revelation must have the final say in relation to the Christian's use of psychology. Just as success, ideology, and experience must not be allowed to run roughshod over biblical theology, so too psychological insights must always be scrutinized by Scripture before they are allowed to pass into Christian use, especially when that science touches on so many issues addressed by Scripture.

The fact that psychology, as a social science, is committed to producing good, moral, and responsible people does not make it an enemy of Christianity, but neither does it render it an ally in public preaching and teaching of the gospel message. A good, moral, and responsible person stands under God's judgment just as squarely as a serial murderer. There are obviously two different levels of self-assessment: before men and before God; in the kingdom of nature, and in the kingdom of grace. On the one hand, the fact that I am a miserable sinner before God whose only ethical worth and acceptance is the gift of someone else (viz., Christ) does not mean that I cannot maintain a sense of self-confidence and self-worth in my work, in my relationships, and in society. "The worker is worthy of his keep" (Matthew 10:10). Further, we do have the worth and value of Christ assigned to us: we are children, and not slaves; coheirs with Christ "created in Christ Jesus to do good works" (Ephesians 2:10).

Since all humans are created in God's image, there is sufficient basis for our realizing the value of every human being, while recognizing that that is not the gospel and that our being so created is not a value or worth God accepts as worthy of His Son's death. That image has only rendered humanity, since the Fall, all the more responsible for its depravity and moral worthlessness before God. For the Christian, this civil righteousness is but hay and straw, or, as

Paul describes all righteousness, merit, and worth outside of Christ, "rubbish."

Thus, the "better way" is to steer a middle course between those, on the one hand, who would reject psychology altogether as a legitimate discipline in the kingdom of nature, and those, on the other hand, who would give psychology a partnership in the kingdom of grace. Jesus Christ does not merely give better answers to psychological questions; He gives the only answers to questions psychology does not even ask, much less answer.

NOTES

1. "Using Self-Esteem to Fix Society's Ills," *New York Times,* March 28, 1990.
2. Ewald Plass, *What Luther Says* (St. Louis: Concordia, 1959), 3:1220.
3. Calvin, *Institutes* (Grand Rapids: Eerdmans, 1983), 2:75.
4. Ibid.
5. Plass, *What Luther Says.*
6. Ibid.
7. Werner Elert, *The Structure of Lutheranism* (St. Louis: Concordia, 1962), p. 80.
8. Viktor Frankl, *The Unconscious God* (New York: Simon & Schuster, 1975), p. 75.
9. Robert Schuller, *Self-Esteem: The New Reformation* (Waco, Tex.: Word, 1982), p. 98.
10. William Kirwin, *Biblical Concepts for Christian Counseling* (Grand Rapids: Baker, 1984), p. 107.
11. Donna Foster, *Building a Child's Self-Esteem* (Glendale, Calif.: Regal, 1977), p. 6.
12. Ray S. Anderson, *The Gospel According to Judas* (Colorado Springs, Colo.: Helmer & Howard, 1991), p. 99.
13. Timothy Lull, *Martin Luther's Basic Theological Writings* (Minneapolis: Fortress, 1989), p. 168.
14. Elert, *The Structure of Lutheranism,* p. 80.
15. C. S. Lewis, *Mere Christianity* (New York: Macmillan, 1943), p. 190.

PART 5

POWER PREACHERS

"I will myself gather the remnant of my flock out of all the countries where I have driven them and will bring them back to their pasture, where they will be fruitful and increase in number. I will place shepherds over them who will tend them, and they will no longer be afraid or terrified, nor will any be missing," declares the Lord.
Jeremiah 23:3

Thus you nullify the word of God for the sake of your tradition. You hypocrites! Isaiah was right when he prophesied about you: "These people honor me with their lips, but their hearts are far from me; they worship me in vain; their teachings are but rules taught by men."
Matthew 15:6b-9

If anyone else thinks he has reasons to put confidence in the flesh, I have more: circumcised, . . . a Hebrew of Hebrews; in regard to the law, a Pharisee; as for zeal, persecuting the church; as for legalistic righteousness, faultless. But whatever was to my profit I now consider loss for the sake of Christ . . . that I may gain Christ and be found in him, not having a righteousness of my own that comes from the law, but that which is through faith in Christ—the righteousness that comes from God and is by faith. I want to know Christ and the power of his resurrection and the fellowship of sharing in his sufferings.
Philippians 3:4b-11a

POWER PREACHERS

11

This Present Paranoia

Kim Riddlebarger

"This world is not my home, I'm just a' passin' through," goes the refrain of a popular American hymn. The world is understood to be a very evil place, and America is no longer thought of as a bastion of moral virtue. Thus evangelicals do their best to exist in a society that they feel is increasingly hostile to their cause. The goal held out to the weary faithful is survival as unwelcome pilgrims in a world and culture that is not thought of as "home," but merely as a place to endure, to just "pass through" while awaiting the return of Christ. In the middle of all this tension many American evangelicals, not surprisingly, reflect a good degree of fear and suspicion of the world around them, a kind of paranoia, if you will.

And, as recent trends seem to indicate, there are several disturbing indications that this hostility may, in fact, be in the process of becoming mutual. Conservative American Christians are viewed with increased suspicion and fear by the secular world around them, and their agenda is increasingly viewed as a reactionary militant barricade on the golden highway toward supposed pluralism and personal freedom. The term *fundamentalist* is applied pejoratively to everything from Islamic revolutionaries holding American citizens against their will to Mormon polygamist sects hiding out on the

KIM RIDDLEBARGER is vice president of Christians United for Reformation (CURE), Anaheim, California, dean of the CURE Academy, and associate professor of apologetics at the Simon Greenleaf School of Law at California State University.

fringes of American society. Evangelicals who attempt to stem the rising tide of secularism in society and who take a public stand against evil are simply dismissed as fundamentalists who have no regard for the moral views of others and are simply trying to impose their own personal values on society generally. Considered leftover Victorians who are out of place in the new vision of America, evangelicals can't help but feel left out, and that produces resentment of the very society in which they live and into which they are sent as salt and light.

But, as this chapter will argue, there are some indications that American evangelicalism actually may be more hostile to secular society than secular society is to the church. It is that hostility and fear that perpetuates an uneasy tension and that, in effect, cuts off many opportunities for fruitful dialogue with a society that is searching for honest answers to life's toughest questions.

This point I think can be demonstrated by a general analysis of the massive evangelical subculture and a more detailed review of one aspect of that subculture—popular Christian literature.

POPULAR EVANGELICAL BOOKS

I am convinced that an important and often overlooked place to take the pulse of the Christian community is the Christian Booksellers Association's list of best-selling books.[1] The kinds of books evangelicals purchase, even if not indicative of what evangelicals actually read, are good barometers of where the evangelicals' heart and treasure really lie.

My chief concern in this essay is not that evangelical literature denies any great doctrines of the Christian faith outright. Indeed, some may argue that the great popularity of evangelical literature in the contemporary marketplace actually exposes an unbelieving secular culture to Christianity. I think that the case can be made that what this generation of popular literature has done is present to modern America great Christian truths that are recast in decidedly sensational and high-tech packaging with less than satisfactory biblical content and emphases. Apart from the recent acceptance of the neo-gnostic Word of Faith literature[2] into the mainstream of evangelical publishing by some publishers, outright denial of classic

266

Christian teachings has not been a significant problem. Instead, those great truths are undermined by redefinition, trivialization, and sensationalized emphases.

WHAT ABOUT THE DOCTRINE OF CREATION?

One theme that recurs in popular Christian literature is the unhealthy and unbiblical fear of the world. To be sure, the Bible does warn us to defend ourselves from the subtle influences of the world and to instead "be transformed by the renewing of [our] mind" (Romans 12:2). Nevertheless, biblical revelation marks Christianity as the most world-affirming and world-embracing religion.

It is impossible to create an atmosphere of trust and friendship with a culture we are trying to win to Christ at the same time we are expressing a profound sense of alienation and even hostility toward that same culture. And yet, the fear of the world has contributed significantly to the face-off between a hostile secular world and an alienated evangelical subculture.

The unifying note this book sounds is this: nearly every problem plaguing the evangelical church today is rooted in the misunderstanding or ignorance of a particular Christian truth. Doctrinal reformation is the goal of this entire volume, and, in the case of the evangelical community's response toward the world, I submit that a misunderstanding and ignorance of the doctrine of creation is at the root of "this present paranoia."

In historic Protestant understanding, the world, which was seen to be created as "very good" by God, is still beautiful even after the Fall. Even in its bondage to decay, pollution, and depravity, the world continues to be the object of God's love, concern, providence, and even redemption (Romans 8:19-22). Even the world's cruelest tyrants bear God's image, though they try desperately to eradicate it. But whereas the world is *morally* depraved and its inhabitants in bondage to sin and death, it is not nature itself but the *corruption* of nature that is the source of evil (see Calvin's *Institutes* 1:14:20). God did not abandon His fallen creation when humanity rebelled. Although He destroyed nearly all living creatures in a flood, He relented and promised not to send such a flood in the future. Instead, He brought His kingdom to earth, centered in the nation Israel, and worked His mighty acts of salvation and redemption in human history, culminating in the incarnation, death, resurrection, and ascension of Christ.

This high view of creation, and the role given God's world as the theater of redemption, has been replaced by a doctrine of creation that is more classically Greek and neoplatonic than biblical. In Greek thought, the point of human existence is to somehow escape matter. The spirit is hostile to the body; the spiritual person is hostile to the physical realm of the world. In classical paganism (particularly Greek and Persian), the point is to be redeemed *from* this world, whereas, in biblical religion, it is to be redeemed *in* this world.

A great deal of best-selling evangelical literature is nothing more than a feeble and reactionary attempt to formulate an apologetic against a vague and undefined enemy. We are not even sure which dimension our enemy occupies—the so-called experts are not in agreement. We do not know if the real enemy is Satan and his demonic minions; the secular humanists who do the devil's bidding; the key players in the current geopolitical scene, who are setting the stage for the coming Antichrist; or those who advocate a left-wing social agenda. Nevertheless, for each proposed enemy there can be found an entire genre of popular Christian books and tapes.

We do not even know if we are to fear what we cannot see, touch, or taste; and each author or authority who tackles this vague enemy simply proposes his or her own diagnosis as to identities he, and apparently he alone, has discovered. All we know for certain is that the enemy is out there, that it is evil, and more important, that it is associated with the world in some way, shape, or form. Therefore, we must oppose this vague enemy at all costs, even if we cannot agree upon who or what it is exactly that we are opposing. In fact, in many "spiritually correct thinking" groups, opposition to those undefined forces is a test of orthodoxy.

One might suppose that this inability to define our enemy might produce a paralysis of sorts. But instead, it has given rise to a mass of books and ministries, *each* claiming to have a scoop on the enemy's identity, tactics, and connections. What has resulted is a hydra of individuals and parachurch ministries who perpetuate that uneasiness. Although each has its own idea of the enemy, all are unified by the certainty that the enemy can be personified, not only in a real devil (the biblical identity of evil's source), but in various individuals and movements. The more cynically minded reader may even draw the conclusion that some Christian publishers thrive on perpetuating this paranoia by marketing the latest call to arms in the ongoing competition to discover the focus of evil in the world.

As a result, corporate marketing strategies rather than serious theological reflection determine the content, style, and morale of the evangelical masses.

THE GROWTH OF THE EVANGELICAL SUBCULTURE

Another factor that demonstrates the depth of the uneasy relationship between evangelicals and the surrounding culture is the massive growth of the Christian subculture.

Since worldly amusements are out, we have *Christian* television, radio, and film. If rock music is of the devil, how about *Christian* rock? We can put catchy biblical motifs on spandex pants and proclaim the glories of God instead of making music for the devil. Since we cannot tolerate senseless violence, the current wrestling craze is probably taboo, but it is very nicely replaced by a Christian equivalent in The Power Team, a group of professional wrestlers who pack auditoriums around the world in an effort to demonstrate that being "plugged in" to Jesus is responsible for their success in breaking blocks of ice with their foreheads. And whereas no truly God-fearing person would have the least bit of interest in horror films and suspenseful science fiction, and conscientious Christians should never be seen reading a Stephen King novel, serious evangelical readers are provided with an excellent alternative in the fiction of Frank Peretti and the enthralling tales of supernatural warfare among angels and demons in the mythical city of Ashton. The unknown god popularly known to Alcoholics Anonymous as "the higher power" is far too secular for us, so we have our own Christian recovery craze, which appears to provide little more opportunity to discover that deity. Yet these alternatives to what the world offers, whether in fiction or nonfiction, are often neither good literature nor good Christian theology. By demanding that good books have an overtly Christian content, evangelicals often do little more than replace *no* theology with *poor* theology.

What may also come as quite a surprise to many is just how large is the massive evangelical subculture and the Christian retailing industry that underlies it. Although exact figures are hard to come by, one report puts the sales of all items in Christian bookstores at $2.7 billion for 1990 alone; sales of Christian books nationwide in all stores logged in at more than $1.5 billion in 1989.[3] By all accounts that is a massive industry, and an industry that grows by leaps and bounds every year. We are selling more books, more Bibles, more tapes, and CDs than ever before, and all the while our beloved America becomes increasingly more secularized and Christians themselves grow biblically illiterate. Clearly something is wrong.

Since Christians generally make little attempt to inform the secular culture with biblical themes in cultural products, many Christians are content simply to react to the "unknown enemy" and throw gospel rocks at the world. Although those products pretend to be evangelizing the lost, they are clearly geared to the choir, which already speaks "Christianese." That is borne out by rather distressing statistical evidence that indicates that only 25 percent of Christians who regularly attend church actually shop in local Christian bookstores. What is most shocking about that statistic is that it means that one-quarter of the Christian population manages to purchase 90 percent of all merchandise sold, a figure that would amount to more than $2.4 billion annually.[4] Despite protests to the contrary, the cold figures demonstrate that Christian bookselling is oriented toward feeding the Christian consumer, not toward reaching out to American culture generally. And although it must be said at the outset that publishers and bookstores are in business for the purpose of profit (which, by the way, is a God-honoring reason to be in business), it seems to me that the time has come to begin asking some hard questions about perpetuating the consumer-oriented evangelical subculture under the guise of evangelistically oriented mission statements produced by many companies.

The amazing paradox in all of this is that the more Christians fear the world, the more they end up actually imitating and even perpetuating the very worldliness that terrifies them. Christian alternative entertainment is often a mere mimicking of pagan culture. The basic philosophical questions about what media can be used to communicate the gospel, and how each media affects the message it communicates, simply are not asked.[5] Because we are so prone to copy the various forms of media uncritically, without any reflection, we may find ourselves baptizing with Bible verses forms of the culture that present inherent obstacles to an accurate communication of a message. Worse, we may take legitimate forms of media and misuse them by turning them into mere Christian propaganda. By "denying the world" and offering alternative entertainment, we may find that, instead of being "in the world but not of it," we are "of the world but not in it." We are "of the world" because we are content to copy the cultural products of a given trend; we are "not in it" because we are selling 90 percent of the cultural products we produce to ourselves.

There are several major turning points in the recent history of Christian publishing that serve to illustrate the type of uneasiness and paranoia with which we are concerned.

FOCUS NUMBER ONE: END TIMES

If you were asked to name the number one best-selling book in America during the 1970s, the answer would probably *not* be Hal Lindsey's *The Late Great Planet Earth,* published in 1970. But, in fact, that sensational end-times account was the best-selling book in America during the tumultuous seventies, selling more than 10 million copies to date and going through 140 printings. The amazing success of *The Late Great Planet Earth* lay not so much in its eschatological perspective as in the timing of its release, proving the adage that "timing is everything."

In the seventies America stood on the brink of war at varying times, with both the Soviet Union and the People's Republic of China. The evening news carried sensational and emotional new film of the previous day's carnage of the best of American youth in the jungles of Vietnam. The Six-Day War in 1967 had already rallied public support and interest in the fledgling nation of Israel through what was truly a great military miracle. It was David and Goliath all over again, only this time on television in our own living rooms. The Yom Kippur War of 1973, while pushing the superpowers to the brink of war, only enhanced earlier favorable opinions of Israel's cause.

International crises were not the only elements at work. In November of 1963 Americans watched as their young president was brutally murdered in Dallas. At the close of the sixties (1968), Robert Kennedy and Martin Luther King, Jr., were both tragically assassinated at what seemed to be the brink of an important turning point in American history. Who can forget the near anarchy that took place at that year's Democratic convention in Chicago? The whole world *was* indeed watching. Lyndon Johnson's promised "Great Society" never did materialize, and instead Americans watched while many of its biggest inner cities burned with race rioting induced by bigotry, hatred, and ethnic violence. Then the nation watched its president resign in disgrace, again on live national television, due to the rapidly hemorrhaging Watergate scandal.

It was in the midst of our loss of innocence and well after the end of the post–World War II optimism that *The Late Great Planet Earth* burst onto the scene. People were desperately seeking answers, and even the most level-headed commentators grew apocalyptic. What would the future hold? Would there be nuclear war? What would happen to America, Israel, and the Soviet Union? What would God do in the midst of these troubles? What would happen to Christians, who already had good biblical reason to be less than optimistic about the future of the world? The evening news had experts who offered educated guesses, but the people wanted more certainty. *The Late Great Planet Earth* gave them their answers and assured them that those answers were predicted in the Bible. This was something that secular prophets such as Jeanne Dixon could not produce.

What answers did Hal Lindsey offer the church at that critical moment? If you are a Christian, you will not be here to experience any of the horrible things that are going to happen on the earth. Christ is going to return, secretly, and remove all believers from the earth before the beginning of the Great Tribulation. After that, Israel will be invaded by the Soviet Union, a ten-nation confederacy mimicking the Roman Empire will arise, and the Antichrist will be ushered to the stage of history. All of those events will take place after Christ has removed His church.

Many Christians saw those end-times events as an incentive to evangelize the world, just as in the nineteenth century a major impetus for the modern missionary movement was the widespread belief that Christ would return and establish His kingdom after the church had Christianized the world. Different end-times scenarios turned out to be responsible for basically the same energetic missionary response. Some evangelistic appeals began to spend more time on the coming Tribulation and the shaping up of world events than on the gospel message itself. Many conversions were due more to a particular understanding of future events (the rapture, Armageddon, and so on) than to a grasp of the past (Christ's Person and work).

The Late Great Planet Earth popularized a common scenario of end-times events and gave birth to a new genre of "Bible prophecy" books. On its heels followed sequel after sequel, and entire parachurch ministries devoted to end-times teachings burst upon the scene. End-times prophecy conferences became popular and influential enterprises in the Christian world. The Jesus-People phenomenon was shaped by that movement as seminars and low-budget films about Christ's return drew enormous crowds.

For some Christians the end-times scenario popularized by Hal Lindsey and others had the side effect of tending to perpetuate antagonism toward the world. Some Christians began to regard every major news item as a signal that they would soon escape this world, and it became difficult for them to be genuinely interested in world events for their own sake. Since the church was not going to be around after the rapture, an event that might take place at any moment, what was to become of the role of the church in the world, society, and the surrounding culture? Since human government was nothing more than a vehicle for the rise of Antichrist, perhaps it would be better if Christians did not get involved. The world itself was to be savaged by nuclear war and horrible plagues and upheaval. Of what use, then, was ecological stewardship? In fact, the poor ecological state of the earth was actually *evidence* that the end was quite near. And since the end was near, of what use was it to urge peace among nations or to work toward the reform of social injustice? The only justification for the earthly existence of the Christian, it seemed, was evangelism.

If our earth is seen as only the stage for the bowl and trumpet judgments of the Apocalypse, and if ecological and economic collapse and crime in our streets are seen only as dramatic signs heralding the imminent return of Christ for His church, there is much less incentive to get involved in causes that work to restrain evil. Apart from involving themselves in certain moral and political issues that directly affect the happiness, security, and values of their own subculture, some evangelicals have sent the message to society that evangelicals are its enemies in the courtroom, the classroom, the media and the arts, and in virtually every other field of endeavor.

It is argued, however, that books like *The Late Great Planet Earth* promote the gospel. They give incentive for people to turn to Jesus Christ in an uncertain time. Yet those books can generate a most unfortunate side effect. It seems that every time a geopolitical crisis occurs a new rash of such books appears. Then, as the crisis unfolds and events do not lend themselves to the interpretations put forward, prophecy pundits are forced to rewrite and rethink the scenarios they had advanced. The Scriptures warn us clearly about speculative investigation of end-times events. Concerning the hour of His return, our Lord expressly warned, "No one knows about that day or that hour, not even the angels in heaven, nor the Son, but only the Father" (Matthew 24:36).[6] Peter tells us that one of the characteristics of the last days will be that scoffers will come, saying, "Where is this 'coming' he promised?" (2 Peter 3:3-4). Unfortunately, we have given scoffers a great deal of new ammunition. The watching world picks up on "this world is not my home" attitude, and the consequences we have helped to create include the scoffing and contempt we see around us.

Yes, Jesus *is* coming back. But will the world listen to that glorious promise with trust and respect? It appears to non-Christians who watch us that many Christians have their own selfish agenda and that they really do not care about those outside the club or about the very world they share in common with those who may disagree with them. That is an unfortunate and unbiblical legacy.

There was a time when Christians were characterized as hardworking, charitable neighbors who were more likely to follow Paul's instructions to those confused about the end: "Make it your ambition to lead a quiet life, to mind your own business and to work with your hands, just as we told you, so that your daily life may win the respect of outsiders and so that you will not be dependent on anybody" (1 Thessalonians 4:11-12). Sadly, many Christians have become so preoccupied with escaping from this world that they no longer are effective communicators to their society. They have forgotten the words of Martin Luther, who when asked about what he would do if he knew that Jesus were coming back tomorrow, replied, "I'd plant an apple tree today."

FOCUS NUMBER TWO: CONSPIRACY THEORIES

Most Americans love a good conspiracy theory, as the recurring debates over the Kennedy assassination remind us. That is because sensational conspiracies are more interesting and offer simplistic resolutions to the complex problems of life. Why should we be surprised, then, that conspiracy theories would be preferred in Christian circles as well?

A major foil for Christian conspiracies came during the late seventies with the secular humanist scare. Do these charges sound familiar? *Those secular humanists took such things as prayer out of our schools, foisting evolutionary teaching on our children. The humanists are behind the immorality that is rampantly sweeping across America.* Christians of an earlier era, undergirded by the doctrine of total depravity, would have attributed immorality to the character of every fallen human being, including Christians themselves. But the new theorists are convinced that Americans are basically good people who have had their institutions stolen from them by a significant minority of intellectuals, artists, and members of the media. It is the secular humanists who have championed pornography, adultery, and sex-education in our schools, it is said. Some conspiracy theories even imply that our major network news anchors are conspirators in a plot to promote unchristian attitudes and perspectives in the general public to prepare the way for the rise of Antichrist.

Again and again, we seem to be blaming the world instead of taking a cold, hard look at our own failures as a church. Must the lack of Christian influence in the arts, for instance, be put to the charge of a group of hostile conspirators? Or is it more the case that we have abandoned the arts because we thought they weren't worth the time since Jesus was coming soon? Are we to blame educators for the predominance of secular outlooks and attitudes in the university, or ought we rather to blame ourselves for fostering an anti-intellectualism that took us out of leadership in that arena in the first place?

Economic hard times and uncertainty brought about by the struggle between international banking interests and third world debt spawned Mary Stewart Relfe's *When Your Money Fails*. Constance Cumby saw the same kinds of international tensions as a New Age conspiracy, now bent on world domination. Satan's tentacles were everywhere, his demons responsible for every crisis, and we became more paranoid, more afraid and distrustful of the world around us.

The effects of the conspiracy theories and their distinctly American slant on things is perhaps best illustrated by Dave Hunt's best-seller, *The Seduction of Christianity*. Dave Hunt did a great service for the Christian church in what amounted to a tremendous act of personal courage. He took some very popular and successful ministries and ministers to task for unorthodox teaching, and that is to be commended. The problem, however, with much of Dave Hunt's work, including *Seduction,* is that woven throughout his research into various doctrinal errors is a recurring satanic conspiracy motif. That motif only serves to detract from the overall research and general impact of the book the reader looking for a serious theological critique. There is an unfortunate tendency in Hunt to respond with a sensational flair to those he opposes. That is what the American audience wants and has come to expect. One gets the feeling while reading the book that lying under every psychiatrist's couch are a legion of demons ready to pounce on any unsuspecting patient. Here again, we find an almost irrational and superstitious fear of the world, evidenced in overt hostility to several legitimate disciplines.

In much of this genre, it is not merely poor education that is held suspect, but education in general; not merely questionable art and entertainment, but art and entertainment in general; not only the narcissism of a therapeutic society and the theories it spawns, but psychology of any kind is seen as part of an end-time demonic conspiracy. Christian thinkers such as Francis Schaeffer called attention to such concerns but took the time to understand the positions instead of finding a bogeyman. Perhaps that is why *Seduction* sold far more widely than anything Francis Schaeffer ever wrote.

Clearheadedness and sober scholarship characterized polemics of the previous generation, such as *Christianity and Liberalism,* by J. Gresham Machen, the evangelical Presbyterian theologian who broke away from Princeton on the grounds of its liberalism. Walter Lippman, an outspoken critic of Christianity, nevertheless credited the orthodox Machen with the most cogent arguments in the debate. In this classic, Machen warned the church in the thirties of what is now known as Protestant liberalism. Though the book is dated, there is nothing in it that would embarrass Machen if he were return to read the manuscript today. One finds no conspiracy theories linking liberalism to an end-times scenario or a plot to overthrow orthodoxy. Machen realized that his rivals were, like he, men with powerful arguments and moved by genuine passion for what they believed to be true. They were simply wrong, and quite seriously so. Machen saw his task as that of establishing his case for that conclusion.

There is no doubt that Satan, the master of lies, is behind all heresy. Nevertheless, for those with prophetic-conspiracy theories the unifying factor is not the character of the heresy itself so much as the setting of the stage for Antichrist. Satan has probably never been given more free publicity than he has by us at the end of the twentieth century. Can it be possible that we are even, inadvertently of course, contributing to an unnatural interest in the occult? That is a distinct possibility. There is a fine line between love and hate. Both are an obsession.

FOCUS NUMBER THREE: SPIRITUAL WARFARE

Other chapters in this book deal with the signs and wonders movement, so I will pass over any discussion of that genre of popular literature. Instead, I will focus on the fiction side of that preoccupation.

The huge popularity of Frank Peretti's *This Present Darkness* and its sequel, *Piercing the Darkness,* reveals a sense of uneasiness and fear of the world in what I consider a disturbing trend.[7] Whereas Peretti endeavored to produce a fictional account of the supernatural warfare revealed in the Scriptures, many Christians who lack basic theological and biblical training have ended up reading Peretti's fiction as though it were systematic theology. Because the intended audience is sometimes ill-informed about the purpose of the genre of fiction and the reasons for telling a compelling story simply to entertain, many who read Peretti's fictional account of spiritual warfare possess little ability to discern between truth and fiction. People have, in many cases, actually redefined their entire worldview based upon a novel, instead of developing a view of the supernatural from the clear *nonfictional* teaching of Scripture.

The result of Peretti's success is that a host of similar books have followed in its wake, many of those less than sound in content. Cumulatively, that has produced a new generation of Christians who are beginning to see the world through a grid that has more in common with Greek and Persian mystery religions than with Christianity.[8] Since many evangelicals no longer view the world around them as Protestants historically have—through the doctrines of creation, the Fall, and redemption—there is no doctrine of original sin left from which to form the category necessary for making sense of evil and suffering. Consequently, we shift to a metaphysical war between the good God and His angels and the bad god and his demons. The problem is no longer viewed as being the inherent sinfulness residing within the shadowy darkness of my own human heart and the resulting rebellion against God and His Word. Instead, the problem is outside of me—conspiracies, secular humanists, demons. There is suffering and evil in the world because of the presence of demons, not because I, too, along with all of my fellow human beings, am guilty with Adam for rebelling against God. Indeed, suffering can never be considered good in this scenario because it is the sign of the demons getting the upper hand, whereas in biblical religion "we also rejoice in our sufferings" (Romans 5:3) because they are part of God's plan for our growth.

Instead of seeing the world as portrayed in the creation account—as "very good"—the model put forward by this view sees the world as merely incidental to the ultimate reality—the spiritual realm. This world, then, is not so much a realm in which God becomes flesh and crushes Satan's head at the cross and in His resurrection claims victory, but an arena of combat where we decide whether the good God or the bad god wins. Spiritual warfare is the dominant model, but the weapons supplied are not the ones called for in the Scripture. In Ephesians 6 the weapons for spiritual warfare are the written Word of God and the knowledge of our justification in Christ. We are nowhere called upon to engage in spiritual warfare as a combat between angels and demons.

Those who see reality exclusively through the lens of warfare between angels and demons will inevitably read the turmoils of life as proof of a struggle between those spiritual combatants. People in the culture around us are looking for answers to the great questions of life in the "spiritual" dimension. Yet many evangelicals are preparing for the wrong kind of warfare. They are being told they should be looking for demons to cast out if they wish to be victorious Christians and liberate our society.

If you think that statement is a bit strained, a recent gathering of noted evangelical and charismatic leaders has begun conducting "spiritual warfare" sessions in which they attempt to bind the demon princes of specific geographical areas. Although there are many Christians who have not abandoned the inner cities, for many in the spiritual warfare crowd even the solution to street crime, drugs, and prostitution is to be found in taking authority over the demonic forces that control a particular geographical area. The superstitious character of all this was pointed out by one of my seminary professors, who cynically remarked, "So what if they bind the demon prince of Pasadena; he just moves his operations over to Duarte"(a neighboring city).

So once again the world watches and shakes its head—not because our gospel is a stumbling block, but because *we* are! And this "devil made me do it" theology will never give them the biblical sense of personal responsibility for sin necessary if they are to understand the meaning of the gospel message. Worse yet, this worldview has more in common with animistic paganism than with biblical Christianity.

FOCUS NUMBER FOUR: THE NEW AGE MOVEMENT

A further bit of confusion results as the church takes a legitimate stand against the influx of the various New Age ideologies.

When one of the networks runs a Shirley MacLaine propaganda film, we rise up in protest, but when one of our own Christian networks runs the same theology daily we protect it.[9] On secular talk shows Christians pop up from time to time to talk about the rise of the occult, another sensational TV topic. But Kenneth Copeland teaches that "Jesus accepted the sin nature of Satan in His own spirit" and "made Himself obedient to the Lordship of Satan at the cross,"[10] assertions not too different from the New Age dogma that humans can be divine. Even when we confront the New Age movement in the secular arena, it often looks as though we have more in common than we think; it's just that we're on the "good side" of the force. And many non-Christian viewers simply walk away from the show thinking we're *both* kooks.

CONCLUSION

From my reading of Scripture, the best method of binding Satan is still the preaching of the gospel (Luke 10:18; Revelation 20:1-3). And although no one who takes the Scriptures seriously can deny the reality of the demonic, there can be little doubt that the great interest in the types of books I have been discussing reveals how uneasy evangelicals are about the world around them. That is clearly demonstrated by the fact that many new Christians know more about the apocalyptic figures in the book of Revelation than they do about Christ Himself. Books about end-times conspiracies outsell books about Christ's Person and work. Peretti's book languished on the shelves until it was "discovered" by a Christian celebrity who recommended it at concerts. The fantasy classics of C. S. Lewis, the Chronicles of Narnia and the Space Trilogy, have not, to my knowledge, seen any increase in sales, as they do not reflect this uneasiness with the world. The one Lewis book that has experienced a renaissance of sorts is *The Screwtape Letters,* which is Lewis's fictional account of a senior devil giving instructions in deception to a junior devil.

Certainly Frank Peretti is not to blame for the current preoccupation. He simply produced an entertaining novel. But there can be no doubt that the success of *This Present Darkness* and the rise of a whole genre of "spiritual warfare" fiction and nonfiction betrays an underlying confusion. The most pressing present darkness is that night into which the evangelical church, along with an increasingly antirational culture, will descend unless evangelicals stop singing, "I can't feel at home in this world anymore."

NOTES

1. These are published on a monthly basis in several trade publications, including *Christian Retailing* and *Bookstore Journal.*

2. As documented in Michael Horton, ed., *The Agony of Deceit* (Chicago: Moody, 1990).

3. Philip Gold, "Getting the Word to a Mass Market," *Insight* 6, no. 51 (December 17, 1990), p. 42.

4. Ibid., p. 42.

5. See Kenneth A. Myers's excellent critique of popular culture in *All God's Children and Blue Suede Shoes: Christians and Popular Culture* (Westchester, Ill.: Crossway, 1989).

6. One recent book goes so far as to argue that Jesus is telling us the exact opposite, that we can know the day and the hour. See Colin Deal, *The Day and the Hour That Jesus Will Return* (n.p.: 1989). This book is distributed by the same prophetic ministry that produced the now infamous *88 Reasons Why the Rapture Will Be in 1988,* by Edgar Whisenant.

7. According to the publisher's advertisements, these two books have sold more than 1.5 million copies as of July 1, 1991.

8. As documented in Horton, ed., *Agony of Deceit.*

9. Ibid.

10. Kenneth Copeland, "What Happened from the Cross to the Throne," tape, side 2, on file with Christian Research Institute (CRI); quoted in Horton, ed., *Agony of Deceit,* pp. 117, 273-74.

12

The Comfort of Conservatism

J. I. Packer

Arose by any other name, we are told, would smell as sweet; and by the same token, mud by any other name would smell just as bad. When evangelicals call themselves conservative, is there anything more to their conservatism than barren, blind traditionalism? Many of our critics think not, and if they are right we are in trouble, for mere traditionalism is a legalistic thing that kills; it does not give life, nor does it give hope for the future. The aim of this chapter is to explore ways in which that kind of traditionalism (or conservatism) can quench the Holy Spirit and cause paralysis and impotence in the church. "Tradition and Tyranny" is the title I might have come up with, had I been asked for one. But "The Comfort of Conservatism" was handed to me, so to speak, on a plate, and I take off my hat to the person who thought of it; its poker-faced ambivalence captures most effectively the elements of the problem.

That ambivalence springs from the fact that *comfort* and *conservatism* are two-tone words. Both carry two distinct sets of associations that contrast sharply with each other, and there is no better way to begin our quest than by spelling these out.

J. I. PACKER is Sangwoo Youtong Chee Professor of Theology at Regent College in Vancouver, British Columbia.

COMFORT

First, take *comfort*. (That, by the way, is not intended to be a joke.) Here is a word that is both noun and verb. The verb, which is primary, comes from the Latin *confortare*, meaning "to make strong" in the sense of imparting energy and resolve so that one stands firm and shows enterprise under pressure. The Bayeux Tapestry captions its picture of King Harold telling some glum Englishmen to fight hard in the battle of Hastings with the statement that in this way he "comforts" (*confortat*) his troops. In the King James Bible, *comfort* regularly renders words that carry this sense of invigoration and renewal of strength. We may call this the comfort of the cordial: it is tone one.

But in ordinary speech today *comfort* suggests rather the providing of support that lets people relax and flop physically, or the expression of sympathy that soothes distress and leaves people feeling easier in their minds. That we may call the comfort of the cushion: in the short term, and sometimes in the long term also, it enervates instead of invigorating: and it is tone two.

CONSERVATISM

Now take *conservatism*. A relatively modern word, with a sociopolitical focus, conservatism also has two tones or meanings, each determined by usage.

One sort of conservatism is a heroic resolve to preserve whatever in one's heritage one sees to be truly valuable: to hold on to it and defend it, come what may, and to call back to it those in the community who are drifting or have drifted from it and may indeed be actively undermining it. Such conservatism calls for a responsible use of one's intelligence and critical judgment and also for the courage to swim against the cultural tide where necessary, in order to safeguard what is right and precious. That sort of conservatism—creative conservatism as I venture to call it—may prove to be the most radical, realistic, hard-thinking, forward-looking, and stimulating option that the marketplace of ideas has to offer. Such is tone-one conservatism.

The other sort of conservatism, however, is a blind, stubborn, "Archie Bunkerish" adherence to what is old and conventional just because it is old and conventional, a knee-jerk reaction of the mind expressing nothing more respectable or responsible than prejudices that one refuses to examine. Jesus noted that no one, after drinking old wine, wants the new, "for he says, 'The old is better'" (Luke 5:39). He was exposing the psychology of that kind of conservatism, namely, a wish to be soothed and massaged and made to feel easy by a constant flow of the familiar. Such is conservatism, tone two: a nostalgic syndrome that buries its head with regard to the future and seeks only to hang on to the past. I label that, in King James language, "carnal conservatism," since the inertia of mind at its heart is flesh-fed, just as it is flesh-pleasing. Both sorts of conservatism exist: the first is praiseworthy and the second pathetic; the first is sometimes mistaken for the second, and the second sometimes kids itself into thinking it is really the first.

THE COMFORT OF CONSERVATISM

I ask my readers now to observe that in my title, both nouns are being used in their two-tone significance, and what I invite them to reflect on is the following pair of facts: (1) that backward-looking fixity, whether demanded by leaders or sought by followers, or both, can of itself make people feel good, safe, and wise; (2) that those feelings can in turn prompt people to gang up in order to impose the same fixity on others, in the belief that such action renders its recipients the truest service. That can happen either with historical movements and figures or with established codes of conduct. Although the people in charge admit that their denominational distinctives, favorite Bible teacher, institutions, and behavioral standards may not have behind them *direct* biblical command, they often insist that in order to render fullest obedience to God we ought to surrender our own thought processes to those who have already made the difficult decisions for us. Peer pressure and group pressure are then exerted, and the persons who act as enforcers of the required conformity, whom I shall call "traditioners" (echoing the late great Sidney Bechet's habit of referring to New Orleans jazzmen as "musicianers"), become truly tyrannical.

In spite of their disdain for "the traditions of men," the insistence of many conservative Christians in demanding that adults accept traditions of faith and practice in the manner of children who are told to shut their eyes, open their mouths, and swallow whatever is tipped in is not a maturing thing; at best it leads to bigotry, at worst it leads to cultism. Let us remember that the mass-suicide in Jonestown in the seventies was the product of an extreme form of just the sort of religious conservatism I have here described.[1] Yet it is, as we shall see, no more, just as it is no less, than a good thing gone wrong, which makes it all the sadder. And in that connection I give notice, here and now, that in nailing the abuse of power that tyrannical traditionalism involves I shall not be making a brief for any of the modes of anarchy, indiscipline, creedal and doctrinal confusion, and moral chaos that also characterize large segments of the Christian world these days. On the contrary, it is my purpose before I am through to point out the genuine enrichment and vital necessity of Christian orthodoxy, responsibly received under authentic authority, and so to affirm the comfort of conservatism in a tone-one sense as one of the true secrets of a healthy Christian and a lively church.

THE NATURE OF THE CHRISTIAN TRADITION

I have already used the word *traditionalism* as a synonym for conservatism, and shall do so again in what follows. It is another two-tone word, as is the word *tradition* itself. In the church, as in the world, there are good and bad traditions, just as there is one sort of traditionalism that is blind and blinding and another sort that is wise and enlightening, and we need to be able to tell which is which. Earlier debates about this between Protestants, Roman Catholics, and Eastern Orthodox believers generated more heat than light, but in this century intensive study has yielded an account of tradition that focuses our understanding of its positive role.[2] The main points of that account are as follows.

Tradition characterizes communities. Nobody can claim to be detached from traditions. In fact, one sure way to be swallowed up by traditionalism is to think that one is immune to it. Very often,

286

those who despise tradition the most escape having to recognize the value of traditions by insisting that the humanly derived practice is Bible-based, even though they would be hard pressed to find chapter and verse. The greatest threat of traditionalism may not always come in the expected form of popes and extrabiblical ceremonies; very often the most dangerous form of traditionalism is the sort that refuses to affirm the positive role of history and community in shaping one's understanding, the sort that refuses to call traditions what they are and therefore refuses to hold them up to the standard of Scripture. Instead, their traditions become merely confused with Scripture, and that is a disaster.

In the church, as in other communities, tradition is best defined primarily as the handing-on process and then secondarily as the sum of what is handed on. Roman Catholic theology distinguishes explicitly between the process (*traditio tradens*) and the content (*traditio tradita*) of tradition. Within that perspective, the New Testament speaks of the handing on of both good (pastoral and apostolic) and bad (Pharisaic and philosophical) traditions (see Mark 7:5, 8-9, 13; 1 Corinthians 7:10; 11:2, 23-26; Colossians 2:6-10; 2 Thessalonians 2:15). In the church, the *process* of handing on tradition takes place through official church pronouncements, pastoral catechizing, preaching and teaching, the words and songs used in worship, the ethos of a particular congregation or denomination, the printed materials and media resources, and personal interchanges between Christian people. All the church's opinion-making organs are involved, and the process goes on all the time. If you think evangelicals are immune to it, think again. We have developed our own in-house language ("Christianese," as it has been called), music styles, favorite books and tapes, and we have even created unique traditions in the way we communicate the Christian message. (Some who scorn tradition would hardly consider it a day at church or a proper evangelistic meeting without an "altar call," and yet that is a tradition invented by Charles Finney in the middle of the last century.) The question, then, is not whether we *have* traditions, but whether our traditions conflict with the only absolute standard in these matters: Holy Scripture.

Traditions began as contemporary ventures. What are now the traditions of the churches began as contemporary ventures in exegeting, expounding, and applying biblical truths, and should be understood as such. Tradition should be viewed as yesterday's church giving today's church a lead in matters of belief and behavior, a lead that is offered as being Bible-based and wise. Within that approach, and on the basis of a common awareness that both the Spirit of God and human sin are always at work in the church, Christian traditions may be expected to be partly correct and partly in error. However, specific differences do appear with regard to the authority of these traditions.

The Roman Catholic and Orthodox churches, on the one hand, claim that particular bits of the totality of tradition are infallible guides to faith and life; but whereas Rome places in this category all doctrines defined by councils in communion with the pope, and by popes speaking ex cathedra (i.e., in their role as teachers of all of Christendom), Orthodoxy limits infallibility to the definitions of the seven ecumenical councils that met before the East and West divided in 1054. It was long supposed that the fourteenth-century notion that the Western church was entrusted with oral traditions supplementing Scripture was defined as true by the Counter-Reformation Council of Trent, but that is now seen not to be so; the idea is only a permitted speculation, which few Roman Catholic teachers today would endorse.[3]

Mainstream Protestantism, on the other hand, while affirming the infallibility of Scripture as God's inerrant word of instruction, denies that any part of the church's expository tradition is infallible. Receiving it as a help to understanding the Bible, Protestantism tests tradition by the Bible and sets it under biblical authority. The principle here is that infallible Scripture itself, rather than supposedly infallible tradition, interprets infallible Scripture. The Bible is not an obscure book. What is unclear in one passage can regularly be sorted out by referring to other, more explicit texts, and on all major matters, biblical teaching proves to be both clear and sufficient. Therefore, Scripture must have the last word on all human attempts to state its meaning, and tradition, viewed as a series of such human attempts, has a ministerial rather than a magisterial role. In other words, tradition allows us to stand on the shoulders of the many giants who have thought about Scripture before us. We can gather from the consensus of the greatest and widest body of Christian thinkers from the early Fathers to the present an invaluable resource for understanding the Bible responsibly. Nevertheless, those interpretations (traditions) are never final; they need always to be submitted to Scripture for further review.

Here, too, a spectrum of opinion opens up. At one extreme are thinkers who make much of tradition as wisdom from the Holy Spirit (often focusing on one or two periods as the "golden age"), to such an extent that Scripture is forced to play a supporting role. At the other extreme are those who deeply suspect tradition as embodying the sinfulness and worldliness of the church rather than its wisdom, to the extent that this or that new movement comes to be represented as a restoration of the church—that is, a refounding of it—out of a state of hopeless corruption. Such groups represent their community as simply recovering New Testament Christianity, refusing to be polluted with "man-made traditions." Between these extremes there are intermediate positions. But the varying assessments of a particular tradition's worth are all based on agreement that the role of tradition is ministerial and not that of an absolute or infallible authority.

Christians benefit from and are the victims of tradition. All Christians are at once beneficiaries and victims of tradition—beneficiaries, who receive nurturing truth and wisdom from God's faithfulness in past generations; victims, who now take for granted things that need to be questioned, thus treating as divine absolutes patterns of belief and behavior that should be seen as human, provisional, and relative. We are all beneficiaries of good, wise, and sound tradition and victims of poor, unwise, and unsound traditions. This is where the absolute "last word" of Scripture must sort the wheat from the chaff. Hence, the apostle Paul's counsel: "Test everything. Hold on to the good" (1 Thessalonians 5:21).

There is, however, nothing ungodly about being shaped, formed, influenced, and guided in our reflection by tradition. Learning from God "with all the saints" (Ephesians 3:18), in a relation of fellowship, is part of the divine purpose, and being helped by the Christian past to understand and know God in the present is merely the historical dimension of that purpose. In fact, the *ungodly* approach would be to try to learn from God as a spiritual lone ranger who has proudly or impatiently turned his back on the church and its heritage: that would be a surefire recipe for weirdness without end!

What we must do, rather, is acknowledge that we are frail children of tradition, good or bad, to a much greater extent than we realize, and must learn to ask by the light of Scripture critical questions about what we have thus far taken for granted. Testing everything by Scripture, while holding on to the good, as Paul commanded, is in fact a life's work, and it is a vitally important habit for us to follow. The only alternative is to be enslaved to human tradition in practice, treating it as if it had divine authority, just as the Pharisees did before us. Whereas it would be most unwise to disregard the accepted beliefs and practices of our community, it would be equally irresponsible to adopt the same with blind devotion. We must never embrace the sentiment that says, "I'm just a layman, and no theologian. I go to church and listen to the preacher and him I believe." That, by the way, is a direct echo of Martin Luther's warning to those who had settled for "implicit faith"—that is, a faith that takes the church's word for things in unquestioning obedience.

It cannot be said too often that to believe and to do what is acceptable in a particular community just because it is acceptable, and without regard to whether it is biblically warranted, is not Christianity.

Secular and religious traditions of the world oppose and corrupt Christian tradition. Christian tradition, offered as elucidation and application of Scripture in subjection to its corrective judgment, faces constant opposition from the secular and religious traditions of the world, which again and again corrupt it. Detecting and countering inauthentic infiltrations of that kind is a permanent task of the church and of the individual Christian. The Reformation slogan, *ecclesia reformata semper reformanda* ("the church that has been reformed has always to be reformed"), expresses proper awareness of that fact. As the church's ongoing battle to maintain the truth of God is one of methodology and ideology, so it is also one of warring traditions: and it never ends this side of Paradise.

THE BENEFITS OF THE CHRISTIAN TRADITION

Partly through ignorance of its breadth and wealth, partly through vehemence against the idea of its infallibility, and partly through absolutizing some features of their own heritage, as we shall see, evangelicals often fail to profit from tradition as they might. A full response to this negativism cannot be made here, but it is worth being specific, however briefly, about four particular benefits that knowledge of tradition can bring.

Roots. First, by knowing tradition the Christian discovers *roots.* That one can draw vision, inspiration, and a satisfying sense of identity from discovering one's origins and appreciating the family out of which one sprang has become a commonplace of our time. A soldier who learns of the past prowess of his regiment knows what he has to live up to, and identifying with its established ideals gives him a sense of personal identity and vocation that he did not have before. When one knows something of the goals and achievements that have distinguished the family of God on earth for nearly two thousand years, the effect is similar. In the contemporary church there is much with which evangelicals can never identify, and from which they cannot but feel alienated; the follies of today's Christians are not, however, the whole story, and conscious solidarity with the stronger, wiser, braver church of the past remains a vast enrichment.

Realism. Second, by knowing tradition the Christian gains *realism.* Knowledge of the past gives a vantage point for assessing the present and frees one from an otherwise inescapable imprisonment in the mind-set and culture of one's own age. There is a sense in which you cannot see any aspect of your own time, however hard you look at it, until you can stand outside your period and measure it by standards that are not part of it. Knowledge of the Christian tradition down the centuries and across cultures imparts that ability in relation to all matters of present-day Christian concern. Although we can never be absolutely objective, testing our contemporary presuppositions by those of other ages can help us toward that goal.

291

Resources. Third, by knowing tradition the Christian acquires *resources*. He or she walks with the giants and gains from the past deeper wisdom than our present-day peers can offer. No age shows equal insight into all spiritual truths and all facets of godliness, but the explorer of tradition finds the wisdom of every age opening up for him to draw on. He sees how the intellectual and moral errors of Christians today were confronted when they arose yesterday, as most of them did. He learns more about the possibilities of the Christian life and the power of the Christian hope than our own pygmy era can teach him. That modern Western culture impoverishes itself by not fostering a sense of history is too plain to be denied, but there is no reason Christians should follow suit, and every reason they should not.

Reminders. Fourth, by knowing tradition the Christian receives *reminders*. In the Old Testament story God often diagnoses His people's present failures to live up to their covenant commitments as due to their not remembering the goodness and severity of His dealings with them in the past, and similar reminders are often in order in the Christian fellowship. To have some knowledge of how the church has in the past incurred God's chastening judgments through barren euphoria, somnolent stagnation, blithe triumphalism, and moral and spiritual corruption, and how by contrast it has found His blessing through fidelity, humility, boldness, and wholeheartedness is most salutary, by reason of the searching admonitions that those facts yield. It has been said, too, that those who will not learn from history are doomed to repeat it, and that is as ominous a warning to Christian people as to any others.

THE CHRISTIAN TRADITION ABUSED

Having come to appreciate the value of knowing our heritage of faith and life, we are now in a better position to understand the false comfort that carnal conservatism imparts and to take the measure of the particular form of tyranny that it begets.

Here, then, is a diagnosis of what seems to go wrong. It is purposely couched in formal and structural rather than in specific and personal terms. My interest is in the size and shape of the cap, rather than in whom it fits or whether anyone is actually wearing it at present. I leave it to my readers to judge for themselves whether carnal conservatism grows anywhere in their backyard: that, after all, is their concern, not mine.

The source of the trouble is the absolutizing of formulations and fashions that are human, not divine, and, because human, provisional and open to change. Carnal conservatism treats those traditions as if they come straight from God and are therefore sacrosanct, and traditioners in leadership roles enforce them as if on that basis. The traditions thus become sacred cows, before which all are required to bow down and show reverence. Tyrannical pressures are put on people to make them do that, and if they really want to fit in, or even remain, in this "uniquely spiritual" community, they will conform. In the circles where that is done, interests are selective and few, minds are narrow and wary, and knowledge of the larger Christian tradition as a whole, as distinct from the improperly highlighted items, is near to nonexistent. But to some the very rigidity of this culture-defying traditionalism ("we stick to the old-time religion") makes an appeal: they see it as faithfulness to Christ and are sure that He approves and blesses it, or else it could not sustain itself. So they wheel into line behind the traditioners, admiring them for their bold eccentricity and orneriness, and venerate them as if they were God (which is not perhaps too surprising, in view of the authoritarian way they sometimes speak). That combination—peremptory leadership, legalistic group distinctives that members receive as from God and as defining their own identity, community conformity, hostile and condescending criticism of others outside the group, and confidence that they alone constitute Christ's faithful remnant— borders on the cultic. Edward John Carnell gave great offense a generation ago when he described American fundamentalism as evangelicalism gone cultic.[4] Whether we agree with his censure, then or now, we can see what he meant.

Samples of that syndrome are not hard to find. There are, for instance, those for whom only the King James Version is the Bible; those for whom only the Anglican Book of Common Prayer is a vehicle of worship; those for whom only hymns in the style of Watts and Wesley, or perhaps Ira D. Sankey, or maybe, more recently, the Gaithers or other praise song writers, are fit to be sung in worship.

The five points of Calvinism, which I myself affirm, can be a cause of strife rather than comfort and assurance. Such doctrines as the secret rapture and particular views of end times become ties that bind over and above the essentials of the gospel.

Then, at a deeper level, there is the magic-word mentality, which insists that revealed truths can only be affirmed by using particular familiar words for them. Logicians and theologians know that no single verbal formula is necessary for expressing a particular truth, as long as the point is made. Yet, agreed formulations always emerge as part of the in-talk of any purposeful group and become a jargon, functioning like shorthand, enabling communication of much in a short compass. That is fine in its place, but the fact remains that anything that is understood can be expressed in more ways than one, and if you cannot express it without using one particular, familiar formula or word, it is proof that you do not really understand the idea. In the recent discussions of biblical inerrancy, for instance, it appeared that some could not grasp that inerrancy might be affirmed without using that magic word for the purpose, and that others who maintained the full truth and trustworthiness of Scripture might choose to avoid the term because they thought it had unfortunate associations. There was no question as to which group understood inerrancy better! The magic-word mentality is a regular symptom of carnal conservatism, just as is the out-of-hand rejection of changing cultural and behavioral styles among Christian people.

Carnal conservatism can and does emerge as soon as a Christian group comes to value something in its tradition as God's ideal, and treats its own embrace of that item as integral to its testimony and its faithfulness to the Lord. It is observable that what a congregation has done (or, perhaps more to the point, *not* done) for a generation constantly becomes a focus for carnal conservatism as soon as a change is suggested. "We never did it that way before." "We would lose our Christian testimony if we allowed freedom in that area." One may sympathize, knowing how familiar patterns of church life give a sense of stability to older people who feel that our fast-changing world is leaving them behind; but at the same time one must grieve that any should look for their security in unchanging church structures rather than in their unchanging relationship through Christ to God, and should as a result greet all thoughts of change with a shocked negativism that can actually obstruct and quench the Holy Spirit.

Already we begin to see that carnal conservatism is a murky mix. There is in it an unwillingness to have one's landmarks of security removed; fear at the threatened loss of something valuable; a muddled but deeply felt loyalty to unquestioned routines that one sees as beneficial; and behind this, a love of power, in seeking to tell others that they need to fall into line instead of letting the people tell you that *you* are the one who needs to change. And behind this, again, is a sense that by the rigidity of one's religion one domesticates God and enlists Him on one's own side, so that one has Him in one's pocket, like a pet mouse. Carnal conservatism is an irreligious sort of piety that is all too widespread, and it is very weakening.

Nor does the absolutizing of a traditional feature have to wait a generation or two before a carnal conservatism builds around it. One example will demonstrate my point.

In what Britishers called the "swinging sixties," when all sorts of Western cultural inhibitions went to the wall, the charismatic movement, oriented to Spirit-baptism and tongues, burst forth in the older churches and spread like wildfire. Charismatics knew, of course, or at least half-knew, that God's faithful people had for centuries tasted His power and love without those particular distinctives, but that did not prevent an imperialistic carnal conservatism from crystallizing immediately around the distinctives. Consider the following indictment carefully:

> During the height of the charismatic movement in the seventies, I attended the "First International Conference on the Holy Spirit" in Jerusalem as a reporter. . . . Since I was not a charismatic, I became the object of much witnessing. People badgered me about speaking in tongues (there is no other way to describe it). One otherwise charming elderly woman told me that God had sent me to the conference just so that I would begin to speak in tongues. And there were others, not quite as charming, who upbraided me for not submitting to the Holy Spirit, for being proud and defensive. These people wanted power over my relationship with God. They used every spiritual tactic they could to shame, ha-

295

rass, embarrass, and propel me into an experience that was for them a mark of a Christian. These people were guilty of spiritual violence and thus of misplaced loyalty: The wrong God was in control.[5]

Cheryl Forbes wrote that paragraph to illustrate how piety can become a power play, and that is the only point she draws from her narrative. But it seems clear that the rest of the murky mix was there, too. I cite this example to illustrate a point, not to indict the entire movement. In fact, charismatics with whom I fraternize today would also find this behavior deplorable.

For leaders, we should note, a carnal conservatism context creates special temptations, for it gives them a role as traditioners that places great power in their hands. We know how pastors as a body love power across the board, and how the desire for total control factors into the decisions of nonpastors to form independent "ministries" of their own, in which they are not accountable to any authority. Now we should note that leaders who commit themselves to uphold as vital bits of the tradition what others have let go seem to their followers, for that very reason, to be persons of superior insight and are praised for "taking a stand." The possibilities of abusing one's power when one finds oneself on this pinnacle of veneration are enormous, and we should not be too surprised when we hear of traditioners of this type seeing themselves as above the law and coming moral croppers.

CREATIVE CONSERVATISM
AND THE CHRISTIAN TRADITION

It is a relief to move from diagnosis to cure, and that I now joyfully do. The cure for *carnal* conservatism (in addition to the priesthood of all believers, which I shall leave Alister McGrath to address in the next chapter) is *creative* conservatism. Creative conservatism uses tradition, not as a final authority or an absolute in any sense, but as an important resource, made available to us in God's providence, to help us grasp what Scripture is telling us about who God is, who we are, what the world around us is, and what we are called to do here and now. The real difficulty in making moral decisions lies in discerning the values involved: here tradition, which encapsulates in itself a vast amount of Christian argument, consensus, and experience, is always of great help. To tap into the great tradition of Christian conviction, contention, and counsel is to be nurtured in ways that present-day Christianity cannot come up to. Education in this heritage, on the basis that conscience is hereby schooled in its required captivity to the Word of God, is urgently needed in most evangelical churches today, and one can only hope that it will become a matter of priority concern over the next generation.

Honesty in self-criticism. What does the pursuit of creative Christian conservatism require of us? Three things, at least. The first is *honesty in self-criticism.* Socrates is reported to have said that the unexamined life is not worth living, and that is as true of mental as of moral life, and for Christians no less than for nonbelievers. Constant, searching assessment of the things we have taken for granted, so far as we are now aware of them, with a willingness to discover that we have been wrong and need to change, is the life-activity with which creative conservatism begins. Ironically, by understanding tradition we may be forced to reconsider our own more recent traditions. In that way, tradition can actually nudge us out of traditionalism. The appeal "We've never done it that way" can be easily countered by someone who points out, "Yes, but if millions of Christians through the centuries *have* done it that way, is it not possible that *you* are the one who has misunderstood Scripture on this point?"

Humility in private judgment. The second requirement is *humility in private judgment.* The Reformation is often misrepresented as having taught the *right* of private judgment of Scripture in terms of the Christian's being privileged to disagree with the church, the Bible, and every external authority if his heart moves him so to do. In fact, the Reformers taught the *duty* of private judgment, in the sense that no adult may take his or her faith secondhand, but all must accept the discipline of verifying from Scripture whether what they have been told is so. The Christian's conscience, as was said above, and as Luther memorably declared at Worms in 1521, is and must be subject to the Word of God—which means the teaching of Holy Scripture, which is God's own teaching about Himself and about us. Humility in private judgment means that one keeps searching the Scriptures until one is clear as to what God says, and that one forbids one's own proud intellect to close issues that the God of the Bible leaves open, or to jump to conclusions on matters about which Scripture does not speak, or to decline to take help in interpreting Scripture from Christian tradition, on the supposition that a godly Bible student gets on perfectly well without such help.

Integrity in moral action. The third requirement is *integrity in moral action:* that is, first and foremost, rejection of thoughtless conformity to the crowd, even the Christian crowd, as a way of living, and a self-imposed insistence on having biblically based reasons for the policy commitments and lines of actions to which one gives oneself. The standard of Christian integrity is Scripture, not what human wisdom legislates. Evangelicals are often justly warned of the peer pressure of an unbelieving world, but there is the more subtle danger of a negative type of Christian peer pressure known to us, and to many who have since left their evangelical upbringing, by the name "legalism." The *fruit* of integrity, faithfulness to one's beliefs, grows out of the *root* of integrity, thoughtfulness as to what those beliefs ought to be.

For churches to move beyond the false comfort of carnal conservatism in which so many evangelical groups are currently trapped to the true strength of creative conservatism would require nothing less than a renewal of Reformation faith, the cradle of evangelical Christianity. Though itself a self-conscious tradition, it not only respects its own past but also insists on continual self-reformation "according to the Word of God." If we do see such a renewal, unwarrantable claims to power will be seen for what they are, and the Word of God will rule, to the glory of the God whose Word it is.

"He who has an ear, let him hear what the Spirit says to the churches" (Revelation 2:7, 11, 17, 29; 3:6, 13, 22).

NOTES

1. On Jonestown, see Mel White, *Deceived* (Old Tappan, N.J.: Revell, 1979).

2. To explore this discussion, see D. T. Jenkins, *Tradition and the Spirit* (London: Faber, 1951); P. C. Rodger and L. Vischer, eds., *Report of the Fourth World Conference on Faith and Order* (London: SCM Press, 1964), pp. 50-60; F. F. Bruce, *Tradition Old and New* (Grand Rapids: Zondervan, 1970); C. O. Buchanan, E. L. Mascall, J. I. Packer, and Bishop of Willesden [G. D. Leonard], *Growing into Union* (London: SPCK, 1970), pp. 29-39; and the following Roman Catholic works: Vatican II, Constitution on Revelation (1964); G. Tavard, *Holy Writ or Holy Church* (New York: Harper, 1959); J. P. Mackey, *The Modern Theology of Tradition* (London: Darton, Longman & Todd, 1962); *Tradition and Change in the Church* (Dayton, Ohio: Pflaum, 1968); and the Protestant-Catholic symposium, ed. J. Callahan et al., *Christianity Divided* (London: Sheed & Ward, 1962), especially the articles by J. R. Geiselmann and Oscar Cullmann.

3. See Geiselmann in *Christianity Divided*.

4 E. J. Carnell, *The Case for Orthodox Theology* (Philadelphia: Westminster, 1962), p. 113.

5. Cheryl Forbes, *The Religion of Power* (Bromley: MARC Europe, 1986), p. 86.

13

A Better Way:
The Priesthood of All Believers

Alister E. McGrath

W ho has authority to speak on behalf of God? Who has the right to claim that he or she has privileged access to the mind and will of God? Who has the prerogative to tell others what God is like and what He wants of His people? Those questions, as we have seen, are fundamental. No Christian community can survive without agreement on those matters. All Christians can agree that it is vital to know the will of God for churches and individual believers, but who can tell us the will of God?

Throughout history, God has made available to us knowledge of Himself and of His will. Before the coming of Christ, God made His will known through the great Old Testament prophets (Hebrews 1:1). At the time of Christ, God spoke to us through His Son (vv. 1-4). But what of our own age? Who speaks for God today? Who has the authority to speak in the name of God to His people? Since "the word of the Lord" appears to be whatever this particular fashion in secular thinking or that particular charismatic preacher is decreeing, there appears to be a cacophony of disparate noises. It reminds us of the Lord's rebuke in Jeremiah 23:34-36:

ALISTER E. MCGRATH is lecturer in historical and systematic theology at Wycliffe Hall, Oxford, England, Brempton Lecturer at Oxford University, and Tipple Visiting Professor of Theology at Drew University, Madison, New Jersey.

If a prophet or priest or anyone else claims, "This is the oracle of the Lord," I will punish that man and his household. This is what each of you keeps on saying to his friend or relative: "What is the Lord's answer?" or "What has the Lord spoken?" But you must not mention "the oracle of the Lord" again, because every man's own word becomes his oracle and so you distort the words of the living God, the Lord Almighty, our God.

Who speaks for God today? Such authority would give a person, or group of people, the ultimate power—power over the lives, futures, and finances of the people of God who, wishing to obey their God, are desperately searching to know His will.

Speaking *for* God can easily degenerate into speaking *as* God. In much the same way, to speak *for* Jesus Christ can rapidly become a matter of speaking *as* Christ. Of course, we have seen this business in its most grotesque form in the so-called "Word-Faith Movement," which has stretched far beyond the shores of North America. In relating an alleged visitation he received from Jesus Christ, Kenneth Copeland, who claims to be an evangelical, reports that Jesus told him, "Don't be disturbed when people accuse you of thinking you're God. . . . They crucified me for claiming I was God."[1] One of the most disturbing tendencies in some of the more irresponsible leaders is a willingness to blur the vital distinction between the will of God and the will of the leader himself.

Copeland is thus able to place himself on the same plane as Jesus Christ, claiming the same divine authority for his actions. In this vision, Copeland hears Christ tell him, "I didn't claim that I was God; I just claimed I walked with him, and that he was in me. Hallelujah! That's what you're doing."[2] Notice the strategy: the uniqueness of Christ is denied. Christ was not God; He just walked closely with God—as, we are asked to believe, does Copeland. The essential distinction between Christ and Christians, so vital as a safeguard against irresponsible leadership and the more grotesque theological developments normally linked to the New Age movement, is denied. And for that reason, Copeland seems to think that he and Jesus Christ have just about the same authority for the believer. And as Jesus Christ does not make personal television appearances, get on the lecture tour circuit, or deliver personalized sermons, those who claim to have authority on a par with Him have a significant advantage over Him. Imagine having the same spiritual authority as Jesus Christ. Imagine having the same charismatic *power* as He. It's irresistible.

Benny Hinn, the author of the runaway best-seller *Good Morning Holy Spirit,* has this to say: "Are you ready for some *real* Revelation Knowledge? Now watch this. He laid aside His divine form. Now these are the seven steps from the glory to the cross. He laid aside His divine form. Why? So one day *I* would be clothed with the divine form."[3] Imagine the power of being able to give people "*real* Revelation Knowledge"! And to do that, he, like Copeland, is willing to alter the biblical and historic view of Christ and step in His place. "We are on the same level as the Son on earth," he adds. "Those who put us down are a bunch of morons. . . . Don't touch a man of God."[4]

That is true not only for those who claim a direct line to "Revelation Knowledge," but for those who demand obedience to their teaching or moral regulations with blind devotion. Very often one may ask a believer in some evangelical circles what he or she believes on a particular point. Then one asks the person why or how he or she came to that conclusion. "Well, that's what Pastor So-and-So says the Bible teaches" is all too frequently the response. Like the medieval Christians, we are all too willing in our day to let the "professionals" do our thinking for us.

The *power trip* connected with this authority is precisely the point made by Max Weber in his famous essay "The Sociology of Charismatic Authority."[5] At a time when traditional power structures seem to be in decline or confusion, people are disposed to seeking authority elsewhere. Where society appears confused concerning its own moral values or where traditional academic institutions seem muddled over questions of truth, people will look for—and find—those who speak with a clear voice and offer them crisp, neat, and authoritative solutions. Power evangelicalism owes some of that power to its force of conviction: perhaps not so much to the *views* that are held or to the *doctrines* that are preached, but to the *conviction* and *authority* which they are held and preached.

There is a vitally important lesson here for the denominations of mainline Protestantism, who are losing members in droves on account of the failure to preach a clear gospel with conviction, or to take the lead in providing moral direction. But there is also a vitally important lesson for power evangelicalism itself. It needs to realize that its power and appeal may rest upon human qualities rather than upon the gospel itself. The force of conviction is not an adequate criterion of truth. One can be forcefully, as well as sincerely, wrong. The appeal to subjective experiences of God, to personal visions, to esoteric and unverifiable words of knowledge, and for forceful, but unsubstantiated, convictions is as powerful as it is dangerous. Power evangelicalism de-emphasizes the objective means by which those revelations and visions may be checked against some criterion available to the general public, namely, the Scriptures. The virtual marginalization of Scripture within certain types of evangelicalism today (including within groups adhering to an official inerrancy position) is one of the greatest scandals of our age.

WHY MODERN EVANGELICALISM IS
ESPECIALLY PRONE TO THE POWER TEMPTATION

Sadly, we are reminded that we live in a sinful world. Human nature, the height of God's glorious creation, is fallen. What God created "good" has, through sin, become frail and weak, vulnerable to temptation and pride. And what is the most fundamental sin of all? What is the *original sin* of Genesis 3? It was the desire to be like God, and the shadow of the sin still hovers over the people of God. Even though we have been redeemed from the penalty of sin, we have yet to be completely liberated from its power and presence.

I remember once reading Betty McDonald's *The Plague and I,* which superbly evokes the atmosphere of a sanatorium for long-term patients. Having discovered that she is ill, McDonald is admitted. Eventually, she makes a full recovery, but it takes a long time. It isn't as if she is ill one day and the next day has recovered. The patient gradually moves from a position that could be described as "ill" to one that could be described as "well." The symptoms of illness do not suddenly vanish. They persist. But their pattern changes. They become less frequent and less intense. But they never entirely disappear. Someone who has had malaria knows only too well how its symptoms can reappear, even though they have been "cured."

Sin is a symptom of our old and unredeemed human nature. It is characteristic of the sinful human tendency to trust in ourselves. What Christ achieved through the cross and resurrection secured the redemption and transformation of our wounded and sinful nature. But even as we are being healed by grace, the symptoms of our illness persist. We remain sinners. The power of sin is waning, but it is still there. Christ was sinless; Christians are being redeemed from sin. But it remains within us, a hostile and threatening force, which continually threatens to break into and disrupt our lives as believers.

Granted, that is not the sort of "positive thinking" our culture demands, but it is essential if we are to know our own ongoing temptations to take the power trip.

The writings of the Puritans are steeped in that realistic attitude toward sin. The Christian life is seen, rightly, as a continuing struggle against the reality of sin. But some modern preachers seem able to deny the continuing reality of sin within believers. They are not satisfied with declaring that the penalty of sin has been paid for once and for all at the cross. Its *power* has been decisively broken, and its *presence* removed from believers: that is the way it is often presented. Through the power of the Spirit, they tell us, we can live a life free from sin.

That is a second-rate gospel, which denies the power of sin and so cheapens the glory of what God did through Christ. Sin is here portrayed as a puny enemy, easily defeated. But in reality, as the New Testament makes clear, it is a powerful and abiding presence within believers. We need to remind ourselves that it was to Christians that John wrote those telling words: "If we claim to be without sin, we deceive ourselves and the truth is not in us" (1 John 1:8). Christians, whether young or old, pastors or laypeople, teachers or those who are taught, are prone to temptation and to actual sin.

Why have I been stressing the reality of sin? Partly because I believe that vast tracts of modern North American evangelicalism have become so obsessed with the idea of the power of the Spirit that they have neglected the other side of the coin—the continuing presence and power of sin in believers. Power evangelicalism often seems to pretend, with phrases such as "the victorious Christian life," that it has disposed of the problem of sin, whereas in reality it has failed to grasp how serious the problem is in the first place. Take Robert

Schuller's declaration that "once a person believes that he is an 'unworthy sinner,' it is doubtful if he can really honestly accept the saving grace God offers in Jesus Christ."[6] Could there be a more obvious case of a person's failing to grasp the nature, reality, and sheer *seriousness* of sin? Or the wonder of grace, which is offered to those who realize that they are indeed, despite the reassuring platitudes of power evangelicalism, really sinners, worthy of divine condemnation?

But my main concern here is that that form of evangelicalism has failed to grasp how its approach to Christian leadership makes it *especially* vulnerable to temptation.

THE CULT OF PERSONALITY

The rise of televangelism and preaching ministries has led to a growing cult of personality within power evangelism. That is true not only of media ministries but also of those rounds that Christian celebrities regularly make to their appointed megachurch destinations. It is not what the Scriptures teach that really matters, but what this celebrity has to share with me about his or her experience or insights. Even for some of the pastors, it is not what Scripture says, but what the preachers say that Scripture says, that is really important. Often, Scripture is ignored altogether: it is what God is saying directly and personally to this preacher that counts. But how can we check out his message? How can we be certain that he is speaking in the name of the Lord and not simply claiming a totally spurious divine authority for his own ideas? Let us remind ourselves that the original sin is to wish to be like God.

I am not suggesting that every preacher within the tradition of what we are calling *power evangelicalism* is deluded or is indulging in some kind of ego-trip. Rather, I *am* suggesting that the emphasis laid upon individual preaching and prophetic ministry is vulnerable to sinful human exploitation. Deep within us, our old sinful desires call us back to ourselves and remain unconquered realms of grace. Power evangelicalism is fatally vulnerable at that point. Why? Because it encourages both preachers and their congregations to *expect* some individuals to be able to declare, with a degree of infallibility that would be the envy of any modern pope, exactly what is the will of God for His people.

How can this difficulty be resolved? How can we acknowledge the reality of human sin, with all of its attending dangers and temptations, while at the same time maintaining that it is possible to know God's will? How can we uphold the idea of prophetic ministry and preaching while safeguarding our people from being misled or exploited? In short: How can we recover a *responsible* attitude toward ministry? Happily, an answer lies to hand in the writings of the sixteenth-century reformers. Let us listen to them, and learn of a better way.

THE REFORMATION

There are remarkable, and disturbing, parallels between the distorted idea of priesthood in the medieval church and the notion of ministry found within modern power evangelicalism. Both are intensely authoritarian. Both rest upon an ideology of power, which places the right to speak for God in the hands of a small and unaccountable elite. Both studiously ignore the possibility that they might get God wrong, and the deeply threatening and humiliating possibility that God might choose to challenge and correct them through ordinary lay folk within their undervalued congregations.

At the dawn of the Reformation the Reformers posed a powerful and biblical challenge to that distorted idea of priesthood. The name given to their challenge has passed into history—"the priesthood of all believers." We badly need to recover that doctrine and explore its consequences. For the simple fact of the matter is that modern evangelicalism badly needs the same kind of clean-up that the Reformers brought to the late medieval church. Astonishing though it may seem, the bad old ways of the pre-Reformation church have surfaced again, even among those who claim to be evangelical. Even someone such as Robert Schuller, who calls for a New Reformation, merely perpetuates the delusions and distortions of unreformed Christendom.[7]

And if evangelicalism has lapsed into pre-Reformational ways of thinking, it needs to be confronted once more with the ideas of the Reformers, which they recovered from Scripture. Why? Because in the first place, we need to see how far modern evangelicalism has wandered from its path, and in the second, we need to learn all over again their solutions to the ills of the late medieval church in an attempt to bring reformation to the modern church. If those problems have merely resurfaced, let us reach for older wisdom in our struggle for a solution. What would Martin Luther or John Calvin say if he knew that the evangelical movement he launched had become the very unreformed church he faced?

Luther's doctrine of the priesthood of all believers served as the foundation for his criticism of the Roman priesthood. Every Christian, he insisted, was a priest on account of his or her baptism. There was no fundamental difference in status between the ministers of the gospel, by whatever name they might choose to be known, and the ordinary believer. The medieval church recognized a fundamental distinction between the "spiritual estate" (that is, the clergy—priests, bishops, popes) and the "temporal estate" (that is, everyone else). Luther declared that distinction to be null and void, a human invention rather than an ordinance of God. He writes thus in the *Appeal to the German Nobility* (1520):

> All Christians are truly of the spiritual estate, and there is no difference among them except that of function. Paul says in First Corinthians 12:12-13 that we are all one body, with every member having its own function by which it serves the others. This is because we have one baptism, one gospel, and one faith, and are all Christians, just the same as each other; for baptism, gospel and faith alone make us a Christian people. . . . And so it follows that there is no true fundamental difference between lay persons and priests, between princes and bishops, between those living in monasteries and those living in the world. The only difference has nothing to do with status, but with the function and work which they perform.[8]

So much for threats about touching the Lord's anointed! There was no place in Christianity, said Luther, for any notion of a professional class within the church (which evangelicals today call "full-time Christian service") that is in a closer spiritual relationship to God.

That vision of the call of the laity has been lost again. When someone says, "So-and-so is called," or, "He got the call," we automatically assume he or she is talking about someone being called to be a pastor, a missionary, a youth worker, or to be involved in "Christian ministry" in some sense. Sometimes we will hear evangelicals say, "Plumbing is my job, but singing in the choir is my ministry," as though one's secular employment is somehow less spiritual or valuable than church-related activities.

The laity, all too often, are seen once more today as little more than financial and practical supporters of the church, who have neither the right nor the ability to discern the will of God for their lives nor for the Christian communities of which they are a part. They are encouraged to listen, not so much to God in His Word, as to those who claim to speak in His name. To question the preacher is to question God Himself. They are encouraged to give and not to ask too many questions about what happens to that money or other resources. In short, they are encouraged to be docile and uncritical, in every way like the laity on the eve of the Reformation.

WHAT THE PRIESTHOOD OF ALL BELIEVERS DOES *NOT* MEAN

Nevertheless, not everyone could be allowed to *act* as a priest. As Calvin put it, "No Christian in his right mind makes everyone equal in the administration of the word and sacraments, in that all things ought to be done decently and in order, and, by the special grace of Christ, ministers are ordained for that purpose." Just as Luther's doctrine of the priesthood of all believers did not entail the abolition of a professional ministry, neither did it necessarily imply the rejection of spiritual direction.

Luther's fundamental principle is that all Christians share the same priestly status on account of their baptism; they may, however, exercise different functions within the community of faith and the community at large, reflecting their individual God-given gifts and abilities. To be a minister is to stand alongside one's fellow-Christians, sharing their status before God; nevertheless, those fellow-believers have recognized the gifts of that individual and have invited the person to exercise that ministerial function in their midst. As someone called to be a doctor is different in terms of the skills and education necessary, so someone called to the ministry of Word and sacrament must have the skills and education necessary for that calling, but both stand before God on an equal basis.

In his treatise *Concerning the Ministry* (1523) Luther argued that the calling that individuals have to the ministry is conditional upon the approval of the people and upon their continued support. Their authority resided in the fact that they were called by God and the people, not in some esoteric vision or voice from heaven.

Contemporary Pentecostal leader Earl Paulk writes, "No man judges a prophet. . . . People cannot put the reed of God into the hand of a man called by God, nor can they take the reed out of his hand." "When people begin tampering with God's anointed servants," warns Paulk, "the road they travel is like the one that Judas traveled. . . . God clearly warns, 'Do not touch my anointed ones; and do my prophets no harm.'"[9] That is just the sort of power trip sought in the medieval system. And it was that authoritarianism that the Reformers confronted with their doctrine.

The idea that prophetic or preaching ministry is conditional upon the support of the people of God seems to have been swallowed up in the personality cult surrounding leaders. So-and-so *can't* be removed, many say, because God called him, and who are we to judge him?

It is here where the Reformation doctrine is seen to be closely linked to its sister doctrine of the *sufficiency of Scripture*. God's will for truth and godliness is there for all to read, and God does not whisper secrets into the ear of the minister. Knowledge is not locked up, available only to the spiritual elite who have the key. It is not the restricted privilege of a self-selected group. Those twin doctrines must once again challenge the religious totalitarianism we see in some quarters of evangelicalism today.

The accountability of ministers to their people rests upon the existence of means by which their preaching, ministry, and teaching may be checked. Scripture is the sole God-given and God-authorized means by which the people of God can claim to speak in the name of their God. We must "test the spirits to see whether they are from God, because many false prophets have gone out into the world" (1 John 4:1). We must "test everything," holding "on to to the good" (1 Thessalonians 5:21). If one loses sight of the objective and public character of the Scriptures, one is defenseless against the power evangelical who declares, "God told me to say this," or, "I had a personal revelation from God authorizing me to behave in this way." The Reformation provides us with vital safeguards against such developments, enabling ordinary Christians to blow the whistle on their leaders. And as recent history has made abundantly clear, Christian leaders are just as prone to sin, failure, and pride as those whom they believe they are called to lead.

The Reformation doctrine of the priesthood of all believers thus gives every Christian believer, male and female, both the *right* and the *means* to ensure that his or her church and pastors remain faithful to their gospel calling—and authorizes the people to exercise them if necessary. The Reformation can be seen as a collective protest of the people of God against the errors, ignorances, and failures of their totalitarian ministers. But with the Reformation came a slogan—a slogan that needs to be splashed onto new banners again today: *ecclesia semper reformanda*—the church must always be reforming itself. In other words, reformation is not a once-and-for-all event, but a continuing process. Those who claim to stand in that evangelical tradition need to return to their roots and rediscover the need for continual correction, reform, and criticism of their ideas and actions.

For the simple truth is that modern evangelicalism has spawned a number of ideas and attitudes that bear a disquieting resemblance to the worst excesses of the corrupt and confused church of the late Middle Ages. Take, for example, the Renaissance popes. They had no difficulty in affirming the world and its values and methods, even occasionally developing new twists. The Borgia pope Alexander VI was chiefly noted for turning dinner parties into a Renaissance version of Russian roulette: you were never quite sure which of the many dishes would contain the poison. Where Jesus counseled talking through difficulties with your opponents, Alexander favored more direct and permanent approaches hitherto neglected by Christian spiritual directors.

The pope who condemned Luther in 1520 was a member of the prominent Florentine banking family of the Medicis, and he had liquidated his bank in order to purchase the papacy outright. There were other, more suitable candidates, most of whom had fewer mistresses and illegitimate children than Leo, and occasionally even none. By all accounts, Leo was a good-natured gourmet, equally fond of the world of high finance, hunting, and extravagant spending. The Renaissance popes had no trouble, at least at the practical level, with sex, money, or power. They knew how to get them and how to make the most of them. They denied themselves no pleasure. There are simply too many parallels for comfort with the financial, political, and sexual activities of certain much-publicized sections of modern evangelicalism. And what about the issue of authority? In his famous reforming work of 1520, Luther argued forcefully against the papal claim to have a final say in matters of faith and practice:

> If we are all priests . . . why should we not also have the power to test and judge what is right or wrong in matters of faith? . . . We ought to march boldly forward and test all that [the popes] do, or leave undone, by our believing understanding of the Scriptures. We must compel the Romanists to follow not their own interpretation, but the better one. . . . Therefore it is the duty of every Christian to espouse the cause of the faith, to understand and defend it, and to denounce every error.[10]

Has God not given His Spirit to ordinary Christians? Luther's question, asked tongue in cheek, seems more relevant and urgent than ever today. Where the German scholar Martin Kähler complained about the "papacy of the professors," perhaps we should be complaining about the "papacy of the prophets and preachers." The Reformation principle is that of the public accountability of preachers to the Word of God and the right of all believers to read and interpret Scripture and challenge their pastors where they appear to deny it, depart from it, add to it, or subtract from it.

Therefore, the Reformation vision has these components:

1. A community of people, each person possessing the right to read Scripture and reflect on its meaning
2. A church whose members are faithfully obedient to God as He has publicly revealed Himself in Scripture, and not to the fallible and frail personality of their charismatic preacher
3. Pastors and preachers who are aware that others could, and might, do their job just as well as they, and who are conscious of their accountability to God and His Word for the safekeeping and spiritual nourishment of those for whom Christ died

4. A church (congregation and its pastors) whose supreme desire is to glorify God, whom they know to be utterly distinct from them and to have come among them in an unmerited act of gracious condescension

5. And above all, a group of people who are conscious of their frailty and sinfulness, and are anxious to place checks in the way of their human tendency to sin. (It is human sin that makes the doctrine of the priesthood of all believers necessary, just as it is the grace of God that makes it possible. If we are to take that human sin seriously, and if we are to be responsible stewards of that divine grace, then we will end up espousing the insights of that neglected doctrine.)

They say that power corrupts, and power evangelicalism too easily becomes a corrupt evangelicalism. The Reformers, our forefathers in our faith, had the wisdom to restrain the potential of sin, in the light of the scriptural declaration that we are indeed a royal priesthood in the sight of God (1 Peter 2:9). We would do well to follow their wisdom in a day when corruption is so newsworthy and power so easily grasped.

NOTES

1. Take Copeland's words as an example: "The believer is as much an incarnation as was Jesus of Nazareth,'" Kenneth Copeland, *Word of Faith* (Fort Worth, Tex: Copeland, 1980), p. 14. Other statements along this line can be found in Kenneth E. Hagin's *Zoe: The God-Kind of Life* (Tulsa, Okla.: Faith Library, 1981).

2. *Believer's Voice of Victory,* August 1988, p. 8.

3. Audiocassette on file with CURE.

4. Benny Hinn, taped from the telecast; on file with CURE.

5. Max Weber, "The Sociology of Charismatic Authority," in H. H. Gerth and C. Wright Mills, eds.; *From Max Weber: Essays in Sociology* (London: Oxford U., 1946), pp. 246-52.

6. Robert H. Schuller, *Self-Esteem: The New Reformation* (Waco, Tex.: Word, 1982), p. 98.

7. Ibid.

8. Martin Luther, *Appeal to the German Nobility* (1520). *Three Treatises* (Philadelphia: Fortress, 1973), pp. 12-14. I have modified the English translation of the German to bring out the modernity of Luther's language at vital points.

9. Earl Paulk, *Satan Unmasked* (Atlanta: K Dimension, 1984), pp. 187-90.

10. Martin Luther, *Three Treatises,* pp. 21-22.

PART 6
POWER SWITCH

This is what the Lord says: "Let not the wise man boast of his wisdom or the strong man boast of his strength or the rich man boast of his riches, but let him who boasts boast about this: that he understands and knows me, that I am the Lord, who exercises kindness, justice and righteousness on earth, for in these I delight," declares the Lord.
Jeremiah 9:23-24

Jews demand miraculous signs and Greeks look for wisdom, but we preach Christ crucified: a stumbling block to Jews and foolishness to Gentiles, but to those whom God has called, both Jews and Greeks, Christ is the power of God and the wisdom of God.
1 Corinthians 1:22-24

POWER SWITCH

14

The *Object* of Contemporary Relevance

R. C. Sproul

Do you find church on Sunday morning boring? Have you ever found yourself glancing at your watch more than once in a given service? Church boredom is not only a modern phenomenon. It even occurred in the New Testament, when someone fell asleep as the apostle Paul was preaching, providing a source of comfort to centuries of ministers. Think for a moment about the event at the Mount of Transfiguration where the glory of Christ burst through His humanity. His countenance changed, and the apostles were enveloped in a bright cloud. A voice from the cloud declared, "This is My beloved Son, with whom I am well-pleased. Listen to Him!" (Matthew 17:5-8, NASB). Peter was not guilty of slack watching that day. In fact, he wanted to build a little shelter so that he could stay there much longer than the ordinary termination point of a one-hour service.

The problem is that we have not seen any clouds lately. We are living in the "already" of the kingdom, as the gospel—and with it, the glory of Christ—reaches the ends of the earth. And still, there is the "not yet" of the kingdom's presence among us. Because Christ is physically at the right hand of the Father, nothing short of His physical return will usher us into the direct experiences such as this

R. C. Sproul is founder and president of Ligonier Ministries in Orlando, Florida, and professor of apologetics at Reformed Theological Seminary in Orlando.

remarkable event. "Now we see but a poor reflection as in a mirror; then we shall see face to face" (1 Corinthians 13:12). Therefore, the means God has chosen for our worship and growth is the testimony of those whom He hand-selected during His sojourn among us.

Although we do not have the benefit of Christ's physical presence day to day, we do have His Holy Spirit and the Word which He left to be proclaimed until He returned. When we read passages such as Romans 8, it is difficult to imagine how on earth we could have made this biblical record so boring in our church life. The apostle Paul, after proclaiming the great doctrines of grace—providence, election, calling, justification, and glorification—exclaims, as if rising from his chair in worship, "What shall we say in response to this? If God is for us, who is against us?" (Romans 8:31). Three chapters later, he does the same thing. After describing the mystery of election and redemption, he is moved to praise: "Oh, the depth of the riches of the wisdom and knowledge of God! How unsearchable his judgments, and his paths beyond tracing out! Who has known the mind of the Lord? Or who has been his counselor? Who has ever given to God that God should repay him? For from him and through him and to him are all things. To him be the glory forever! Amen" (Romans 11:33-36). No one fell asleep while *this* letter was being read.

But surveys tell us that our neighbors find church boring and irrelevant. And that creates a tension: will we glory in our irrelevance, confusing boredom with faithfulness? Or will we glory in a relevance that compromises not only the old wineskins but the sacred wine itself, confusing excitement with faithfulness? It will be the purpose of this chapter to offer a better, more biblical alternative to both options. Whether our particular part of the vineyard is inundated with pop-psychology, an unhealthy preoccupation with signs and wonders, carnal conservatism, political and moral utopianism, or a pragmatic disregard for truth in the pursuit of church growth, this chapter aims to refocus our attention on the God we worship. In the end, after all, the church of Christ above all is a *worshiping* community. The service, the outreach, the fellowship, and every other activity of the church flows out of its worship. A great God who is known is a great God who is served, praised, and proclaimed.

Part of our problem is the disdain for theology that abounds in Christian circles. Although theology is taken from two words that, together, mean "the study of God," many brothers and sisters prefer shortcuts to "relevance." To say that theology is boring is really to say that God is boring. And yet, part of the problem is that the average person in the pew is not likely to get a steady diet of theology that is proclaimed with excitement and relevance. How can we think about God's character and actions in history and yawn? Who would dare say that the God of the Bible is irrelevant for the modern world? The Creator of heaven and earth, the One who has all of history in His hand, the Lord of history, is relevant to everything we do. And yet people still find it boring to come into His presence for the purpose of adoration and reverence. Or is that the purpose of church anymore? Perhaps the shift from the character of God and His grace to attempts at relevance is to blame for boredom, as the excitement of last week's meeting wears off by Monday.

WORSHIPING IMAGES

Lest the reader fear that I am suggesting that we worship images, let me state emphatically what I mean. Each of us has been created in the image of God. Therefore, we are image-bearers of the Creator. We exist to reflect His praise and glory, and His image in us directs us to worship. We are incurably *homo religiosis,* that is, religious in our very nature, so that even in our natural state our corrupt desires are not enough to root out the passion and the drive for worship entirely. In fact, the most fundamental sin according to Scripture is idolatry, which comes from two words, *idola* and *latria,* meaning "the worship of idols." The apostle Paul tells us in Romans 1 that idolatry is practiced when we exchange the glory of the immortal God and begin to serve and worship the creature rather than the Creator. The difference between our natural and regenerate state, then, is not a difference in the *practice* of worship, but in the *object* of worship. The worship of unbelievers is distorted worship, sinful worship, corrupt worship—but it is worship all the same.

Everywhere one goes worshipers are found. They may be falling before a totem pole, a sacred cow, a rock star, a religious leader, or an abstract concept of the philosophers, but worshipers are to be found everywhere. In fact, it seems that people are worshiping everywhere *but* in church on Sunday morning.

It has become a cliché that in America worship begins every Sunday at one o'clock in the stadium of one's choice. That is where our heroes are; that is where we express our adulation and excitement about what really matters to us. If Paul Tillich was right when he said that God is that which concerns us ultimately, then it may be the standings of the National Football League that are the deities of our time.

In any case, let us direct our attention to Mars' Hill, in Athens, where the apostle Paul is presenting the claims of Christ: "While Paul was waiting for them in Athens, he was greatly distressed to see that the city was [fully given to idolatry]" (Acts 17:16). At the zenith of the cultural and intellectual progress of the ancient world, the city of Plato's Academy, of Aristotle's Lyceum, Athens is found by the apostle to be a superstitious and idolatrous center. "Therefore he disputed daily in the synagogues and in the marketplace with those that met with him" (v. 17). Paul could not stop talking about Christ, and he used both religious and nonreligious forums as an opportunity to explain the Lord's Person and work. By verse 19, we read, "Then they took him and brought him to a meeting of the Areopagus, where they said to him, 'May we know what this new teaching is that you are presenting? You are bringing some strange ideas to our ears, and we want to know what they mean.'" Luke adds, "All the Athenians and the foreigners who lived there spent their time doing nothing but talking about and listening to the latest ideas."

Here is a case in which a fairly impressive group of unbelievers found the proclamation of the Word anything but boring. The gospel was placed by the Athenians in the category of "the latest ideas." And yet, you will notice, Paul did not compromise the message in order to gain this access. His message was considered relevant precisely because it was *not* like anything they had heard before. Too often today, what Christians hear in church is merely a biblical gloss on what they hear every day in popular culture. Then, in verse 22, Paul gives the Athenians a backhanded compliment: "Men of Athens! I see that in every way you are very religious. For as

I walked around and looked carefully at your objects of worship, I even found an altar with this inscription: TO AN UNKNOWN GOD." An altar to an unknown god? Now *that's* religious. To be so circumspect in one's religious devotion that one will even worship an unknown entity is a sign of remarkable, if foolish, piety. The altar was there, but who were those people worshiping? In fact, they were not worshiping at all when Paul arrived, but were merely sitting around having a social meeting, talking about the latest ideas. The scene has far too many associations with the modern church for comfort.

Most of the churches that keep their members in the United States are churches that have a vital social life. Sometimes it is even disparagingly said of this or that church, "Well, that's not a church, but a country club." Although we could only hope that churches would be places where people felt at home and were able to meet others, isn't it easy to turn the church into a social club under the guise of "fellowship" and "community," erected in His place and featuring other attractions to bring the people together? If the churches are boring today, it could hardly be because they are preaching too much theology.

HOW EXCITING IS THE UNKNOWN GOD?

The question I want to raise is, How in the world can we worship God in a way that is exciting and passionate and moving if we do not know anything about Him? Of course, we can manufacture excitement. We can create synthetic passion. If the rock stars can move audiences, surely we can have moving productions. But how can we get excited *about God* if we do not know what He is like? Who is going to want to sing praises or pour out one's soul in confession before an unknown God? Who wants to get up, get dressed and spend the better part of the day off paying respects to someone he doesn't even know? It's like going to the funeral of a distant and unknown relative. You feel out of place and awkward.

No wonder the church is perceived as irrelevant. It is because the people don't hear the message of the character and saving action of God in history. If we are communicating who God is, people might be angry, they might try to drive us out of town, as they did the apostles time and time again, but there is one thing they are guaranteed *not* to be, and that is bored. Nobody, I mean nobody, ever called Martin Luther a bore. No one ever thought what he had to say was irrelevant. There were powerful people who were all too anxious to carry out the imperial death warrant on Luther. John Calvin spent his early years as a reformer holding crowded services in the caves of southern France under a pseudonym. Meanwhile, their brethren in England and elsewhere across Europe were being burned at the stake as dangerous subversives. The Reformation was a period of recovering the forgotten truths about God, about Christ's Person and work, and about the way sinners are accounted just before God's righteous tribunal. In other words, while others were proposing moral, political, mystical, and philosophical reformations, the Reformers were demanding a theological reformation. The Reformation amounted to a group of biblically literate ministers and laypeople calling the church to inform the masses of the identity of "the unknown God." It may have caused a mess, but it was not irrelevant; it was not boring.

In the eighteenth century, Jonathan Edwards began preaching a series of sermons on justification by grace and on the sovereignty of God, the same doctrines that formed the core of the Reformation message. George Whitefield and others joined in proclaiming those truths that had once again been forgotten, and the result was the Great Awakening. Edwards and Whitefield were criticized for rocking the boat, but never for being boring. They were not irrelevant.

WORSHIP IN SPIRIT AND IN TRUTH

We are familiar with the New Testament mandate: "God is spirit, and his worshipers must worship in spirit and in truth" (John 4:24). In other words, Jesus is saying, "Genuine worship requires both the involvement of the heart and the head." You have seen worship that some would characterize as emotionalism. I have seen religious leaders who understand how to generate enthusiasm in a crowd. I was at a tent meeting once where a fellow came out with a tambourine and started pounding on it very slowly, and the rhythm intensified. Then he moved the people to begin clapping. It was just like being at a rock concert, with everybody getting into the beat.

Then this leader said, "OK now, turn around and tell your brother the devil is a liar!" One of the ushers came up to me, since I was completely unmoved by this, and he said, "What's the matter, brother, don't you feel the Holy Spirit?" I replied, "If that's the Holy Spirit, I'm going to sleep in tomorrow morning." I had to get out of that tent, because it was plain to me that the emotions of the people were being whipped up by manipulation and that the service had nothing to do with the character of God.

That is not only true of the more emotional segment of the evangelical movement. Church growth techniques can become means of manipulating superficial growth that has nothing to do with God. Very often evangelicals even fall prey to political manipulation, the likes of which Chuck Colson describes in his chapter in this volume. There is the psychological manipulation of superficial slogans and "feel good" affirmations about ourselves that move us even further away from any serious knowledge of God and His character. Legalism or unquestioned and unchallenged authorities can become extremely manipulative. In short, the exercise of power can be manipulation, and we see it replacing the knowledge of God and His Word in our churches.

It is impossible to avoid manipulation unless we return to a rational Christianity. God Himself is rational: He speaks, He explains, He argues, He answers. The Bible is rational: its teachings are interrelated and logically consistent; its reports of historical events are being increasingly verified by modern discoveries. It is possible to excite the heart without informing the mind. The excitement will not last long, but it is possible to have at least momentary excitement by circumventing the mind. That, however, is not worship, for those who worship must do so "in spirit and in truth."

However, there are those who simply take the "truth" part of the mandate and ignore the spirit of worship. Expositions are doctrinally precise (even though many in the congregation were lost by the time the preacher reached his second point), and the teaching is accurate, but there is no sense of enthusiasm from the preacher or from anybody else, for that matter, in response. In some settings, the truth is presented as a lecture rather than as a proclamation of good news to sinners. Further, some Christians have become excessively suspicious about the "spirit" part of worship because of the excesses they perceive in group number one. But the Scriptures, not the abuses of our brothers and sisters, must be our guide in these matters, and the Scriptures command not only true worship, but spiritual worship. Jesus commanded, "Love the Lord your God with all your heart and with all your soul and with all your mind" (Matthew 22:37). Worship of the heart, without the mind, is an inappropriate form of worship, according to the Lord Jesus Christ. We are so constituted as creatures made in the image of God that both dimensions are to be engaged in worship.

No wonder, then, that so many of our contemporaries judge the church as irrelevant and boring. How can the heart really respond to that which it does not know, without the employment of manipulative devices to get people whipped up? There is a content to the revelation that God has given to us, and that content is addressed to our minds so that we might be called to understand it, and the more we understand the revelation God has given us about Himself, the more we ought to be moved to worship and praise Him in response. However, those who stop just before allowing themselves to get too excited about what they have just discovered need to melt before the Word of God as they perhaps never have before. Impossible as it is to truly be excited about God without understanding who He is, it is no less impossible to really understand who God is and what He has done without being moved in a variety of ways.

CONCLUSION

The book of Hosea is a lawsuit God levels against His people. "There is no faithfulness, no love, no acknowledgment of God in the land," He charges (4:1). After lamenting, "My people are destroyed from lack of knowledge" (v. 6), He warns that "a people without understanding will come to ruin!" (v. 14). Notice the connection at the beginning between faithfulness, love, and knowledge. Many believers want a shortcut to faithfulness and love, praise and worship, fellowship and service of God without having to do the hard work of thinking about God. But without knowledge, there is no faithfulness, no genuine love, no deep, heart-felt praise and adoration; there is only noise and momentary manipulation.

As far as I am concerned, the greatest issue facing the Christian church as we near the twenty-first century is the character of God. Unless we understand what God is like, nothing else in the Bible will make sense. Apart from understanding God's justice, wrath, mercy, and holiness, there is no way we can understand the gospel. The cross will make no sense to us if we do not understand why God's character required it.

If you understand the character of God, then the doctrine of Scripture, the doctrine of Christ, and everything else falls into place. On the other hand, everything else can be correct apart from your doctrine of God and you are still a pagan. You are still an idolater. You may be an inerrantist; your eschatology might be right on target; you may never miss a quiet time or an opportunity to go to church. But if you do not worship and serve the *right* God, you worship and serve a *false* one. Therefore, we *must* "press on to know the Lord" (Hosea 6:3, NASB). "For from him and through him and to him are all things. To whom be the glory forever! Amen."

15

The *Subject* of Contemporary Relevance

Michael S. Horton

The gospel of power is an enemy of the power of the gospel.

It was Tom Wolfe, author of *The Bonfire of the Vanities,* who dubbed the seventies the "Me Decade." The eighties, he said, could be regarded as the decade of money fever. I would like to suggest, if Wolfe is accepting submissions for what we ought to call the nineties, that this decade's most obsessive expression of narcissism is its quest for power. And that quest has not been without its effect on the church, from naming and claiming prosperity from the "pool of power" to "power ministries" in church growth, advocated by C. Peter Wagner and the Vineyard Fellowship, to "the power released by our Self-Talk" advocated by an evangelical pastor, and the blending of psychology, magic, and religion in Robert Schuller's remark, "You don't know what power you have within you! . . . You make the world into anything you choose. Yes, you can make your world into whatever you want it to be."[1]

We are seeing Christianity become a technology for power in the hands of those who, when talking about Christian mission, frequently sound more like marketing executives, CEOs, psychologists, scientists, and politicians than shepherds of God's flock. I am not

MICHAEL S. HORTON is the founder and president of Christians United for Reformation (CURE), Anaheim, California, and is currently engaged in doctoral studies at Wycliffe Hall, Oxford, England.

suggesting for one moment that this quest for power is deliberate. Many of those leading the movements we have been describing are absolutely convinced that their work is contributing to the advance of Christ's kingdom. And in some instances, I do not doubt that that goal is achieved.

Nevertheless, a great many Christians at the end of the twentieth century appear to be interested in everything *except* the gospel. Motifs of political liberation, "spirituality" (with dozens of subheadings), celebration of sexuality, creation as sacrament, radical feminism, self-esteem and inner healing, signs and wonders, church growth, spiritual gifts, moral crusades: you name it, we've got it! But the one thing we no longer believe in is the gospel. There's no room for irrelevant dogmas about original sin, total depravity, guilt, atonement, propitiation, substitution, justification, the sovereignty of God, regeneration and sanctification, judgment, heaven, and hell. In our day nearly every one of those doctrines is up for grabs; one does not have to hold a "narrow" position on these issues to wear the evangelical label.[2]

However, an evangelical must be absolutely certain about how to tackle issues such as abortion, pornography, socialism, affirmative action, homosexuality, the gifts of the Spirit, and the precise chronology of end-times events. Whereas the Bible does indeed have something to say about our behavior, spiritual gifts, and eschatology, often issues barely (some never) discussed in the Bible have become the standard tests of orthodoxy at the same time the most obvious biblical motifs are largely unknown.[3]

In this concluding chapter I want to tie together the themes we have addressed and demonstrate that the various forms of the "power religion" by which the contemporary church has been seduced amount to more than different *emphases* or *models;* they are substantial and fundamental. As R. C. Sproul has demonstrated that theology (the study of God) is more relevant than the distractions, so I hope this chapter will present a sound case for a renewed confidence in the gospel itself as "the power of God unto salvation." To do that, I would like to take a closer look at one of the most important challenges an apostle presented to a congregation.

THE CORINTHIAN POWER RELIGION

The commercial capital of Greece, Corinth was the quintessence of metropolitan sophistication in the region. Athens was the center of academic life, but the practical Corinthians liked to think that they, too, were up on the latest ideas. Temple prostitution was big business at the shrine of Aphrodite (goddess of love). Down the street was the shrine of Asclepius, the god of healing. In fact, even decades later, after all of the twelve pagan temples were converted to churches in Corinth, the healing shrine continued to be frequented.[4]

The purpose of Paul's letters to the Corinthian believers was to respond to news the apostle had received about divisions in the church (1 Corinthians 1:11). "Super-apostles," as Paul called them, had gained access to the congregation, bringing confusion in their train, and the apostle's patience was wearing thin: "For if someone comes to you and preaches a Jesus other than the Jesus we preached, or if you receive a different spirit from the one you received, or a different gospel from the one you accepted, you put up with it easily enough. But I do not think I am in the least inferior to those 'super-apostles.' I may not be a trained speaker, but I do have knowledge" (2 Corinthians 11:4-6).

Indeed, Paul did have knowledge. Not only was he a well-educated Pharisee, he demonstrated a remarkable facility with secular literature and philosophy by quoting pagan poets and writers from memory.

In fact, when in Athens, Paul addressed his audience in terms of comparison and contrast between Christianity and Greek wisdom. Against the Epicureans, he argued God's sovereignty (Acts 17:24-26); but against the fatalistic Stoics, he presented a personal God who took account of people for their actions. Paul quoted from the Cretan poet Epimenides, from the Cilician poet Aratus, and from *The Hymn to Zeus,* by Cleanthes. This he also does elsewhere, to the Corinthians (1 Corinthians 15:33) and to Titus (1:12). Notice that Paul took the time to become familiar with the culture he was addressing (and quite possibly not simply for evangelistic purposes), and yet he used that familiarity as a bridge for communication, not accommodation: "In the past God overlooked such ignorance, but now he commands all people everywhere to repent. For he has set a day when he will judge the world with justice by the man he has appointed. He has given proof of this to all by raising him from the dead" (Acts 17:30-31). The result was not overwhelming, but "a few men became followers of Paul and believed," while others conceded, "We want to hear you again on this subject" (vv. 32-33).

But in Corinth, the simplicity of the gospel was being undermined by those who sought to turn it into the speculative mysticism of Greek philosophy. Combining Christianity, folk religion, and esoteric wisdom, the "super-apostles" attracted the metropolitan upper classes much as Eastern philosophy has gathered a following among professionals in our time. Silver-tongued speakers would put on seminars and promise the keys to success and happiness. Because they made at least some appeal to Christ, the super-apostles convinced some of the Corinthian believers that they were simply bringing together the best of secular wisdom and Christian belief. The gospel was not enough; to make Christianity relevant in a pagan commercial center like Corinth, in order to really market it well, the church had to promise answers to questions the Bible never answered and solve riddles about which the Bible was not the least bit interested. Where the Scriptures were silent, secular wisdom threw in its two cents worth.

The sophisticated Corinthian, confident and self-assured, had little time for sin and judgment, guilt and grace. Religion was supposed to supply social glue, give people a philosophy of life and a way of living a happy and meaningful life. In that sort of setting, the gospel was probably viewed as an answer to a question the people were not even asking: How can I, a condemned prisoner of my own depravity, ever have a relationship with a holy and just God?

But Paul's response was clear. Instead of taking a marketing survey of Corinthian attitudes and developing a gospel that would address "felt needs," he told them what the real needs were, whether they *felt* them or not. In fact, said Paul, if they did *not* feel within them the need or were not asking the right questions, it was not because the gospel is irrelevant, but because "the message of the cross is foolishness to those who are perishing" (1 Corinthians 1:18). "The

330

man without the Spirit does not accept the things that come from the Spirit of God, for they are foolishness to him, and he cannot understand them, because they are spiritually discerned" (2:14). In other words, if people were not asking the question, "How can I be right with God?" it was not because the gospel was dead, but because *they* were "dead in . . . transgressions and sins" (Ephesians 2:1). Although the gospel is "foolishness to those who are perishing, . . . to us who are being saved it is the power of God" (1 Corinthians 1:18).

Thus, Paul launches on his classic defense of the gospel:

> God was pleased through the foolishness of what was preached to save those who believe. Jews demand miraculous signs and Greeks look for wisdom, but we preach Christ crucified: a stumbling block to Jews and foolishness to Gentiles, but to those whom God has called, both Jews and Greeks, Christ is the power of God and the wisdom of God. For the foolishness of God is wiser than man's wisdom, and the weakness of God is stronger than man's strength. (1 Corinthians 1:21-25)

The super-apostles were more powerful than Paul in terms of popular appeal. They appeared to be more relevant, offering the recently converted pagans something familiar, and they made it sound captivating. They could really sell the product, and Paul was being put on the back burner a bit. In fact, their success suggests that the super-apostles spoke more directly to the felt needs of the Corinthians. And what were those felt needs? Probably not much different from those about whom Paul warned Timothy: "People will be lovers of themselves, lovers of money, boastful, proud, abusive, . . . rash, conceited, lovers of pleasure rather than lovers of God" (2 Timothy 3:2-4)—and these were professing Christians!

This is the problem, isn't it? By preaching to "felt needs" we are often preaching to selfish and idolatrous cravings. What will be the "felt needs" of people who love themselves, money, and pleasure? Our job is not to preach to felt needs, but to expose such felt needs as sinful cravings that must be supplanted by Christ. Only in that way can unbelievers see their truest, deepest need for the One whose absence those distractions have sought to soothe.

In the meantime, Paul responds to the problem with the super-apostles by telling the Corinthians they are shallow and immature, captive to "the wisdom of this age," which did not even have the sense to recognize the most remarkable triumph of divine wisdom in history: the satisfaction of God's justice and mercy in the cross of Christ.

But Paul didn't let the Corinthian Jews off, either. Whereas Greek culture-Christianity turned Christian discourse into a combination of magic, self-reflection, and speculation, Jewish sympathies led to a different distraction: the miraculous. In both cases, power was the key. Through understanding esoteric mysteries of life and knowing the secret "laws" that governed the spiritual realm, Greek religion promised Christians power through magic; the Jews promised power through miracle; and Paul said both promised what God considers weak.

We see the weakness of the miracles, even of those performed by our Lord himself. Well into His ministry, after scores of miracles, the Pharisees asked Jesus whether He was the Christ. "Jesus answered, 'I did tell you, but you do not believe. The miracles I do in my Father's name speak for me, but you do not believe because you are not of my sheep" (John 10:25). Indeed, seeking signs and wonders was not considered by our Lord to be a sign of faith, but of unbelief: "As the crowds increased, Jesus said, 'This is a wicked generation. It asks for a miraculous sign'" (Luke 11:29).

The cross was a stumbling block to the Jews also in that accepting its message meant coming to terms with the fact that they could not save themselves, not even with God's help. They were helpless to participate in their own redemption, and this public picture of Christ hanging on a cross, carrying the weight of our sins, meant that all of their works had been for nothing. Salvation by grace alone, through faith alone, because of Christ alone, was a scandalous notion to a religion that had become increasingly legalistic by the time of Christ.

The magic wisdom of the Greek and the miraculous signs and legalistic "righteousness" of the Jew are for Paul, therefore, *stumbling blocks,* not *power encounters.* The gospel does not step into the ring with such challengers. The gospel is not like a shy, physically retiring boy who needs his big brother to stick up for him—whether the big brother is the miraculous, secular wisdom, marketing, business, psychology, politics, legalism, or traditionalism. Although miracles, philosophy, corporate and psychological insights, and political positions may well be part of the life of any Christian, they are weak substitutes for the gospel.

Part of the problem is that, as fallen men and women, we want power not only for the advance of the church in a secular culture, but even for ourselves. There is something exalting about being a part of something that is respected by society. If we can build larger buildings, have larger gatherings, create larger enterprises, and compete with other mass-marketed products, we will be a part of something powerful, something relevant, and the world will have to sit up and take notice of us for our impressive technological, philosophical, psychological, and financial sophistication.

That is what was driving the Corinthian believers, too, who had forgotten their roots. That is what Paul points out immediately after he describes the gospel as a stumbling block:

> Brothers, think of what you were when you were called. Not many of you were wise by human standards; not many were influential; not many were of noble birth. But God chose the foolish things of the world to shame the wise; God chose the weak things of the world to shame the strong. He chose the lowly things of this world and the despised things—and the things that are not—to nullify the things that are, so that no one may boast before him. It is because of him that you are in Christ Jesus, who has become for us wisdom from God—that is, our righteousness, holiness and redemption. Therefore, as it is written: 'Let him who boasts boast in the Lord.'" (1 Corinthians 1:26-31)

The Corinthian believers did not want to *win* their sophisticated neighbors as much as they wanted to be *like* them. In a culture that idealized power, strength, wealth, wisdom, and nobility, Christianity made little sense. After all, the saviors of Greek mythology and philosophy redeemed by example. They displayed heroic qualities that wise followers emulated to their own immortal conquest. Although the gods were worshiped for each deity's unique role, all of them shared a common attribute: power. They made mistakes, misjudged, miscalculated, miscarried, waged wars among themselves, and committed adultery, but they were *all* powerful.

In the face of all of that, Paul expects the Corinthians to tell the neighbor next door that their Savior-God was sentenced to death by (1) His own people, (2) the Roman authorities, and (3) God the Father Himself. Thus salvation in this scheme is the result of a shameful death on a cross that, for Romans, had the equivalent criminal associations we would make with the electric chair. No wonder many cultures have found it difficult to understand this core message of Christianity! Our culture worships power. Even if power is stolen or used manipulatively, it is respected by our society. Strength is reverence, if reverent *hatred* on the part of those who get the brunt of it.

Nevertheless, at the point Christianity is least salable, it is the most powerful. The resurrection was such an overwhelming concept that those gathered in Athens to "hear the latest ideas" told Paul, "We'll hear more from you again on these things."

But today, we hardly say enough to provoke the slightest interest. In bending over backwards to be relevant, we have actually become politely irrelevant, mumbling when we get to the bit about judgment, hell, wrath, condemnation, human helplessness, and our utter dependence on the grace and righteousness of someone outside of ourselves. "Give us a god who shows us an example of greatness—power, virtue, wisdom; not a god who dies for us, but one who shows us how to live!" That is what the modern Greeks demand, just as others demand miraculous signs. But Paul continues his defense with the following:

> When I came to you, brothers, I did not come with eloquence or superior wisdom as I proclaimed to you the testimony about God. For I resolved to know nothing while I was with you except Jesus Christ and him crucified. . . . My message and my preaching were not with wise and persuasive words, but with a demonstration of the Spirit's power, so that your faith might not rest on men's wisdom, but on God's power. (1 Corinthians 2:1-5)

In other words, the apostle Paul could say today, "When I came to you I didn't have a lot of clever insights and tips for successful living, child-rearing, and inner healing. I didn't give you a political agenda or a building program." Paul even declines a "power encounter" between himself and the super-apostles. In addition to what we have already seen about Paul's superior education, he himself adds, "I am not in the least inferior to the 'super-apostles'" (2 Corinthians 12:11). And yet, "I did not come with eloquence or superior wisdom" (1 Corinthians 2:1). There was not going to be a test to see whose gospel was the cleverest, whose gospel was the most relevant, whose gospel could attract more attention. "For I *resolved* to know nothing . . . except Jesus Christ and him crucified" (2:2; italics added).

We want to stand out, to be relevant and "in touch," but when we don't talk about sin, judgment, grace, and redemption enough for even regular churchgoers to be able to articulate their theology, we couldn't be *more* irrelevant.

OF LADDERS AND TOWERS

Another way of making the point Paul makes in 1 Corinthians is to turn to the biblical image of ladders and towers. That idea was picked up by the Reformers as they distinguished true and false religion in terms of whether one knelt at the foot of the cross or tried to climb the cross or some other ladder into heaven. False religion builds ladders to heaven for us to climb; true religion teaches that God built a ladder from heaven to earth for Himself to descend. As Paul challenged *stumbling blocks* (speculation and miracle seeking), the Reformers added the Old Testament idea of *false ladders and towers.*

Most of us are familiar with the story in Genesis of the building of the Tower of Babel (Genesis 11). The ambitious project was tackled when various leaders of what was then a united culture said, "Come, let us build ourselves a city, with a tower that reaches to the heavens, so that we may make a name for ourselves and not be scattered over the face of the whole earth" (v. 4). Excavations of the Mesopotamian basin have turned up evidence of such temple-towers (called "ziggurats") as central features of the ancient Babylonian landscape. By uniting religion and culture, it was believed, humanity could reach the heavens. Nothing would stand in the way of progress. The desire expressed in terms of their reaching the heavens was met with the contrasting line, "But the Lord came down" in judgment of that proud attempt. As a result, the culture was scattered and the languages confused.

There is another ladder in Genesis important to our story. Jacob "had a dream in which he saw a stairway resting on the earth, with its top reaching to heaven, and the angels of God were ascending and descending on it" (Genesis 28:12). The Lord God stood at the top of the ladder and renewed the Abrahamic covenant to Jacob and his descendants. The pagans called their ziggurats by such names as "House of God," "Gate of Heaven," and "The Platform Which Leads to Paradise." But Jacob responded to his dream by exclaiming, *"This* is none other than the house of God; *this* is the gate of heaven" (v. 17, italics added).

In much of popular evangelical preaching and Sunday school classes, Jacob's ladder is normally presented as a metaphor for our climbing toward God. In fact, in one frequently sung Sunday school chorus we sing, "We are climbing Jacob's ladder." And yet it is clear from the context that Jacob has his head firmly planted on a rock and is asleep the whole time (vv. 10-11). God was at the top of the ladder, and angels were ascending and descending the ladder. But here is the interesting part: Jesus tells Nathanael, in John 1:51, "I tell you the truth, you shall see heaven open, and the angels of God ascending and descending on the Son of Man." In other words, not only is Jacob *not* climbing the ladder, Jesus Christ is Himself the ladder from heaven to earth. *He* is the "gate" of heaven (John 10:7); *He* is the house of God (see Matthew 2:6).

The point of all of this is to offer the possibility that we as evangelicals have been doing precisely what we used to find suspicious in others: building towers and ladders to heaven with bricks of ambition, pride, morality, pragmatism, and power. You can hear it in the background at evangelical conferences and conventions as speaker after speaker and celebrity after celebrity appears to overwhelm us with the latest figures of our successes, state-of-the-art multimedia shows, and guest appearances by United States government officials.

Just six years ago the evangelical media establishment was the pride of the movement. There was a euphoric sense of relevance:

"We're in the headlines!" cheered one speaker, to the applause of the guests during a banquet at one evangelical convention I attended. The last thing one expected to hear about was the gospel—that messy message about a Savior redeeming us, not by showing us the way to power but by dying *for* us and showing us the way to die *to* ourselves.

In the sixteenth century, the Reformers faced a similar crisis. Martin Luther distinguished between biblical, evangelical Christianity and medieval corruptions in terms of two ladders: the *Via Crucis* (way of the cross) and the *Via Gloriae* (the way of glory). What Luther meant by glory we mean, at least in part, by power. That is what makes this historical illustration so relevant for our own situation.

Luther believed that the medieval church followed the way of glory rather than the way of the cross. In other words, the saint wanted a direct encounter with God "in the nude," as only the German Reformer could put it.[5] The ladders of glory were mysticism, speculation, and merit.

The ladder of mysticism. There was first the ladder of mysticism, often preferred by the monk. By throwing oneself into devotions and pious exercises, one could climb up and peek into God's private chamber.

We are all inquisitive, and we want to have direct, intuitive supernatural experiences. But God has determined that we derive all of our knowledge of Him, not through direct encounters, but through the written Word, the Bible, and in the Person and work of His incarnate Son.

Today, once again, mysticism has swept even the evangelical world into its scope. "The Lord told me," "The Lord spoke to my heart," "I don't know, I just felt that's what He wanted me to do"—those phrases occur all too frequently for people whose watchphrase is "Scripture alone." How often do we hear those who defend their particular brand of faith or piety in the following terms: "You'll never convince me it isn't true. Why, I *know* someone who . . ," or "God gave me a peace about this idea"? Our own experience has often replaced the objective, historical details of Christ and His death, burial, and resurrection in our evangelistic witness. In our evangelism, our own personal experiences with the ascended Christ (usually called "testimonies") often replace the testimony of the inspired prophets and the apostles who were eye-witnesses of His incarnate ministry. We recommend Christ because of "the difference He has made in my life," even though the hearers (and in too many cases, the speakers) don't have the faintest idea about the objective nature of Christ and His saving work.

Classics of medieval and Counter-Reformation mysticism have now been republished by evangelical presses; devotionals and guides to spirituality far outsell books on God Himself. Morton Kelsey, a minister and family counselor, seeks to merge the psychological mysticism of Carl Jung with classical Christianity,[6] not unlike the curious blend offered by the "super-apostles" in Corinth. Why not adopt Jung's occultic psychology? His views are "compared to the Christian view of the progress of the soul."[7] But, as we have seen, the "progress of the soul" up the ladder of mysticism is not as Christian as the medieval monks and modern mystics would have us believe.

Devotional and meditation guides roll off of evangelical presses with such titles as *Deeper into God,* as though the He were a swimming pool rather than a Person. Jesus "in my heart" (i.e., "the Christ within") has largely replaced the centrality of the cross as Christ outside of my own personal experience, in time and history.

Today, many Christians once again climb the ladder of mysticism.

The ladder of human opinion. The second ladder was speculation. The "sophists," as the Reformers called them, after the ancient Greek relativists, gloried in resolving the "deeper" questions God never saw fit to answer. Instead of accepting God's revelation in Christ as sufficient, many medieval theologians simply chose to turn the Bible into a book of mysteries and riddles, like a code that only the professionals could crack. That led the average believer to concede, according to Luther's report, "I'm a layman and no theologian. I go to church, hear my priest, and him I believe."

Calvin elaborated on the point as well, pointing out the dangers of "seeking God . . . with bold curiosity to penetrate to the investigation of his essence, which we ought more to adore than meticulously search out." We should be seeking God, Calvin continues, "in his works whereby he renders himself near and familiar to us, and in some manner communicates himself."[8] What is God like? The sophists *speculated,* whereas God had already *communicated.* "Anyone who has seen me," said Jesus, "has seen the Father" (John 14:9). "I and the Father are one" (John 10:30). We are not left to opinion or speculation.

But isn't that what we do today? How often do discussions even among Christians interject the phrase "Well, my idea of God is . . . " or "I think of God as being more loving than that." We create idols of opinion and imagination rather than serving the one true God of revelation in Christ and Scripture. Bible studies easily degenerate into "what this means for me" instead of a discussion of what the text actually means, objectively, as the author intended it for his original audience. Sermons are often direct applications to the believer's current experience. David and Goliath become metaphors for victory over trials and sins. Bible characters become mere moral examples rather than key actors in the drama of redemptive history. Biblical stories often are reduced to the level of Aesop's Fables, with a moral offered for practical application.

Not only is there a popular form of this speculation. Often the impression is given that because the preacher has gone to seminary and knows Greek (or at least enough of it to be dangerous), he has an inside track on biblical revelation. Surely academic training offers a tremendous (and, for that vocation, essential) advantage in terms of being prepared to minister God's Word to the congregation, but the gospel is so clearly taught that anybody can understand its major themes. There is a great need, especially in our time, for learned scholars and theologians, but their duty is not merely to the clergy but to the whole church, and whenever theology leaves the ground floor and moves exclusively into the ivory tower, the great truths of the Word become the property of the professionals all over again.

A final form of the ladder of human wisdom we seem to have today is pragmatism. The gospel tells us what is true; pragmatic wisdom tells us what works. The two could not be operating on more conflicting principles.

And yet, C. Peter Wagner defends church growth principles on the grounds that pragmatic wisdom is often primary: "What Christians experience about God's work in the world and in their lives is not always preceded by careful theological rationalizations. Many times the sequence is just the opposite: theology is shaped by Christian experience."[9]

So, for instance, Wagner himself points out the tension between the "traditional theologians," who expect converts to be willing to cross racial, social, and economic barriers, and the church growth leaders, such as the late Donald McGavran, who concluded that "people like to become Christians without crossing racial, linguistic, or class barriers." Nobody doubts that for a moment. In fact, that is in part what two books of the Bible (Galatians and James) were written to redress. The difference is, the Scriptures (divine wisdom) consider such discomfort selfishness; and pragmatism (human wisdom) creates churches around this narcissistic tendency (which, at least in North American church growth tends to be white, suburban, middle-class yuppies) rather than around a common faith (Acts 2). Perhaps one observer captured the movement best with his editorial "Evangelism Without the Gospel."[10]

The ladder of merit. The third ladder for Luther was merit: "The monks have taught and persuaded the whole world of this, that they can, by that hypocritical holiness of theirs, justify not only themselves, but also others to whom they communicate it."[11]

The medieval church believed that salvation was by grace, but that it was by God's grace *infused* to help us live a new life. By being born again and walking with the Lord, one believed he or she would be accepted by God on that final day. But for Luther and Calvin, as well as for the New Testament writers, that simply was not enough. Even if God *did* give me new life and His Holy Spirit, I still could never cooperate with His grace to the extent that I could eradicate my sinful nature and, therefore, my sinful actions. No, God demands perfection, and anything short of it is fatal.

Then Luther had his breakthrough. He realized first from Romans that righteousness is not only something God *is* and *demands,* but that it is also a *gift* that He *gives.* In other words, we are accepted not by God's righteousness *making* us righteous, but by God's righteousness *declaring* us righteous; not by holiness imparted, but by holiness imputed. As Paul told the Romans, "The judgment followed one sin and brought condemnation, but the gift followed many trespasses and brought justification" (Romans 5:16).

And what is that gift but "the gift of righteousness" (v. 17)? God not only demands perfect obedience; by substituting His own Son in our place, there is what Luther called "this marvelous exchange": the sinless Christ is judged by God's court as guilty of condemnation, and the sinful believer is judged righteous in God's court as worthy of eternal life. The innocent Man is condemned so that the guilty could not only be pardoned but be accepted as though he *had* earned eternal life by perfect obedience to the law.

Today, there is a lot of traffic on the ladder of merit. John Wesley and the emphasis of the pietists on Christian perfection turned believers back in on themselves, looking to their growth in holiness, measured in legalistic terms. Human wisdom dictated that, in Wesley's words, "God will punish no man for doing anything which he could not possibly avoid; neither for omitting anything which he could not possibly do."[12] Whereas the Reformers had echoed the Scriptures in regarding the believer's being "at the same time justified and sinful," Wesley, like Rome, could not accept the idea that a person's righteousness could be "alien," that is, a gift of perfect righteousness from someone else. After all, wrote Wesley, does not the doctrine of justification tend "to mislead men; almost naturally leading them to trust in what was done in one moment? Whereas we are every moment pleasing or displeasing to God, according to the whole of our present inward tempers and outward—behaviour."[13] Human wisdom says, "It just can't be that simple. Such a teaching would eliminate the motivation for right living. There *must* be balance between grace and works as God's method of accepting sinners so that people will not be too lax in their obedience."

People move up and down on the ladder of merit in the way they reflect on prosperity and suffering, often concluding that reward and punishment are responsible for each.

When Paul tells the Corinthians, "I determined to know nothing while I was among you except for Christ and him crucified" (1 Corinthians 2:2), that is what he was getting at, for he even says a few verses earlier, "It is because of him that you are in Christ Jesus, who has become for us wisdom from God—that is, our righteousness, holiness, and redemption" (1:30).

341

In other words, Paul is saying, "Look, you can climb the ladders of power and glory, but you will discover one day that the goal you have in mind—be it direct spiritual encounters with God; trivial, esoteric speculations; or reward for services rendered—is hell, not heaven." The only wisdom that counts for eternity is the wisdom that causes me to regard my own experience, my own reasoning about what is true and fair, and my own righteousness and holiness as worthless in spiritual matters. For *Christ* is "our righteousness, holiness, and redemption," says the apostle.

True wisdom, therefore, is not the world's wisdom. The world wants religion to answer "practical" questions about relationships, child-rearing, self-image, lifestyle, "how to do" this or that. God must not interrupt; He must never get in the way. Religion must never tell a person what he or she must believe or do. It must simply help the world solve its practical problems. But true wisdom from above considers these "practical" issues as secondary; true wisdom is anxious to get to the part about God's descending the staircase to become flesh, live a perfect life, die a sacrificial death, and rise from the dead as the guarantee that our flesh, too, will be raised to new life.

The wisdom from below fashions an idol who will render willing obedience to the manipulation of its worshipers. If God will not give me self-esteem, I'll get it from another god. If the wisdom from above will not promise a practical program for a successful and happy life, I will find a god who can deliver what I want. Thus, our wisdom is constantly shaping new and improved idols of technique, method, spirituality, inner healing, celebrity, morality, and ideology.

Evangelicals might pride themselves on not venerating statues of saints, but when churches cater to these idolatries of the sinful nature, a nature that is hostile to God, they set up a shrine that makes the Reformation debate appear almost slight by comparison.

One final reference to the ladder motif comes from Friedrich Nietzsche, the German nihilist of the last century. After Christian theology has dissipated, said Nietzsche, there will be a need for a replacement, the Superman, the product of the will to power. Wrote Nietzsche:

> But this is my doctrine: . . . By ladders of rope I learned to climb
> many a window and with nimble legs I climbed high masts. To sit

upon the high masts of knowledge seemed to me no small bliss—
to flicker on high masts like a small flame. . . . By many ways and
modes I have come to my truth; not on one ladder only climbed I
to the height whence mine eye searcheth my distance. And ever
unwillingly have I asked my way of others. That hath ever offended
my taste! Rather I have asked and tried the ways themselves.
. . . Not good, neither evil, but *my* taste, as to which I have neither
shame nor concealment. Here lies *my* way—where lies yours? I
answered them which inquired of me "the way." For *the* way—ex-
isteth not! Thus spake Zarathustra.[14]

Beyond experience, utility, or success, *taste* has indeed become the rope of which most ladders are made these days. Instead of
worshiping the God who exists and accepting Him as He has revealed Himself, we place our own will to power in His place and fashion ropes of taste, pleasure, experience, and passing fancy. If the
church is to be "relevant," it will have to learn to make ropes. Or will
it?

THE PRICE WE WILL PAY

If evangelicals do take the path (or paths) to power there will
be a tremendous cost to every major heading of systematic theology.
Here are some examples, although I am certain each heading could
be significantly enlarged.

The doctrine of God. All of these movements share a common human-centeredness, revealing a thirst for happiness rather
than holiness; self-fulfillment rather than the glory of God. If God
can service these "felt needs," He retains His place, as any successful
product might.

But what happens when one doesn't experience "power encounters," or discovers that the deeper one goes in the search for his
or her "inner child," the more confused and anxious one becomes?
What happens when the church doesn't grow, or what does a pastor
do after the building program is completed? What kind of God do we
end up with after the right-wing and left-wing ideologues have
tamed Him into becoming their mascot? Surely the doctrine of God

is reshaped also in the hands of authoritarian ministers who emphasize only the side of the biblical doctrine that especially impresses them. Undoubtedly, human-centeredness is bound to force us to worship someone or something as foreign to Scripture as the "Unknown God" Paul met up with in Athens. More often than not, that elusive deity is our own mirror's reflection.

The doctrine of salvation. These movements also have tremendous implications for soteriology. Since that has been my central point in this chapter (and perhaps the central point of the entire book), suffice it to make a few brief comments in this regard.

The signs and wonders movement runs the risk of proclaiming salvation by an experience of naked power, such as the event reported by the Vineyard's John Wimber, where a man was "saved" simply by passing the evangelist on the street and being struck by the power of the Spirit that was upon him. Wimber even emphasizes that there was no presentation of the gospel that accounted for the "power encounter."[15] Peter Wagner refers to a Latin American "power evangelist" whose crusades are so power-charged that passersby outside the stadium (presumably, non-Christians) fall to the ground under the power of the Spirit.[16] (It is a curious theology that argues that Christians can be demon-possessed, whereas non-Christians can receive the Holy Spirit's anointing.)

The church growth movement is often perceived as approaching growth as a manager approaches the potential market for a new fast-food franchise. It is *assumed* by many of those experts that the preaching of the gospel is a normal aspect of a congregation's witness and that their growth principles are merely tools to use in addition to, not in the place of, that witness. However, we must say with the Protestant Reformers, "Christ alone!" We must recover the conviction that the gospel really is "the power of God unto salvation." We must no longer assume that growth principles merely supplement the preaching of the gospel; for many entrepreneurial pastors, they *are* the gospel.

Obviously, the legalism often prevalent in carnal conservatism presents a challenge to a biblical doctrine of salvation. So also does the moralism of recent political involvement. The justification of sinners as righteous and holy before God depends not on moral or even spiritual transformation but on the acceptance of "Christ and him crucified," publicly posted in history on a hill outside Jerusalem nearly two thousand years ago. Any message that confuses that central Christian proclamation of an "alien righteousness" is another gospel.

The doctrine of the church. The signs and wonders movement, like much of its lineage, borders on a gnostic doctrine of the church. Like the Anabaptists during the Reformation, many evangelical and charismatic Christians today so emphasize the invisible or spiritual reality of the Body of Christ that the visible or physical aspect of the church is understated or even denied. That affects the church in the following ways. First, it creates an undisciplined church. That was one of Paul's frustrations with the Corinthians. Their services were not being conducted "in order and with decency," but were free-for-alls for individual self-expression and experience. Second, it creates a divided church. Of course, there are many scandalous divisions within Protestant denominations; however, when, for instance, evangelicals were forced out of liberal mainline denominations in the twenties and thirties, the Protestant evangelicals wept as they emptied their desk drawers. But for the fundamentalists and Pentecostals institutions were suspect anyway. The call to leave the mainline churches and form new denominations was almost cheerful and self-righteous for those whose background had little room for the visible church.

The church growth movement, too, has a miserable ecclesiology. Though I realize that is a broad-brushed charge, it is difficult to overgeneralize the point. Rarely does one come across in church growth literature the theological question that so concerned evangelicals since the Reformation: What *is* a true church? According to the Reformers, it was defined by two chief marks: the Word of God rightly preached and the sacraments (ordinances) rightly administered. Later, Reformed theologians added church discipline as the third mark. At a time when ministers who are not faithful to the basic biblical message and who do not uphold the integrity of that message are nevertheless regarded as respected evangelical church leaders, it seems to me that that fundamental question ought to be addressed before even discussing growth principles. Unless we are settled on this issue, how will we know that the church we are build-ing is the same one Christ is building?

Furthermore, the unbiblical foundation of contemporary evangelical ecclesiology is recognized in the fact that there is no such thing as an evangelical *church,* but only an evangelical *move-ment.* Swept along by the movement-oriented century in which we find ourselves, evangelicalism is often led these days more by suc-cessful businessmen, sports stars, or political figures who have be-come Christian spokespersons and entrepreneurial executives than by theologically trained pastors, bishops, elders, and theologians. Pop-psychological approaches, too, often take persons out of the community of faith and treat them instead as isolated souls. The in-dividualism and subjectivism of the movement undermine a solid sense of belonging to a community that is larger than oneself and one's own problems. A biblical ecclesiology insists that we do not have an identity apart from our relationships. None of us alone is the Body of Christ; none of us constitutes the church. Together, we form the people of God.

Carnal conservatism can undermine a biblical doctrine of the church, too, by setting up authoritative figures or a special caste of authorities (a Protestant "priesthood"). As Alister McGrath pointed out, the priesthood of all believers is the antidote to this sort of thinking. We *together* form the body of Christ, and we all are grow-ing up together into maturity in Christ. The personality cults so fre-quent in evangelical and charismatic circles represent a vacuum in our understanding of the doctrine of the church. For that reason, it is easy to become a leader of the evangelical movement without hav-ing much accountability beyond one's local setting.

Political activism can undermine a healthy doctrine of the church as well. A perfect example is that of pastors who identify with a particular political party and platform and encourage Christians to embrace it as the "Christian" agenda. The church then becomes a political action committee and a special interest group. As Ken My-ers argued so persuasively, in this scheme the church loses the in-tegrity of its claim to universal truth. When we demand our rights and act like a special interest group, we become a minority to be pla-cated rather than a prophetic community declaring the good news of Christ and the expectations of God for this new community.

Eschatology. What all of these enterprises share, in addition to a basic human-centeredness, is some form of a realized eschatology. We are well aware of the debates over the Millennium. Premillennialists argue that Christ will come to set up a physical, geopolitical utopia after all human attempts have failed, and postmillennialists insist Christ is already building that physical, geopolitical utopia through the success of the gospel (historic postmillennialism) or through the success of the gospel and Old Testament civil and moral law (Christian Reconstruction). Amillennialists, however, counter both positions with the assertion that the kingdom of Christ is a spiritual kingdom that is, as Christ said, "not of this world." It is a kingdom that does not come by political, economic, or military force. Like salvation itself, it comes to us from the outside. It is not a kingdom created by human beings, but by God Himself. We do not come into the kingdom so much as the kingdom comes upon us.

That concept has, of course, tremendous implications for the movements we have been discussing. This is why I stated that these movements all share a *realized* eschatology. Although all three views (historic premillennialism and postmillennialism, as well as amillennialism) have affirmed the presence of the kingdom in some sense already, they have also been agreed that there is a "not yet," or a future anticipation, to that eschatology. Christ has come, the promises have reached fulfillment, the shadows have become reality, but that does not mean that all is well. There is still more to be done. Redemption has been accomplished, but the consummation and recreation of the heavens and the earth await us.

A *realized* eschatology cannot wait for things to take place. It cannot rest with hope, but must have something more. Adam and Eve had a realized eschatology. God promised everlasting life at the end of the probation, but they wanted power here and now. Satan tried it out again on Jesus in the desert, but this time had no success. Faced with two roads, the short road to power and immediate gratification (i.e., realized eschatology) on one hand, and the long road to suffering and sacrifice, Jesus chose the latter. He "humbled himself and became obedient to death—even death on a cross! *Therefore* God exalted him to the highest place and gave him the name that is above every name" (Philippians 2:8-9, italics added).

Every one of the "heroes" listed in Hebrews 11 was held up for his or her patience. They were willing to wait for the fulfillment of promises. Although they expected redemption at any moment, they were content to die without having realized their eschatology. Hebrews 11 begins with a definition of faith: "Being sure of what we hope for and certain of what we do not see." This matter of faith as being certain of what we do not see appears to be in direct conflict with the proposition that for the success of the kingdom there must be visible signs of power. Noah spent years building a boat in the middle of a desert, anticipating a redemption *and* a judgment that rested on nothing more than a promise. Even in the theocracy, with God's presence among the people in the Promised Land, Abraham lived "like a stranger in a foreign country," because "he was looking forward to the city with foundations, whose architect and builder is God" (v. 10). "All these people," says the writer to the Hebrews, "were still living by faith when they died. They *did not receive the things promised;* they only saw them and welcomed them from a distance" (v. 13, italics added). An earthly utopia was not their goal. "Instead, they were longing for a better country—a heavenly one" (v. 16).

One wonders how much we Christians today long for a better country—a heavenly one.

But the people of God in general have not been very good at waiting. In the wilderness, they longed for Egypt's comfort; in the land, they wanted more than they had in worshiping God, so they worshiped the idols of surrounding nations. Biblical history is littered with people who couldn't wait, people who simply refused to glorify God unless He provided the fish and the loaves (John 6).

The signs and wonders movement has a realized eschatology in the sense that it considers any form of evangelism not accompanied by miracles as not being true evangelism. In the more extreme teachings of the "faith movement," eschatology is almost entirely realized. Ignoring the New Testament calls to turn our suffering into opportunity to reflect on the consummation and restoration of all things *after* this age, these evangelists promise delivery without birth pains. Although the Vineyard movement has distanced itself from the "faith teachers," it nevertheless evidences the same sort of triumphalism with regard to the "already" aspect of the kingdom, while downplaying the "not yet."

The church growth movement tends to work with an implicit realized eschatology in the assumption that technology will usher in the kingdom. On numerous occasions I have heard Christian leaders give pep talks at evangelical conventions with triumphalistic slogans about reaching every unreached people group by the year 2000 so that Christ may return. Certainly, no one argues with the worthy goal of reaching every unreached people group by the end of the century, but one can almost hear the orchestra in the background, playing some Wagnerian piece. The Great Commission included nothing about conditions for Christ's return. Jesus did not offer a reward for reaching every people group by the year 2000, and there would be nothing magical about reaching that goal which would require Jesus to return when it is accomplished. Similarly, church growth ought to be steady growth, not an artificial sprint manufactured by eschatological triumphalism, as though church growth principles could usher in the consummation.

Pop-psychology offers a realized eschatology by looking within. One eventually reaches a point of self-knowledge and self-esteem, and this goal can be reached by following the teachings or principles spelled out by various schools of thought. We want to be absolutely free of guilt—not only the objective fact, but the subjective feelings—and we often cannot wait for the ultimate psychological freedom won for us at the cross, believing what we do not always feel. We do not want to be unhappy, and we will pay an extraordinary amount of money to become happy, since our society equates happiness and healthiness as virtual synonyms.

Those who are carnally conservative or legalistic are utopians, too. They must have a perfect church or a perfect life. If they are a part of a denomination with some problems in it, they must lead a party of the truly committed to the Promised Land. Often, that is not a "denomination," such as the one they left, but a "New Testament church." Many of these individuals also maintain the realized, utopian eschatology of perfection in personal terms. Romans 7, where Paul says, "I am unspiritual," and repeatedly finds himself doing the very thing he hates and failing to do the very thing he wants to do, is taken by such people to refer to Paul before his conversion on the grounds that that is hardly the way the apostle would describe the Christian life. "What a wretched man I am! Who will rescue me from this body of death? Thanks be to God—through Jesus Christ our Lord!" (Romans 7:24-25). Although Paul's experience right now is not only imperfection, but wretchedness, he waits for the promise of deliverance from the presence of sin and evil.

When he challenges the Philippians to press on toward the goal, Paul adds, "Not that I have already obtained all this, or have already been made perfect," for, "I do not consider myself yet to have taken hold of it" (Philippians 3:12-13). Likewise, he tells the Corinthians, "Now we see but a poor reflection as in a mirror; then we shall see face to face. Now I know in part; then I shall know fully, even as I am fully known" (1 Corinthians 13:12).

If the apostle Paul had no room for triumphalistic language about what we are experiencing in "this evil age," why should we claim greater victory? The fact is, until the day we cross the Jordan into the Promised Land and see our Redeemer face to face, without the presence of sin and temptation, sickness and sorrow, we will remain pilgrims looking for a better land who can truly say, "I still haven't found what I'm looking for."

In short, if we do not examine the theological ramifications of such a megashift now, we will be in a difficult position to repair the damage later on. There is no question that such a shift will transform evangelical theology (as it already is transforming it). If evangelical theology is in error on these points, and these movements offer a more biblically directed course, then let us take that course; let us bring evangelicalism into greater harmony with the Word of God. But it is most dangerous to ignore the theology over which we are stepping as though the issues are issues of practice rather than issues of belief.

CONCLUSION

A few years ago it was reported that a man who had become obsessed with the secrecy, majesty, and power of the Queen of England slipped undetected through the security shield at Buckingham Palace. He climbed over the wall, made his way through two layers of soldiers and officers, and then gained access to the palace itself. Queen Elizabeth arrived in her bedroom to find a crazy, if clever, worshiper.

No one climbs into God's bedchamber, either for secret wisdom or revelation, or spiritual power, or experiences, or by accomplishments, as though he or she had earned the right to enter by great feats of holiness or political skill. All of Christianity depends on a downward movement of God, not on an upward movement of humans—even Christian humans, either individually or corporately. We desperately need to abandon this self-confident ladder-building to the gates of Paradise, to spiritual or earthly utopias.

The hope of success for the future of the Christian church is not to be found in power evangelism, power growth, power within, power preachers, or power politics, but in the power of the gospel. Paul said, "I am not ashamed of the gospel, because it is the power of God for the salvation of everyone who believes" (Romans 1:16). But I wonder, if we are to judge by the most common themes in evangelical preaching and publishing, whether we *are* ashamed of the gospel. Perhaps it is not as up-to-date or relevant as we need it to be. It presents stumbling blocks to the miracle-seekers and wisdom-seekers of the age. Yet the gospel is not about our seeking, but God's; is not about our ascent, but His descent.

That has an effect on the way *we* go about business, too. As our Savior came "not . . . to be served, but to serve, and to give his life a ransom for many" (Matthew 20:28), so let us who have no glory to leave behind, no power to conceal, no majesty to put aside become servants again. Instead of *manipulating* God, others, and ourselves, let us begin *serving*. And we do that by asking God what the real needs are.

Without fleshing out our doctrine of God, the Person and work of Christ, and the Holy Spirit; the nature of the gospel, the church, and the Christian view of history and the future, and arriving at some consensus before we act in these other arenas, we will not only be unfaithful to the gospel, but we will also be poor stewards of God in our culture. These doctrinal issues not only shape our proclamation of Christ but also inform our relationship to this world. Because we have rushed in without that theological reflection, our signs and wonders are often superstitious and sensational, our church growth programs pragmatic and mechanical, our pop-psychology superficial and subjective, our conservatism trivial and irrelevant, and our political involvement narrow and naive.

It is true that the world needs peace and relief from hunger and unjust governments; it is equally true that the world needs morality—a sense of right and wrong, settled on the foundation of family and community. The world needs a church that understands it (but in more than statistical terms), and the world needs wisdom for facing the future when the stakes are high. But what the world needs more than anything else is peace with God. While *that* war rages, all successes in other areas pale in significance. Just as the world set out to build its tower of progress to the heavens in Genesis 11, so we are living at a time when our culture (especially our particular nation) is convinced that nothing will be impossible, that nothing will stand in the way of her strength and wisdom. At a time of glory, power, strength, and success, the temptation is to sell the gospel and the church as partners in progress. But also like the Tower of Babel, our towers and ladders will be met on that final day by God's descent—this time, not as a Savior born in a manger but as a Judge riding on a horse. And He will do a great deal more than confuse languages.

The evangelical church *must* leave power behind; it must speak less self-confidently and begin declaring its confidence in God's sovereign grace. There must be a recovery of the riches of mysteries that have been finally revealed in the living and written Word. Until the gospel is clearly known again in our ungodly culture, we must put every other pursuit, every other distraction, every other interest or fascination in abeyance, declaring to the sophisticated foolishness of our age, with the apostle Paul, "I resolved to know nothing among you except Christ and him crucified."

> Almighty and everlasting God, who, by thy Holy Spirit,
> didst preside in the Council of the blessed Apostles,
> . . . save us from all error, ignorance, pride, and prejudice;
> and of thy great mercy vc·ıchsafe, we beseech thee,
> so to direct, sanctify and govern us in our work,
> by the mighty power of the Holy Ghost,
> that the comfortable Gospel of Christ may be truly preached,

truly received, and truly followed, in all places,
to the breaking down the kingdom of sin, Satan, and death;
till at length the whole of thy dispersed sheep,
being gathered into thy fold,
shall become partakers of everlasting life;
through the merits and death of Jesus Christ our Saviour. Amen.
(From the Book of Common Prayer)

NOTES

1. Robert Schuller, Introduction to Paul Yonggi Cho's *The Fourth Dimension* (Plainfield, N.J.: Logos, 1980).

2. See James Davison Hunter, *Evangelicalism: The Coming Generation* (Chicago: U. of Chicago, 1987). This is a University of Virginia sociologist's sobering survey of students at evangelical institutions. The data he presents offers a substantial portrait of the shifts that are taking place.

3. See George Gallup, Jr., *The People's Religion* (New York: Macmillan, 1990) and also his earlier study *The Search for America's Faith* (Nashville: Abingdon, 1980), esp. pp. 18-20.

4. Eugene Ferguson, *Early Christianity* (Grand Rapids: Eerdmans, 1988).

5. Philip Watson, *Let God Be God!* (London: Epworth, 1947), p. 94.

6. From the back cover of Morton Kelsey, *Christo-Psych^logy* (London: Darton, Longman and Todd, 1982).

7. Ibid.

8. Calvin *Institutes* 1.5.9.

9. C. Peter Wagner, ed., *Church Growth: State of the Art* (Wheaton, Ill.: Tyndale, 1986), pp. 33-36.

10. Ibid., p. 34.

11. Watson, *Let God Be God!*, p. 96.

12. John Wesley, *Works*, 10:349.

13. Ibid., 10:325.

14. Friedrich Nietzsche, *Thus Spake Zarathustra!* (London: J. M. Dent, 1933), pp. 174-75.

15. John Wimber and Kevin Springer, *Power Healing* (San Francisco: Harper & Row, 1987), p. 26.

16. C. Peter Wagner, "Spiritual Power and Urban Evangelism: Dynamic Lessons from Argentina," on file with CURE.

Moody Press, a ministry of the Moody Bible Institute,
is designed for education, evangelization, and edification.
If we may assist you in knowing more about Christ
and the Christian life, please write us without obligation:
Moody Press, c/o MLM, Chicago, Illinois 60610.

For more information on the work of
Christians United for Reformation (CURE),
address correspondence to

CURE
2034 East Lincoln, #209
Anaheim, CA 92806.

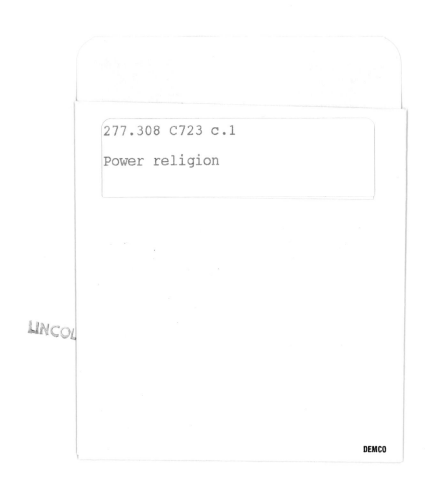